Endorsements for

A **FORCE** FOR
GOOD

Finally, we have a needed sequel to all the management books about building "good to great" companies. Coco Sellman's *A Force For Good* delivers what women founders and entrepreneurs have been longing for—a primer on how to build a successful company that fully embodies the heart, soul, and integrity of the founder AND delivers on its promise to all stakeholders. Coco's own experience has taught her that building great companies requires you, as a leader and entrepreneur, to show up as your best self, fully in your power, connected to a purpose greater than yourself. Not only will *A Force For Good* inspire you. It will guide you with a road map and practical tools to support your journey. Grab this book now and let Coco accompany you on the path to fulfill your dreams.

—Carolyn Buck-Luce, Managing Partner, Imaginal Labs,
Founder of The Decade Game, and Bestselling Author
of *EPIC! T Women's Power Play Book*

A Force For Good by Coco Sellman is an essential guide for visionary women founders eager to amplify their impact and profitability. Drawing on her own remarkable journey, Coco provides a practical toolkit and strategic insights that inspire women to build high-growth enterprises. With themes of transformation, purpose, and leadership, this book not only equips readers with actionable plans but also fosters a community dedicated to societal change. Join Coco in redefining business norms and making a lasting impact!

—Julie Castro Abrams, Founder & CEO of How Women Lead,
How Women Give, and General Partner of How Women Invest

"*A Force for Good* is a powerful source of inspiration as well as practical advice for women entrepreneurs who want to grow and scale their businesses. If you're an Entreprenista committed to building and leading a high-impact business while cultivating a team that will thrive, you must read this book!"

—Stephanie Cartin, Co-Founder of Entreprenista

I enthusiastically endorse Coco Selman's *A Force for Good*. This empowering book offers a fresh perspective on how individuals, especially women founders and executives, can build companies and organizations that drive meaningful, positive change while fueling growth and profitability. The Force for Good website further enhances this mission by offering interactive toolkits and valuable resources to help turn your impact-driven intentions into actionable strategies. It's a must-read for anyone committed to making an impact and driving transformative change.

—Fran Maier, Founder BabyQuip
and Co-Founder, Match.com

If you own a business, or are thinking of starting a business, *A Force for Good* is a must-have resource. The practical and instructional step-by-step guide is full of vital tips and relevant examples that will bring your roadmap for success to life. Keep it within close reach, you will refer to time and time again.

—Emily Dalton, Co-Founder, Jack Black

"Integrating the growth mindset with a step-by-step roadmap, Coco Sellman provides a tangible path to exponential business growth that amplifies the strengths of women. *A Force for Good* is a must-read for women founders who want to *go big,* in both impact and profit."

—Julia Pimseur, Founder, Million Dollar Women,
Best-Selling Author of *Million Dollar Women* and *Go Big Now*

A **FORCE** FOR GOOD

A **FORCE** FOR
GOOD

Empowering Visionary Women to Build High-Impact, High-Growth Businesses

COCO SELLMAN

A Force for Good
Empowering Visionary Women to Lead High-Impact, High-Growth Enterprises

For information about this title, contact the publisher:

Wisdom of Women Media
wisdomofwomen.net
service@wisdomofwomen.net

ISBNs:
979-8-9907225-0-7 (softcover)
979-8-9907225-1-4 (eBook)

Printed in the United States of America

Cover and Interior design: 1106 Design and Jill Skillton Designs

To Amelia and Ella Pearl

FORCE FOR GOOD GROWTH READINESS ASSESSMENT

As you embark on the journey of building a high-impact, high-growth company, first take a moment to assess where your company is today.

The Force for Good Growth Readiness Assessment helps you discover whether your company is ready to GROW or PLATEAU.

You'll receive a score in each of the Four Crucial Areas of Alignment. Companies scoring 80+ in each area—and overall—are not only primed for growth but also have teams that feel supported, valued, and ready to give their best.

More Than Just a Score—It's a Blueprint for Empowerment

Beyond the score, this assessment offers a personalized roadmap for growth, with access to four targeted tools tailored to your results. These tools will help you foster a culture where your team's brilliance can emerge, empowering both personal and business growth.

Ready for Breakthrough?
Take the free *Force for Good Growth Readiness Assessment* today!
www.aforceforgood.biz/quiz

CONTENTS

Contents

Contents

Contents

INTRODUCTION

Entrepreneurs are a *Force for Good.*
At least, they can be. They should be.

Businesses and organizations founded by visionary leaders—women who care deeply about their customers, team members, and community, and who are ready to model new, enlightened ways of relating to one another—have the power to shape, heal, and elevate society.

These purpose-led, innovative entrepreneurs are devising new ways of building and nurturing teams who lead in both impact and profit. Purpose-led teams overcome challenges. They are inspired to greatness every day and gravitate toward a purpose larger than themselves. Purpose-led teams support one another as well as their constituents in transformational, heartfelt ways. Purpose-led businesses have the power to reinvent the way we relate to each other and to change the way we all see the world, all while making it a healthier, more prosperous place for all.

A Force for Good™ was founded on the belief that entrepreneurs have a duty to themselves, to their constituents, and to society as a whole to succeed and prosper. Our purpose is to empower more and more visionary women to operate in a space where they are not only serving their purpose to its fullest potential but are also well-funded, scalable, profitable, and well-positioned to continue long into the future.

**Your mission, should you choose to accept it,
is to join us in being a Force for Good.**

Who am I to be making these claims? Let me share some of my history.

I have launched many businesses over the course of my career. My first all-in attempt was in 1997. My business partner and I had a good concept, and I trusted the strength and purity of my motivation so much that I borrowed money from my grandmother—money it would take me a long time to pay back. We closed things down about two years later. The partnership wasn't working out, and we were out of money.

This is what most entrepreneurs go through. This is often the reality of launching a business. That's also how we learn: "Well, I failed at this one because of this. And I only got so far with that one because of that." At the time, I didn't know yet what it meant to be a partner; I didn't yet know how to create an actionable business plan; I didn't yet know how to figure out and account for all my costs. But, perhaps even more crucially, I didn't know what I was worth.

A few years later, in 2003, I launched a training and consultancy business, called WorldChangingBusiness, which catered to solo entrepreneurs. Soon, we expanded services to include businesses that were a little bigger. Much of the Force for Good System™ began during that time. I was committed to educating myself, taking classes and doing my own work on marketing and sales, and always considering: *What would work? How would it work? If it did work, how do I measure it? How do I put it on a page and systemize it and codify it? How do I create a business that does great, while doing good? How do I create a business that aligns purpose with profit?* I held a lot of trainings where I'd work with groups of 20 entrepreneurs at a time. The workshops were held in New York City, but we offered remote-format classes, and this was long before the days of Zoom!

That segued into my next business, the Trust Leadership Institute. There, I offered training on how to develop self-trust in a business context—and beyond, really. That was a personal journey in many ways. For years, I had felt I wasn't good enough. Through deep, hard, self-focused work, I eventually claimed and rooted my life in the gift of self-trust. When I felt the way that shift was revolutionizing my existence, it ignited a spark. It became crucial for me to help others walk down the same path.

I created and facilitated a 30-Day Trust Challenge™ that included a series of guided visualizations. I wanted the women who participated to leave feeling that they were now able to hear and listen to their inner guidance—and use it to take action in their next right direction.

I would consider both of my businesses in the early 2000s to be meaningful and successful, and yet they were both 100% dependent on me. I was the product. It dawned on me that I wanted to create a business that still did the kind of good I was passionate about, but one that was both scalable and sustainable without relying almost entirely on my active involvement. Finding myself unexpectedly pregnant only heightened my desire to build something that could thrive with my care—but be powered by much more than just me. I had been an entrepreneur and worked with entrepreneurs for years by that time; I had gone through all the ups and downs. I had found success, but it wasn't the rocket-speed success people like to talk about. I paid my bills, and I ran into a few walls. Some things had worked well, and others hadn't. Now, I was ready to put it all together.

I turned to my own method, one that I had cultivated at my training and consultancy business. In 2016, I put together a business plan, and then I followed it.

That's how I was able to do what I did at Allumé: the whole, shiny, overnight-success thing. We'll talk more about that later. But then the pandemic hit in the spring of 2020, and everything changed. That May, I took stock of the situation: *I'm responsible for hundreds of people's welfare, I'm barely able to break even, and I'm worried the pandemic is going to wreck us. What do we do?*

And then I had the thought: *What would I do if I were a man?*

I reflected. *Well, a man would bring in capital from somewhere else.* The thing is, I would never have entertained this thought earlier in my career. And that seems to ring true for of a lot of women founders. We're more likely to place the burden solely on ourselves, believing we must handle everything alone. We have fewer model that show us how successful, visionary businesses leverage external funding to scale their visions. In fact, women are twice as likely as men to shut down their business because they ran out of money.

I didn't want to shut down Allumé. So, I raised the money through investors. Their resources not only helped me weather the pandemic and come through on the other side, but it introduced a new level of account-ability to the process. I was responsible for other people's money, and I had to report on every decision I made. It *also* meant there were other parties who had a vested interest, who could share in both the stress *and* the strategizing of running the business. It was with their encouragement and support that I eventually looked for acquisition targets, and, in the end, I decided to negotiate a successful merger.

These experiences taught me I don't have to go it alone, which is a common trap for women founders. Learning that others' wisdom, brilliance, skills and resources are the key to building lasting high-impact, high-growth enterprises able to live on without you, the founder.

It's been a tremendously positive success, made possible because of all of the experiences I had under my belt. It helped me to consider the challenges and opportunities this business encountered in ways I wouldn't have—*couldn't have*—with the businesses I was operating 20 years before. It is these decades of experience that inform the Force for Good model.

I have never been more passionate about helping women step into their unique opportunities and prosper. American women are starting twice as many businesses as men, and yet only 3% of women-founded companies have $1 million or more in revenue. At the writing of this book, just 2% of venture capital makes its way to women founders.

These statistics don't sit well with me. I am committed to doing all I can to create the knowledge and the access to change this, to help as many women founders as possible find their way to resounding success.

This is why the Force for Good System™ and tools are readily accessible, affordable, and available to any and every founder who wants them.

When you and your team commit to being a *Force for Good* in the world, something amazing will happen. Together, you will step forward into an enriching and soul-satisfying journey of building something profitable, something that endures, and something that matters. And it's not just about where you end up; in the process, you will find tremendous growth, opportunity, prosperity, and even transcendence.

That may sound exciting to you, or it may sound overwhelming or perhaps even incomprehensible. It doesn't have to be. The Force for Good System™ will lead you step by step toward actualizing your vision, realizing your success, and inviting the best within you to shine through.

If you've picked up this book, you are a visionary who sees a brighter future. You have heart. You are driven by purpose. You are gritty, determined, and courageous. You long to create a business and lead a team capable of overcoming anything. You are not interested in *surviving*. Your goal is to *prosper*—to make the world a better place not only for yourself but for all those around you. You are an entrepreneur. Deep down, you know you are unstoppable.

You also recognize that you want help. You are facing a roadblock or two. Maybe you are underfunded, understaffed, overworked, or just plain overwhelmed. Maybe you have begun to doubt the viability of your endeavor. Maybe you need help in one specific area of your business. Wherever you may be on your entrepreneurial journey, I bet you are asking yourself the same questions that have guided me throughout my 25+ years as a businesswoman, corporate coach, and entrepreneur.

- Which processes guarantee remarkable impact, scale, and profit through the creation and elevation of a company?

- How can I integrate what matters most to me as a human—purpose and values—to build greater prosperity than ever before, for both the company and for everyone on the team?

- How can I elevate team collaboration so that it creates a meaningful, transformative journey of growth for everyone involved—individuals, customers, partners, and investors?

During my quest to answer these questions for myself, I have risked it all. I have experienced both crushing failures and resounding successes. Either way, I have never looked back. Each experience has led me toward perfecting A Force for Good™, my blueprint for building profitable, sustainable businesses that are rooted in altruism. Consider this book an invitation to get your own journey started. The chapters ahead will guide you step by step toward conquering every single challenge, one breakthrough at a time. The process will, of course, engage your rational mind, but, more importantly, it will engage your heart and your soul as you tap into your own, unique wisdom and entrepreneurial spirit.

As a Force for Good entrepreneur, you will make magic. You will invent. You will create. You will bring forth what lives on the horizon. You will identify opportunities, solutions, and social models for collaborating. You will articulate and solve challenges, deliver sustainable transformations, and discover abundant prosperity.

You will be a Force for Good.

THE FORCE FOR GOOD VISION: AN OVERVIEW

"The world will be saved by the Western woman
who is willing to step into and own her power."

—CAROLYN BUCK LUCE

EPIC!: The Women's Power Play Book

Business is an incredibly powerful, innovative force. And in our complex, interconnected, ever-changing world, it needs a new approach. The old command-and-control, conveyor-style model no longer fits. Modern business requires a new way of leading, where purpose and profit align, and the brilliance of every member of your team can be harnessed. But this book is more than philosophy; it is a step-by-step road map, complete with easy-to-use tools that will help you embody this new way of leadership and success.

Over the past 25 years as an admirer, coach, and consultant of entrepreneurs, and as a five-time founder myself, I have been driven by the belief that an altruistic purpose can align with scaling and growing a world-class business and, at the same time, be the wind in the sails of sustainable, ever-growing profits. Over the years, I have studied and tested what breeds the kind of businesses so many of us dream of building, businesses known for their:

- Remarkable products and services that customers cherish

- Beloved workplace culture, where team members thrive and never want to leave

- Wholehearted drive to make the world better through intentional business practices

- Longevity, with a certainty that what they're building will last well beyond their original founders

- Commitment to always growing, evolving, and elevating the industries around them.

WHO THIS BOOK IS FOR

This book is dedicated to all visionary leaders, the women who see a bright future ahead, including:

- Founders—Those of us who create something out of nothing, building a business from nothing more than an idea

- Entrepreneurs—Visionary leaders who build business, sometimes from the ground up, like founders do, and sometimes elevating an existing one to ever-higher impact and prosperity

- Intrapreneurs—Leading visionaries within existing, large-scale companies who drive new ideas, innovation, and transformation from inside a corporate environment

- Leaders and Teams—While this book speaks to a founder, it is also valuable for leaders and teams within an existing business. The tools and approach are meant to guide elevated empowerment, collaboration, and personal enrichment for everyone within a company. It is designed to cultivate leaders.

- Nonprofit Leaders and Teams—While this book is aimed at both impact and profit, the framework is also ideal for leaders and teams of nonprofit organizations. In fact, I have used these tools and methods with several NPOs over the years.

HOW TO GET THE MOST FROM THIS BOOK

While this book was designed to be read from front to back, beginning with this comprehensive overview, the methods within can be approached in whatever order is most relevant to your entrepreneurial journey. If you feel drawn to explore one topic or another, go for it! You know what you need. That said, the Force for Good System™ is an integrated model that, when built and used together, produces the greatest cumulative results.

HOW WILL THE FORCE FOR GOOD SYSTEM™ HELP YOU?

The Force for Good System™ is designed to help you, your team, and your company grow. It is designed to help visionary founders and teams actualize the high-impact, high-growth company you envision.

The Force for Good System™ empowers companies at any stage to foster the next level of breakthrough results. The system accelerates the pace at which an organization can progress through each of the company growth stages: existence, survival, scale, and impact.

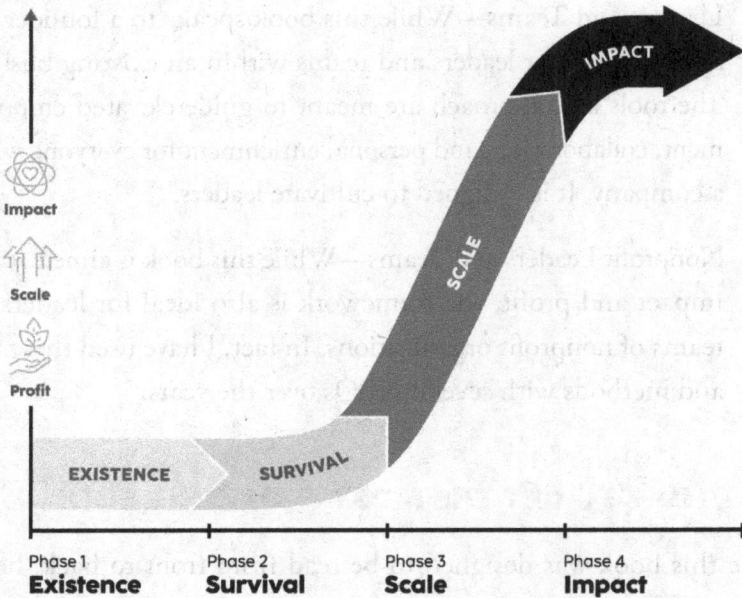

Stage 1—Existence

This is the startup stage. This is when an idea starts to get off the ground. The Force for Good System™ empowers companies at this phase to clarify what is most important and make crucial decisions faster. The Tools empower Existence-Stage companies to create traction and achieve early wins faster. Founders and teams will align more quickly, make stronger decisions, clearly see what's working, pivot, and arrive at the next stage of Survival more efficiently.

Stage 2—Survival

At this point, a company has customers, but it is not generating enough or consistent profits. A majority of companies get stuck at this stage. Most fold and disappear, while others continue on for years, under-resourced and barely able to pay the founder.

Survival isn't just about profitability, however—as we will discuss later—it's also about you, the founder, finding meaning, prosperity, and freedom. Even if your company is consistently profitable, it is still in Survival if you can't go on vacation for a month feeling confident that the business will be fine. You know you are leading a company in Survival mode if it can't run without you.

Another sign of being stuck in Survival is minimal or no growth. If your people, products, balance sheet, and impact in the world are flat, the company is in Survival Stage. Not growing means you are not ready for changes in the market, changes in technology, and not likely to retain the smartest members of your team, who thrive on new rockets to launch. A business *not* constantly growing and evolving will soon be left behind.

Stage 3—Scale

This is the stage when a business is experiencing at least high double-digit annual growth and generating consistent, abundant profits. The Force for Good System™ helps companies at this point identify and accelerate what's working, see what still needs fine tuning, and empower a growing team to bring their best to work from the day they're hired. The bigger your team, the more powerful the Force for Good System™ becomes as it accelerates collaboration, innovation, and transformation. It also attracts and retains high performers because it provides exactly what high performers love:

- Clear goals

- Accountability

- Acknowledgment

- Constant enrichment

- Personal growth

- Freedom to speak up

- Safety to take calculated risks and overcome setbacks

Companies in the Scale Stage can expect high double-digit growth (and even 2X, 3X, or more) annually, due in large part to discovering more clearly where your company is truly remarkable.

Stage 4—Impact

This is where the company delivers on its purpose and values every day and has achieved its first 10-year vision and goal! These businesses have the resources and teams in place to expand purpose and vision in ever-more impactful ways. Companies at this point benefit from the Force for Good System™ by staging the next evolution of their long-term vision.

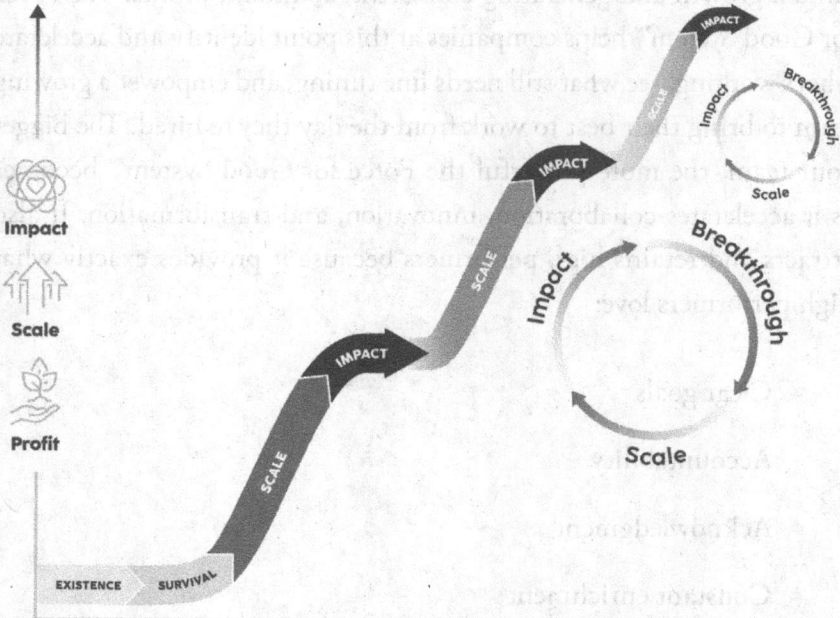

With a strong leadership team in place, the founder can choose where she most wants to be involved—or if she even still *wants* to be involved, or if it's time to relinquish control to the leadership team she has carefully assembled and trained. The Force for Good System™ empowers ongoing, continuous cycles of virtuous scale and impact advances.

GROW IMPACT, SCALE, AND PROFIT

This book is centered around three critical pillars that facilitate the progression from Stage One to Stage Four: impact, scale, and profit. While these three outcomes don't define "success" in its totality, they *are* at the heart and soul of what drives long-term success for any high-impact, high-growth business.

Why Grow Impact?

Impact is the measure of good you bring to those you serve: your customers, employees, partners, your larger community, the industry as a whole, and the wider world. Impact is the measurable progress of a company's purpose, the results that demonstrate the good your company is creating for the people you serve. Impact feeds your company and team direction and passion, and provides them a reason beyond profits to go through all the necessary challenges of building a great company.

Why Grow Scale?

Bigger isn't necessarily better. Scale within our Force for Good™ context is grounded in purpose. Within these parameters, scale is important for two reasons.

First, scale is the manifestation of your vision. It is the realization of what you hope to deliver to the world, en masse. If you don't have a big vision, then stop reading right now. The Force for Good System™ is not for you. It is designed for women who are unapologetic about the size and scope of the good they envision through their business.

Second, practically speaking, you will need a certain level of scale to create the funding (gross profit) necessary to support your purpose. Without an adequate number of customers or units sold, you will not be able to keep the lights on, let alone hire the brilliant team, implement state-of-the art technology, or build the most elegant solutions for customers.

Scale is needed for impact. It is also needed for profit.

Why Grow Profit?

Profit is the life force of your company. It allows you to create prosperity for your team, your shareholders, and yourself. Profit also broadens horizons, leads to new levels of breakthrough, and drives more good in the world. Profit is meant to be a Force for Good™.

TRANSFORMATIONAL FLYWHEEL

The Force for Good System™ is partially inspired by Leonardo DaVinci's idea of a perpetual-motion machine. This is a hypothetical device that is designed to operate indefinitely and continuously, without requiring any external-energy input. In other words, it would generate enough energy to sustain its own motion without ever stopping or needing additional fuel or energy sources.

While no perpetual-motion machine has ever been created, it has been my personal quest to build businesses that contain the momentum, energy, team alignment, and frictionless systems that make such ongoing success possible.

The Force for Good System™ is an elevated model of leading and growing companies and organizations, in building both positive impact and sustainable prosperity.

- It is a Transformational Flywheel, designed to accelerate impact, scale, and profit in your business.

- It also simultaneously builds trust with customers and employees alike.

- As time goes on, the richness of purpose, culture, innovation, and high performance creates sustainable growth and momentum.

That's when you know your Flywheel is spinning.

Four Crucial Areas of Alignment

The Flywheel consists of the Core Growth Elements that empower everyone on your team to participate in the discovery, clarification, and ever-deepening awareness of the **Four Areas of Crucial Alignment.**

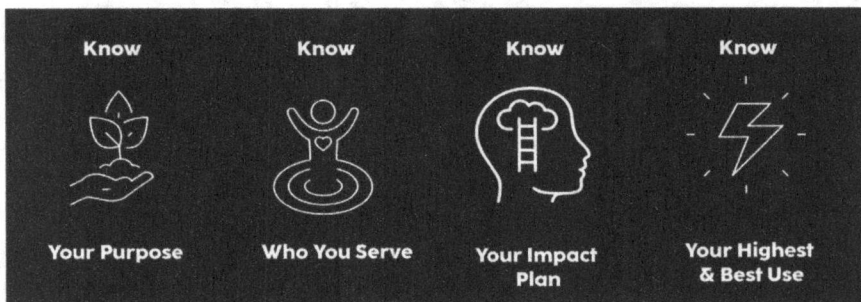

Know	Know	Know	Know
Your Purpose	Who You Serve	Your Impact Plan	Your Highest & Best Use

When everyone on your team is aligned and clear in these specific ways, (inner and outer) growth occurs.

First—Build Flywheel

In the first three parts of the book, you and your team focus on the first three of the Four Areas of Crucial Alignment (Purpose, Who You Serve, and Your Impact Plan), where you define and decide on the Core Growth Elements of the Flywheel. This provides the opportunity to create (or reinforce) an atmosphere of intention and community, which are fundamental needs for any team driven toward creating impact.

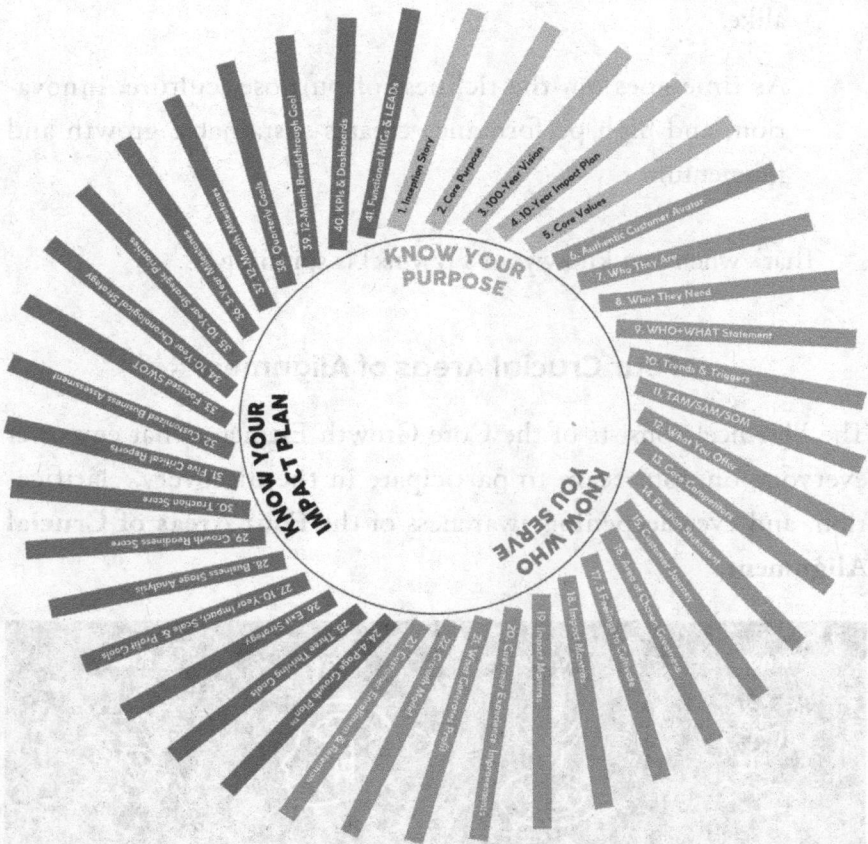

1. **Part 1: Know Your Purpose.** This includes Inception Story, Core Purpose, 100-Year Company Vision, 10-Year Impact Goal, and Core Values.

2. **Part 2: Know Who You Serve.** This includes the Authentic Customer Avatar, Who Your Customer Is, What Your Customer Needs, your WHO+WHAT Statement, Triggers & Trends, What You Offer, Core Competitors, Position Statement, What Generates Profit, your Area of Chosen Greatness, the Customer Journey, Three Feelings to Cultivate, Impact Mantras, Three Customer Experience Improvements, your Growth Model, and the Customer Enrollment Funnel.

3. **Part 3: Know Your Impact Plan.** This includes Three Prosperity Goals, an Exit Strategy, Business-Stage Analysis, Five Critical Reports, 12+ Key Metrics Dashboard, 10-Year Impact, Scale, and Profit Goals, Customized Business Assessment, Focused SWOT, Chronological Strategy, Strategic Priorities, 10-Year Milestones, 3-Year Milestones, 12-Month Milestone, 12-Month Breakthrough Goal, Functional Most Important Goals (MIGs), Functional LEADs, Quarterly Goals, 12-Month Breakthrough Plan, and Pro Forma Forecast and Budget.

As you and your team bring clarity and definition to each of the Core Growth Elements (legs of the Flywheel), the magic of the system starts to create progress. Alignment and clarity emerge. You and your team begin seeing new ways to elevate your common goals. Quickly, you begin to identify ways to move the needle toward progress.

Second—Spin the Flywheel

After constructing your Flywheel, the next step is to get it spinning by implementing the Seven Rituals of Innovation. Rituals are beliefs in action; they are the outward signs of trust we have in a system we believe will uphold its promise. By engaging in Rituals, we are sharing with each other our ongoing commitment to the process we developed, collectively, and which we trust.

Part Four of the book, specifically Chapter 17, will address each of the Seven Rituals. Each Ritual has a unique purpose and agenda. These regular Rituals constantly reconnect the team to the purpose, vision, and goals of the company, while also keeping everyone moving in the same direction. Each Ritual builds momentum, creating perpetual cycles of innovation, acknowledgment, connection, and celebration that lead to actualized breakthroughs in the business. The Seven Rituals include:

1. Annual Retreats

2. Quarterly Reviews

3. Monthly Dashboards

4. Weekly Most Important Goal Sessions

5. Daily Huddles

6. Town Halls

7. Board Meetings

These Rituals become the backbone of your company culture, the mechanism through which you develop leaders, and the place where innovation and transformation happen.

Third—Be a Force for Good

The final section of the book is directed toward you, the leader.

First, your most essential leadership role is implementing the Force for Good System™. In Chapter 17, we cover the Quick-Start Implementation, where you craft the Flywheel and Launch Rituals in just 7 days, and then tune and refine the system over 90 days.

Next, in the remaining three chapters of the book, we discuss *"Who do you need to be as a leader?"* Rather than just what you need to do, here we address the qualities to cultivate and bring to your team daily:

- Be Wise

- Be Transformative

- Be of Highest and Best Use

These crucial qualities make it possible to lead authentically, purposefully, and effectively. Implementing the Force for Good System™ and Rituals with these essential competencies brings the system to life.

THE FFG TOOLKIT

Before we go further, I would like to direct you to the Force for Good (FFG) ToolKit found at: www.aforceforgood.biz/book-bonuses/

This is everything you need to create a WorldChangingBusiness in one downloadable document. The book and Tools complement one another. What you find at that link is more than just standard templates. Each Tool is designed to lead you to answers that, in turn, lead to breakthroughs, helping to build one or more elements of the Flywheel as you move forward.

Throughout the book, you will be directed to the Force for Good Tools, templates, and processes. These are all available in the FFG ToolKit. Some might choose to read the book and explore and implement each Tool as they go along. Others might opt to read the book straight through and explore the Tools later. The system is here for you. Use it in the ways that best support you and your team.

Throughout the book, you will find the "Growth Flywheel" symbol at the left, indicating that there is a Tool, template, or resource available in the FFG ToolKit.

Download the FFG ToolKit now: www.aforceforgood.biz/book-bonuses/

While the FFG ToolKit is a growing set of resources to help founders and teams grow, at the center of them all live the Essential Three—the heart of the Force for Good System™:

1. FFG 4-Page Growth Plan™ (4PGP™)

2. FFG Transformational Map™

3. FFG Innovation Rituals Handbook™

All the other Tools in the FFG ToolKit support the Essential Three. Even if you use *only* the Essential Three and never touch another Force for Good Tool, you will see remarkable growth.

FFG 4-Page Growth Plan™ (4PGP™)

In four pages is everything you need to know to unlock the puzzle of growth in your business. All Core Growth Elements of the Force for Good Flywheel live on the 4-Page Growth Plan™. In one document, you will define and iterate the essential information needed to foster growth. It is the visual summary of the Transformational Flywheel.

The 4-Page Growth Plan™ restores your power as a leader. It reminds you that you and your team already have what you need to take the next brave step. *You* are enough. *Your team* is enough. *Your resources* are enough. It transports you from overwhelm and frenzy to clarity and empowerment. It acts as a daily reminder of the power and brilliance of you. You have what you need, each and every day, to take the next step.

The 4-Page Growth Plan™ focuses your energy and brilliance on the elements of the Transformational Flywheel. It empowers you to pour your wisdom into the areas of your company that will most amplify growth. These are areas that might otherwise go neglected and not receive the attention, alignment, and innovation needed to foster remarkable growth.

Chapter 11 is dedicated to the 4-Page Growth Plan™. However, along the way, the specific areas of the 4-Page Growth Plan™ will be indicated.

Draft Your 4-Page Growth Plan™ Now!
www.aforceforgood.biz/book-bonuses

If you are itching to get started, go to www.aforceforgood.biz/book-bonuses, where you can get immediate, free access to the following:

- 4-Page Growth Plan™ Template
- 60-minute training video, where you will create the first draft of your plan
- Ten ways to use the 4-Page Growth Plan™ to help you and your team foster growth

Transformational Map

Growth requires change. Ponder this for a moment. Every result you have in your business is the cumulative outcome of all the habits, actions, thinking, mindsets, systems, and people in place in the past and currently. New results (aka, growth) require shifts in all of these areas.

A FORCE FOR GOOD

FFG 4-Page Growth Plan (4PGP™)

A living, breathing reminder of what is most important for growth

A FORCE FOR **GOOD**

KNOW YOUR PURPOSE

Inception Story

Core Purpose	100-Year Vision

10-Year Impact Goal	Core Values

KNOW WHO YOU SERVE

Total Available Market	Serviceable Addressable Market	Serviceable Obtainable Market

Authentic Customer + Offering + Go-To Market

Who They Are	What They Need	WHO + WHAT Statement	Why—Trend & Triggers

What You Offer	Core Competitors	Position Statement	Area of Chosen Greatness

3 Feelings to Cultivate	Impact Mantras	3 Customer Experience Improvements	

FFG 4-Page Growth Plan (4PGP™)

A living, breathing reminder of what is most important for growth

A FORCE FOR **GOOD**

Products & Services (Update Monthly)

Core Product & Service Lines	Unit Price ($)	Unit Cost ($)	Unit Gross Margin ($)	Unit Gross Margin (%)	TTM Units Sold (#)	TTM Customers (#)	TTM Revenues Booked (#)	Avg Rev. Per Customer ($)	TTM COGs ($)	TTM Gross Margin ($)	TTM Gross Margin (%)
TOTALS:											

Growth Model:

☐ Whale (ARPC=$100K+)	☐ Deer (ARPC=$10K+)	☐ Rabbit (ARPC=$1K+)	☐ Mouse (ARPC=$100+)
Current ARPC/Yr ($)	#Customers for $100K	#Customers for $1M	#Customers for $10M

Customer Enrollment & Retention Funnel

Shine Your Light—Channels

Experience—Methods

Ask Them to Be Your Customer—Methods

Connect & Nurture—Methods

Everyone in the World Who Doesn't Know Your Company Exists

1 Shine Light — SUSPECTS
2 Profound Experiences — PROSPECTS
3 Make Invitations — QUALIFIED PROSPECTS
4 The Ask — CUSTOMERS
5 Nurture — SATISFIED CUSTOMERS & LOYAL AMBASSADORS

12-Month Customer Enrollment Goals By Date ____ / ____ / ____

How Many Suspects?		How Many Prospects?		How Many Customers?	
Per Month?	Per Year?	Per Month?	Per Year?	Per Month?	Per Year?

% Suspects to Prospects: _____   % Prospects to Customers: _____

FFG 4-Page Growth Plan (4PGP™)

A living, breathing reminder of what is most important for growth

A FORCE FOR **GOOD**

KNOW YOUR IMPACT PLAN

10-Year Goals & Milestones by Date ____/____/____

10-Year Impact Goal	10-Year Scale Goals	10-Year Profit Goal
	Customers/Yr Goal (#):	Gross Profit Margin Goal (%):
	Unit Volume/Yr Goal (#):	Gross Profit Goal ($):
	Revenue Goal ($):	OpEx Goal ($):
	Avg. Revenue/Customer Goal ($)	Net Profit Margin Goal (%):
		Net Income Goal ($):

Assess Where You Are

☐ Stage 1—Existence	☐ Stage 2—Survival	☐ Stage 3—Scaling	☐ Stage 4—Impact
Growth Readiness Score:	Know Purpose Score:	Know Who You Serve Score:	Know Your Impact Plan Score:

Customer Discovery Score:	MVP Score:	Customer Validation Score:	Product Market Fit Score:	GTM Strategy Score:	Scaling Score:

Profit & Loss History (Update Monthly)

	Actuals: Last Year	Actuals: YTD	Actuals: TTM Monthly Avg.	Actuals: TTM Annual Run-Rate	Forecast & Budget (Current Year)	Forecast & Budget (Next Year)
Total Units Sold (#)						
Revenue ($)						
COGs ($)						
Gross Profit ($)						
Gross Profit (%)						
OpEx ($)						
Net Income ($)						
Net Margin (%)						

SWOT—Strengths, Weaknesses, Opportunities, Threats

Our top three strengths to amplify...	Our top three weaknesses to overcome...
1.	1.
2.	2.
3.	3.

Our top three opportunities to leverage...	Our top three threats to mitigate...
1.	1.
2.	2.
3.	3.

xl

FFG 4-Page Growth Plan (4PGP™)

A living, breathing reminder of what is most important for growth

A FORCE FOR **GOOD**

10-Year Chronological Strategy

Years 1-3 (By __/__/____)	Years 4-6 (By __/__/____)	Years 7-10 (By __/__/____)

10-Year Strategic Priorities

3-Year Milestones by __/__/____ /   12-Month Milestones by __/__/____ /

Q1 Goals by __/__/____ /	Q2 Goals by __/__/____ /	Q3 Goals by __/__/____ /	Q4 Goals by __/__/____ /

Company-Wide 12-Month Breakthrough Goal:

Key Performance Indicators—TTM Monthly Dashboard Metrics (Update Monthly)

	Months Ago →	12	11	10	9	8	7	6	5	4	3	2	1
METRIC	90-Day GOAL/Mo Month →	_/_	_/_	_/_	_/_	_/_	_/_	_/_	_/_	_/_	_/_	_/_	_/_

So often we make a plan and don't follow through. We create a strategy, but nothing changes. Why is this? This is because growth requires a new way of looking at ourselves and our teams. Often what stops you or me from doing "the thing" that would produce the new result isn't logical, rational, or even visible.

To be midwives of growth, we must learn to *be transformative*. We must learn the architecture of change and become stewards of this profound and often-tangled journey. As we do, we set free whatever holds us (and our teams) back from living our brilliance.

Chapter 19 is dedicated to this essential mindset needed for growth. At the heart of "being transformational" lives the FFG Transformational Map™, which is a visual model for understanding what we go through as humans to change.

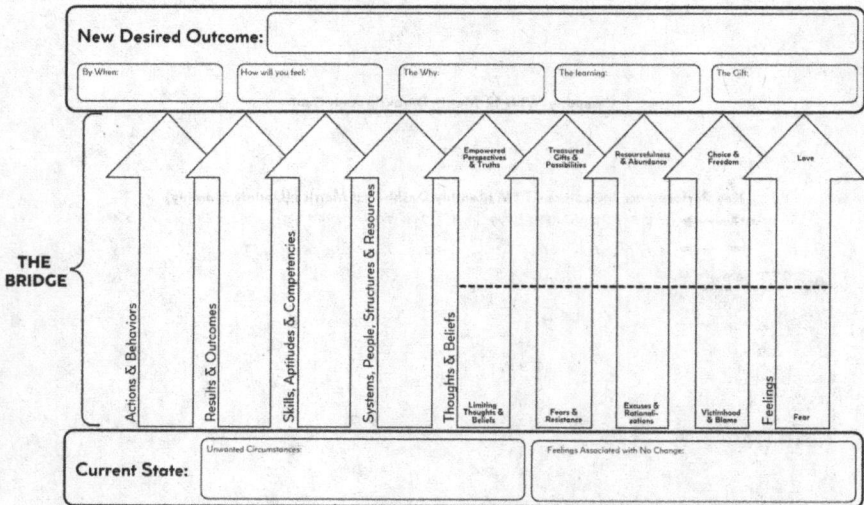

INNOVATION RITUALS

Innovation Rituals are the last of the Essential Three. These important daily, weekly, monthly, quarterly, and annual Rituals are the backbone of the high-impact, high-growth culture you long to build.

Draft Your Transformational Map Now!
www.aforceforgood.biz/book-bonuses

If you are chomping at the bit to get started, go to www.aforce-forgood.biz/book-bonuses, where you can get immediate, free access to the following:

- The Journey of Transformational Process FFG Transformation Map™
- Training video, where you will create the first Transformational Map

Chapter 17 goes into depth on the Seven Rituals of Innovation that will keep your Flywheel spinning. There is depth, nuance, and purpose inlaid in each of the Seven Rituals, however, the best way to start is simple:

- Set up a weekly 30-minute meeting with your leadership team (or just yourself), pull out the 4-Page Growth Plan™, and talk about it. Do this for 6 months; you'll see that growth is not just inevitable but that it becomes a veritable cycle.
- Bonus challenge: Every week, re-write the 4-Page Growth Plan™ together. The act of writing it again each week will produce astounding new results. It will keep the puzzles of growth active in your mind throughout the week. Each week, you will find new clarity, specificity, and insights.

A simple 30-minute gathering of the minds—focused on what's most essential for growth—will transform your business in a very short time.

Later, in Chapter 17, you'll discover the depths and magic of these Rituals.

> **"Growth comes not from doing 1,000 things, but from doing these Seven Rituals 1,000 times."**

THE GROWING FFG TOOLKIT

As of the time I was writing this book, there were more than 100 Tools in the FFG ToolKit. Each Tool is meant to help you and your team connect together, focus on topics that facilitate growth, and update your 4-Page Growth Plan™. All are meant to help you listen to your inner wisdom, discover where change is necessary, and take the action that serves your company most impactfully.

To receive free access to each of the new FFG Tools as they come out, go to www.aforceforgood.biz, and sign up for our mailing list.

WORKING *ON* THE BUSINESS

The holy grail of entrepreneurship is to focus more time and attention working "on" the business, rather than "in" the business. But crossing the chasm of doing everything from cleaning toilets, to closing sales, to delivering services, and processing invoices yourself over to the green magical pastures of working *on* the business can be daunting. Even the most talented leaders struggle with the transition. But this is exactly what separates good leaders from great ones. The journey from being the hero who has all the answers to the wise, silent steward who holds the space for everyone else to shine is worthwhile and necessary if you want to create something remarkable.

One of the wonderful benefits of implementing the Force for Good System™ and its Rituals is that it naturally provides this path. The system itself is how to work *on* the business, rather than *in* it. Over time, the system trains you to elevate yourself from many-hat wearer, to unflappable CEO, to visionary board member, to the wise visionary who sparked a movement. The evolution happens on your own schedule. It happens naturally. As you grow into these ever-more-impactful roles, so, too, will the company grow into greater evolutions of its purpose and vision.

Let's begin our remarkable journey together!

PART 1
KNOW YOUR PURPOSE

"I alone cannot change the world, but I can cast a
stone across the waters to create many ripples."

—MOTHER TERESA

"When you take a stand, you ignite a spark that can
become a beacon of hope and inspiration for others."

—LYNN TWIST

*Living a Committed Life: Finding Freedom and Fulfillment
in a Purpose Larger Than Yourself.*

Whether you are forming a new company or are already well established, knowing your purpose is the first important step toward surviving, thriving, and being a *Force for Good*. In the chapters ahead, you will have the opportunity to reflect upon and build the five important elements we at Force for Good refer to as "your purpose":

1. Your Inception Story

2. Core Purpose

3. Company Vision

4. 10-Year Impact Goal

5. Core Values

This section will help you not only define in words what you stand for but also discover specific ways to bring these ideals into every aspect of your business. With clarity about what is most important, you set the stage for building a run-through-walls team, committed to moving mountains to achieve goals, overcome challenges, and, ultimately, create the positive impact your organization longs to create.

In this section, you and your team will engage in the exciting and elevating work of contemplating these important questions:

1. What do you stand for?

2. What is important to you?

3. What is the impact you want to lead as a company?

4. How does it look to embody these ideals in every aspect of your business?

CHAPTER 1
INCEPTION STORY

"Through the art of storytelling, we can communicate our deepest truths and connect with the hearts of others."

—SONIA CHOQUETTE

*Your Heart's Desire: Instructions for Creating
the Life You Really Want*

I temporarily invested in a hair-salon franchise a number of years before I started Allumé. It met the parameters of what I was looking for at the time: a business where *I* wouldn't be the product or the service—as I wouldn't be the one cutting hair but would instead be empowering other female stylists to do so—and a business with real scalability. I'd gone so far as to buy into the franchise and select a location, and was about to start the salon build when I realized, "This isn't right."

We ended up selling the franchise to someone else before we ever even opened it. That experience helped me clarify for myself that any business I'm involved with not only needs to have a purpose, a mission larger than just making money, but it also has to be one that I connect with in a deep and meaningful way.

I want to be clear that the issue was not with the *type* of business. You can be providing any product or service with purpose and vision. In fact, there is a woman enrolled in our Force for Good Growth Accelerator who owns multiple purpose-led hair salons. Her true desire, her true purpose, is empowering women through helping them feel good about who they are. For whatever reason, I didn't feel that same calling—and it behooves female founders to listen to the voice inside to find the thing that most resonates. That is what I *am* saying here; it's crucial that what you choose is something you have a very personal connection to—and something that matters to you. This is where purpose arises.

As women, we are taught from a young age not to trust ourselves. We are trained to ignore the voice inside that warns us of danger, spots a red flag, or feels uneasy. But that voice is our power! That voice knows us deeply, and she wants only the best outcome for our efforts. Finding faith in our own, inner voice is a journey within, wrapped in this entrepreneurial journey.

You need that purpose *from the beginning* if you hope to get your company off the ground. You need it so you can keep asking after the first 100 pitch funders you pitch say "No." You need it when a regulatory rule comes out, and suddenly your profits are cut by 30% overnight. You need it every morning, to show up ready and excited to do the hard work. When you want to give up, that purpose is the thing that will keep you going. In moments of acute challenge, your purpose will carry you through.

Now, there are plenty of companies out there that don't have a purpose, or they project a purpose or market themselves as having a purpose, but it's a hollow echo. In reality, they're driven by profit. They might even be "successful" enough with that approach to generate enough money that they chart continued progress. But for purpose-led entrepreneurs, it just isn't enough to grow for growth's sake. They need more, in order to give more. That's what we're here to talk about.

YOUR COMPANY INCEPTION STORY

Now that I've shared a time when I realized it was missing, let me tell you about a time when purpose was right at the heart of it all. On my first few dates with Frank, I heard about his daughter Amelia's incredibly hard journey. She had been born at 26 weeks—14 weeks shy of the usual 40. She'd had a twin brother, Luke, who did not survive. Amelia spent her first 90 days fighting for her life in a neonatal intensive care unit. Her organs, especially her lungs, were underdeveloped. She had surgery when she was only a few days old, during which she experienced a stroke that damaged her brain and resulted in cerebral palsy. I knew all of these facts ahead of time, but when I actually met Amelia, when she was five years old, it was her bright smile that immediately stole my heart. From that moment, her energy radiated life and joy.

Amelia, my sweet stepdaughter, is the inspiration behind Allumé, the company I founded in 2016.

Because, while she was able to come home after 90 days in the hospital, Amelia required—and still 23 years later requires—around-the-clock nursing support. She receives no fewer than 20 medical treatments every single day to make sure that she continues to breathe properly and has enough oxygen to survive. She is fed through a tube. She is non-ambulatory and nonverbal.

As Amelia grew, her medical complexities grew. By the time she was 9 years old, she qualified for 16 hours a day of nursing care at home, which was covered by our health insurance. We were grateful to be granted this intensive medical support, but finding a home health provider proved to be more difficult than we imagined. We called more than 20 nursing agencies, but none of them provided that kind of around-the-clock nursing care—something that shocked and appalled us.

Thankfully, we eventually did find an agency that would take us: All Pointe Home Care—a name that will return later in the

Allumé story—was a personal blessing to our family. We worked together with them to build a team of nurses, which transformed Amelia's life—and ours. Having at-home, around-the-clock nursing care changed the trajectory of her life. The ability for her to receive medical interventions at home has kept her out of the hospital for 12 years straight.

Frank and I felt strongly that more families with medically fragile loved ones should be able to access the same kind of remarkable service that had reshaped our lives.

It was in 2016 that I sat down at my dining table with Christine and Stefanie, my first two teammates. We began by thinking about the big picture, and what we dreamed could be possible with the organization we wanted to build.

We knew firsthand how many patients remain stuck in the hospital because they don't have access to safe, high-quality nursing care at home. We wanted to change that by making the option of in-home complex nursing care more accessible. We wanted to help the families who were struggling at home with loved ones whose medical fragility was overwhelming for them on their own. Our aim was to expand access to patients and families who needed it, with a funding source in place through either their own private insurance plan or through Medicaid.

Amelia's story, the story behind why we started Allumé, was built into the heart and soul of everything we did from the start and continues to drive the actions of our merged company and the ongoing advocacy work with which I personally remain connected and involved.

Our Inception Story is told over and over: at interviews, orientations, and to every new patient and family. It is woven into the fabric of every interaction we have and everything we do. When I hear my teammates tell the founder's story, it touches my heart. It means the story has transcended beyond being *my* story . . . now it's *our* story.

This transcendence from *you*, the entrepreneur, to *our*, the collective, is an indicator that you've built something with the power to live and breathe in the world, independent of its creator.

THE STORY OF YOUR COMPANY NAME

Your Inception Story is just one of the many stories that you must craft, tell, and re-tell, in order to create a company that can exist in perpetuity as a Force for Good. At Allumé, for example, another important story passed around is how we chose our name.

At that initial brainstorming session with Christine and Stefanie, we asked ourselves how our home health company would be different from the other available options. We knew right away that we wanted what we offered to be about more than just medical care for our patients; we wanted to bring *something more* into the home. As such, we quickly homed in on how important the quality of our team of nurses would be.

I had seen firsthand how, after some trial and error, finding the right team of extraordinary nurses had transformed Amelia's care. These women changed Amelia's life, and ours. All while they deliver her care, I hear Moombi telling her jokes, Kathleen singing energetic show tunes, and Peggy reading *Page Six* out loud and talking about boys with her. When we talked about what would set us apart, I pictured Amelia grinning ear to ear, giggling, and filled with joy as we discussed how we wanted each of our patients to experience more than just a clinical, medical focus. We wanted to give them something *remarkable*.

The nurses became our focus. From day one, we knew that finding the right nurses and taking excellent care of them would be our special sauce.

This is why we named our company Allumé, which means "lit from within." We would attract and hire nurses who had light within them. Through our nurses, Allumé would bring light into people's homes.

Again, hearing our team tell the story to others lands on my heart like nothing else. Not because they are re-telling *my* story, but because *the story has become theirs.* Each nurse is claiming herself as the light as she enters her patient's home.

If your company name has a special story or meaning behind it, be sure to have it available in written form, and share it whenever possible. If you haven't yet articulated your origin stories, contemplate what your company Inception Story might be. It doesn't have to be a dramatic health-crisis situation like mine. The key is telling the truth of why your company exists, how what you do is meaningful, and how it serves others.

Take, for example, Title Nine, the first big women's athletic clothing company. It was named after the ninth amendment to the U.S. Constitution, which came into effect in 1972 and requires gender equality in all aspects of publicly funded education, including sports and athletic activities. From the space opened by that piece of legislation, teams were formed, careers launched, colleges reformed, markets made, and businesses built. And yet, in the spring of 1989, Missy Park noticed that no one seemed to be interested in athletic gear specifically built for women. She set out to rectify that wrong, and Title Nine was born in her garage in Berkeley, California. Now more than twenty years old, Title Nine Sports is still led and fully owned by Missy. Her company generates $55 million in annual sales, has 250 committed teammates, and has made a tremendous impact on women's sports. No doubt, both Missy and Title Nine are forces for good.

Lean into the lore or mystique of what makes your company special. Know what these stories are, write them down, and share them whenever you can. They should embody your deepest values, articulate your unique perspective, inform teammates' service and commitment, or tell about the transformed lives of your customers. Fostering such stories will lead to the creation of more, all capturing and furthering the essence of your company on an individual and team-wide level.

WHAT ARE YOUR COMPANY STORIES?

Now it is time to craft and share the important stories of your company, beginning with the most important: the tale of your inception. New employees and customers love to hear why you began this company. Everyone wants to be part of a heroic and purpose-filled journey. Having your story packaged in the right way and shared throughout the walls of your company will create an enduring state that transcends any one person or founder. It creates a certain kind of folklore that everyone can own.

Company Stories Builder
Use the Company Stories Builder as we walk through these steps in the remainder of this chapter:

If you are itching to get started, go to www.aforceforgood.biz/book-bonuses, where you can gain immediate, free access to the following:
1. **Answer a series of preparation questions** to help you unearth your company Inception Story.
2. **Draft your Inception Story,** inspired by the answers to the preparation questions.
3. **Share your story** right away in three simple ways.
4. **Gather other stories** that help make up the fabric of your company.

Access the Company Stories worksheet in the FFG ToolKit:
www.aforceforgood.biz/book-bonuses

1: Preparation Questions

Using the Company Stories Builder, consider the story of why and how your company was created. Contemplate these questions:

- What is the story of how your company began?

- What were the hopes and dreams the founders imagined?

- Why was the company founded? What was the deep, profound reason, beyond profit?

2: Draft Your Company Inception Story

Inspired by the answers to the preparation questions above, go ahead and write your Company Inception Story.

Here are a few tips for crafting your story:

1. **Create a real scene.** Rather than speaking generally about wanting to create a company that does what you do, describe the morning in July of 2001 when you were sitting at breakfast with your friend, Martha, and the specific conversation that sparked it all.

2. **Include names and places.** The more you can use concrete nouns, the better (e.g., the person to whom you dedicate your company, the place you were sitting when you had the idea, the person you keep in mind every day going forward).

3. **Anchor it to the present.** Within your story, include how it inspires the way your company has operated from the beginning and how it continues to do so today.

4. **Touch on the desired transformation.** Your story should paint a picture of the way your company was built to transform people's lives and bring good into the world.

Now, take a moment to draft your Inception Story using the Company Stories Builder. In the second section, you can utilize a straightforward mad-lib to craft your initial version.

3: Share Your Story

Congratulations! You have drafted the first Flywheel element of the Force for Good System™! Now that your Inception Story is written down, it can be easily shared, retold by others, and made a part of the fabric of your organization. Your company can transcend you, the founder, when others have the power to tell these stories.

Using the third section of the Company Stories Builder, brainstorm and select ways to share your newly minted Inception Story. There are hundreds, if not thousands, of ways you could share what you've come up with, but here is a list of ideas to get you started:

1. **Post on your website as part of your "About Us" section.** This will make it easy for everyone in your company (including you) to refer to it and utilize the language again and again.

2. **Share it on social media.** I recommend doing this at least monthly. Using a social-media-scheduling tool like Loomly, Hootsuite, or Buffer, you can set it up to be shared every week or month on an ongoing basis.

3. **Email it to all employees.** Distribute the written story to your team, and encourage them to share it whenever they meet a new customer or employee. It's easy, fast, and valuable.

4. **Create a video.** Infuse an additional layer of personalization and warmth onto your written story by recording yourself telling it. Add the clip to all social-media channels, your website, etc.

5. **Post it on the wall.** Create a poster with the key points of your story, and have it hung on the wall of your company entryway or conference room (or both).

6. **Add it to your email signature.** That's right! You won't forget to tell the story if it is already embedded in your signature. It could be either the whole story written out or a link to a web page, blog post, or the video you created in #4 above.

7. **Add it to your new employee-orientation program.** Ensure that each new member joining the team knows the story of why and how it all began from their first day.

8. **Add it to your sales and marketing process.** Ensure your sales and marketing presentations have the story built into them. Ideally, the story should appear and be told repeatedly along the customer journey.

There is no limit to the ways you can invoke your company's origin story into the everyday life of your business, but go ahead and select three to focus on for now.

4: Gather Other Stories

It doesn't stop there. I encourage you to collect stories on an ongoing basis. Since we first began to gather around fires millennia ago, humans have been drawn to storytelling as a way of connecting with the tribe, sharing experiences, learning from each other, and motivating the young who listened. Storytelling is one of the most powerful methods of communicating; it resonates with us on a cellular level.

Telling stories to your team and customers allows your company to come alive and develop its own personality. Each story should embody the ideas and beliefs of what your company is about and collectively demonstrate the good it's creating in the world.

Looking for great stories to tell will deepen the love and commitment your team feels for your company. As a leader, it's wise to get into the habit of telling a story each week, to model storytelling behavior and enrich your team's journey with your company. In time, they will understand the stories don't come only from you. Starting meetings with questions like, "What good happened this week?" or "Who would you like to acknowledge for delivering great work?" invites others to be the storytellers. As this occurs, your team will become more and more clear about what is important, valued, and cherished in the company, and feel empowered to bring the best of themselves each day to building a company that is a Force for Good.

CHAPTER 2
CORE PURPOSE—*WHY* YOUR COMPANY EXISTS

"Purpose illuminates your path and guides your every step."

—SHAKTI GAWAIN

Living in the Light

"Purpose is a spiritual and moral call to action;
it is what a person or company stands for."

—INDRA NOOYI

My Life in Full: Work, Family, and Our Future
Former CEO, PepsiCo

WHAT IS A CORE PURPOSE?

Nothing is more powerful in igniting commitment, alignment, and loyalty in your team than having an authentic Core Purpose for your company. Your Core Purpose is the primary, unchanging guidepost of your organization.

Your Core Purpose is the reason your company exists.

Sit with that for a moment. Your Core Purpose is the reason you created your company. It is the reason why the blood, sweat, and tears are completely worth it. It is the reason you work to foster its survival and success. It is the reason you took the risks, put everything on the line, and made all those sacrifices. It is powering the real work of your company. It is the heart-and-soul intention behind every hard thing you do, every big leap you take, and every moment you rise up.

What is the deep, true, unchanging reason your company exists?

SELECTING THE WORDS

The purpose of Allumé was to surround patients, families, employees, and our community with Remarkable Care™.

Why these words? Back at my dining-room table, it was important to Christine, Stefanie, and me that we chose the word "surround," because we wanted to provide more than just medical care. We wanted our company to encircle our clients with light—the same light referred to in our name, Allumé, meaning "lit from within." A team member in scheduling, a clinical manager, one of our hands-on clinicians caring for the patient, a social worker, the administrator, or me, the owner—all of us, the whole company, existed to surround those in our care.

We defined *those in our care* as four equally important groups:

- Our patients
- Our families
- Our employees
- Our community at large

Next came the question of *What specific kind of care?* And this is where we dug deep. We spent weeks considering to which specific transformational quest we wanted to devote our hearts and souls. We wanted to find the exact words that would best connect with and inspire the hundreds of nurses we would work with in the future, making it clear to them the unique brand of care we were talking about.

We brainstormed for weeks, trying on a parade of adjectives . . . excellent care, kind care, responsible care, authentic care, loving care, reliable care, exceptional care, elevated care, illuminated care, extraordinary care. None seemed to hit the mark—until we got to Remarkable Care™. We took a breath and sounded it out like a mantra. It felt right.

The word "remarkable" communicated several important things for us. It was professional. It instilled confidence. It wasn't too woo-woo. It wasn't too cold and clinical. More than that, "remarkable" had us thinking about the *distance we would be inspired to go to live up to the word.*

Recall from the Allumé Inception Story that we wanted to create "special" or "remarkable" moments with our people. I was inspired by our family's own outstanding team of remarkable nurses, who created special moments every day they worked with Amelia. I thought about sitting with Amelia at a parade, watching cute boys walk by and hearing her nurse, Karen, say as she was filling her feeding bag, "Isn't he cute? Right? What do you think of that one, Amelia?" and Amelia howling with girlish laughter. To me, that was remarkable.

There it was. The reason Allumé was founded. Its purpose for being in the world. To create subtle, remarkable care in the lives of our patients, families, team members, and our community. Moments where you would say to yourself and whoever was around, "Wow, that was really special." Moments of heartfelt connection, when someone experienced relief, joy, love.

Our team latched on to this concept of a Core Purpose, and our word, *remarkable*, was something that the community of nurses and families nurtured and loved. Even when we later decided to merge with another company, All Pointe, one of the questions that a family posed to one of our nurses was, "But will we still get Remarkable Care™?"

Remarkable Care™ became both a Core Value and the Core Purpose of our company. This incredible, layered commitment and focus allowed Allumé to develop deep roots in defining who she was, what she stood for, and, by golly, what she was here to do.

INSPIRING EXAMPLES

Great companies have a clear Core Purpose that directs everything they do. A great example that comes to mind is the company SPANX, which has reinvented shapely undergarments for women, offering bras, underwear, leggings, and activewear. SPANX was founded in 2000 by the inspiring entrepreneur Sarah Blakely, with the Core Purpose of "Elevating Women." As it reads on the website, "We obsess with comfort, deliver results, and ensure you look as good as you feel. We think forward, and give back. We believe women can do anything. And together, we believe we will make the world a better place . . . one butt at a time!"

Here are other examples of a Core Purpose:

- BabyQuip (founded by Fran Maier): To delight traveling families while empowering Quality Providers to build a rewarding business.

- Gotara (founded by Dr. D. Sangeeta): To close the gender gap by elevating performance of STEM teams.

- Hello Alice (co-founded by Carolyn Rodz and Elizabeth Gore): Aimed at supporting the new majority of business owners, including women, people of color, veterans, and other underrepresented entrepreneurs through democratizing access to resources and opportunities.

- MenoWell (founded by Julie Gordon White): Focused on producing plant-based meals specifically designed to improve the health of menopausal women.

- Inclusively (founded by Charlotte Dales and Sarah Bernard): Helping employers access a diverse pool of candidates and integrate them into existing workflows, thereby building a more-inclusive culture.

- Rebellyous Foods (founded by Christie Lagally): Developing a whole new plant-based food-manufacturing system that is cleaner, more efficient, and better for the people who operate it.

FOUR INSPIRATIONS OF PURPOSE

When contemplating what your Core Purpose might be, look to the Four Inspirations of Purpose to inspire you: good, knowledge, beauty, and change.

The Purpose of Good

A purpose based in delivering good seeks to deliver authentic service to others. A business with a purpose based on good holds a genuine empathy for those they serve. These are businesses rooted in expressing love, care, and compassion. Here are a few widely known examples:

- Lovevery (founded by Kellee Khalil)—To create educational toys and products that support early childhood development, helping parents foster their children's growth.

- Cora (founded by Molly Hayward)—To provide organic, sustainable menstrual products, and to give back by providing pads to girls in need around the world.

- The Honest Company (founded by Jessica Alba)—To promote safe, non-toxic products for families, with a commitment to health, sustainability, and transparency.

The Purpose of Innovation

Businesses who seek solutions, knowledge, and ideas that improve the lives of customers have a purpose based in innovation. These are companies obsessed with finding new ways of doing things and devoted to achieving that which has never been done before. It could be advancements that improve the quality or sustainability of life, animals, healthcare, nature, the environment, or the world at large. Examples include:

- 23andMe (founded by Anne Wojcicki)—To help people access, understand, and benefit from the human genome.

- Ginkgo Bioworks (founded by Reshma Shetty)—To make biology easier to engineer, transforming how we manufacture everything from food to medicine.

- HopSkipDrive (founded by Joanna McFarland, Carolyn Yashari Becher, and Janelle McGlothlin)—To innovate child transportation by providing safe, reliable rides for children, with a platform built around safety and convenience for families.

The Purpose of Beauty

The purpose of beauty is often seen through organizations dedicated to creative arts, including design, music, painting, film, and handicrafts, as well as through methods of creating a better life through laughter, play, fun, adventure, travel, or other intentional experiences. These can also be seen through companies dedicated to achieving a level of excellence that might be seen as beautiful. Here are a few examples:

- Away (founded by Jen Rubio and Steph Korey)—To elevate the travel experience by designing beautiful, functional luggage that inspires adventure and makes travel more enjoyable.

- TOMS Shoes (founded Blake Mycoskie, later led by Heather Mycoskie)—To improve lives through creative, sustainable, and beautifully designed products.

- The Wing (founded by Audrey Gelman and Lauren Kassan)—To design inspiring and beautiful co-working spaces for women, fostering community, creativity, and empowerment in environments that celebrate women's aesthetics and needs.

The Purpose of Fostering Change

Some companies dedicate themselves to a desire to change the world, not necessarily through service to others, or through discovery and pursuit of knowledge, or through the quest for perfection, but through the desire to *make a real change.* These are wonderful examples:

- Blueland (founded by Sarah Paiji Yoo)—To eliminate single-use plastic and create a more sustainable future.

- Noonday Collection (founded by Jessica Honegger)—To create meaningful jobs for artisans around the world and alleviate poverty.

- Girls Who Code (founded by Reshma Saujani)—To close the gender gap in technology and empower girls to pursue careers in coding and computer science.

CRAFT YOUR CORE PURPOSE

Core Purpose Creator

It is time to create your very own Core Purpose! Go ahead and download the Core Purpose Creator, and use it for the rest of the chapter.

Access the Core Purpose Creator in the FFG ToolKit: *www.aforceforgood.biz/book-bonuses*

If you already have language for a purpose, great! Utilize the steps below to help you deepen your connection to your existing Core Purpose, and discover new ways to bring it to life in your organization.

I will now walk you through the three-step process of creating your Core Purpose:

1. Discover Your Reason Why

2. Elicit Your Core Purpose

3. Activate Your Core Purpose

1: Discover Your Reason Why

To help you see the deep, inspiring reason why your company exists, reflect upon the questions in part one of the Core Purpose Creator. Reflect on the intentions for good, innovation, beauty, and change.

Notice that a purpose is not *what* you do. It is a broader, deeper, more-expansive reason *why* your company exists. Rather than a mission statement that articulates *how* you deliver, a purpose expresses your heartfelt driving force behind *why* you deliver and what it means in the world.

2: Elicit Your Core Purpose

Take the Leap

When you're ready, go ahead to part two of the Core Purpose Creator and craft a first draft. After you've captured a draft of your Core Purpose on paper, pat yourself on the back. This work you are doing is profound. It will enrich and deepen every aspect of your business. Your effort is worth it. Well done!

The Litmus Test

Congratulations! You have taken the first step in crafting a Core Purpose that will provide your entire team with the opportunity to align and row in the direction that matters most.

Take a moment to reflect on your drafted Core Purpose. Ensure that it passes the litmus test below:

1. **It is already true.** This is a declaration of your current and ongoing purpose. You can say it now and know it to be true. It is not something you *strive to become*—it is something you *already are*.

2. **It states who you are and implies who you are not.** It heralds who you are and who you will continue to be. It is a strategic choice. It helps you know what you are not, and it will direct what you do and don't do, now and in the future. It should be open enough to allow your organization to grow and evolve, while also maintaining a boundary about the work that isn't for your company to do.

3. **It inspires the best in everyone.** The words should do more than just state what you do. It should move and inspire your team to bring forth the best in them each and every day.

4. **It stands the test of time.** It is something you know will be at the heart of your company now and 100 years from now.

Take a moment to reflect on your drafted Core Purpose. Ensure that it passes the litmus test above. Should it not, take a moment to tweak it until it does. Or better yet, live with it as is now, and iterate with your team later. Remember: Perfection isn't necessary. Getting a first draft down is all that's needed to get you started on the Force for Good journey. In "Part Four: Be a Force for Good," I will share the ongoing system that offers built-in opportunities to update your draft and launch the new language to your team and beyond.

3. Activate Your Core Purpose

Brava!! Now that you have a Core Purpose, next is the step of putting it into action. Your Core Purpose is the seed for the most essential work of your company.

10 Steps of Remarkable Care™

Very early on at Allumé, we designed the 10 Steps of Remarkable Care™. It was our blueprint for showing up, our touchstone for being of service. The 10 Steps embodied our Core Purpose and were steeped in our Core Values.

1. **Fill up your cup.** Self-care is the secret ingredient of Remarkable Care™ providers. If you don't care for yourself, you won't be able to care for others.

2. **Be prepared.** Review your goals, schedule, and plan before you begin your day to get into the mindset of delivering Remarkable Care™.

3. **Be on time. Early, even.** Arrive smiling wherever you're scheduled to be, exactly on time or a few minutes early.

4. **Enter as preferred.** Enter the home, office, or meeting with a warm, gentle greeting, in the way your audience (the patient, family, or team members) would prefer.

5. **Anticipate and fulfill wants and needs.** Follow the schedule, plan, or agenda. Listen for spoken and unspoken wants, needs, and preferences of your audience (patient, family, or team members).

6. **Tidy, brighten, and en-"light"-en.** Your job is to bring light to every person, situation, and environment you touch.

7. **Prepare your departure.** Complete your tasks, commitments, and goals. Ensure that you leave everyone and everything better than you found it and that those you serve (patient, family, or team members) have everything they might need in your absence.

8. **Review, report, and innovate.** Review your day's progress, completions, and incompletions. Make a plan for tomorrow to be even better. Identify new ways to bring Remarkable Care™ to those you serve (patient, family, and/or team members).

9. **Fond, caring farewell.** Express a warm goodbye to everyone in your environment. Say farewell in a way that is respectful and doesn't disrupt others.

10. **Acknowledge yourself.** Give yourself loving acknowledgment for the care you provided to another. "I acknowledge myself for . . ."

We explored the depth of these 10 steps, implementing them in a host of ways:

- The system was further fine-tuned for clinicians in the field.

- A 30-minute training was developed on each of the steps and rolled out to everyone on the team.

- A self-reflection practice was developed for each of the 10 steps.

- Social media, blog posts, and marketing materials elaborated on the 10 steps.

- The 10 steps were regularly referred to in meetings.

- The 10 steps were printed on beautiful posters and hung throughout our physical space.

- They were printed on index cards and handed out during the recruiting process.

In other words, the initial, simple recipe for our Core Purpose became alive and actionable through the subsequent 10 Steps of Remarkable Care™.

Your Core Purpose System

Now it's your turn. Using the third section of the Core Purpose Creator, go ahead and craft a system that will bring to life your Core Purpose. As with anything new, give yourself permission to start small. Create a simple edict that articulates an example of what your Core Purpose means.

Draft something, and try it out. Iterate with your team. Write it down, and then talk about it, teach it, model it, demonstrate it, and lead it. This step will give you content to help you implement and lead your Core Purpose. It will give life, structure, and direction to your team.

DECLARE YOUR CORE PURPOSE

It takes courage to declare your commitment to something larger than yourself. Promising to provide Remarkable Care™ was not always easy. You can be certain our patients, families, and our employees pointed it out to us any time we didn't meet our incredibly high standard. We believe that is a good thing! Because being an entrepreneur is about being a Force for Good, about claiming your highest level of both responsibility and accountability.

To be an entrepreneur, to go out into the world and create a business out of nothing, you need to have the ovaries to declare what you stand for—that's what your Core Purpose is. When you and your team stand tall and declare, "This is the reason we exist," it sparks a willingness in each person to remain committed to a purpose even when it becomes unpopular to do so, even when it becomes hard to do so, financially, strategically, emotionally, or otherwise. We commit to this purpose because it is at the very core foundation of who we are and is what we believe is most essential and important.

THE PURPOSE OF ALIGNMENT

Crafting your Core Purpose and your Company Stories all help to build alignment within your organization, resulting in a powerful Force for Good.

Consider the importance of alignment during the moments you need your team to pull together to meet a goal, overcome an obstacle, or achieve a dramatic breakthrough. If everyone is buried in the silo of their individual job and there isn't a common purpose to unite them, your team will not have the scaffolding to rise up and direct their brilliant ideas and energy where they're most needed. A Core Purpose, well articulated and actively used in your company, provides that scaffolding.

It gives your team the ladder to climb up to the top of the building, so that they see the horizon and know where they're headed. Without that ladder, they will stay slumped unenthusiastically at their desk, doing whatever their job description tells them to do, with no heart. A Core Purpose gets them out of their chair, moved by a company's highest ideals, and excited to lend a hand.

CHAPTER 3
COMPANY VISION—*WHERE* YOU ARE HEADED

"A vision is not just a picture of what could be;
it is an appeal to our better selves, a call
to become something more."

—Rosabeth Moss Kanter

SuperCorp: How Vanguard Companies Create
Innovation, Profits, Growth, and Social Good
Professor, Harvard Business School

"It's not just about being big,
it's about changing the world in a fundamental way."

—Susan Wojcicki

CEO, YouTube

WHAT IS A COMPANY VISION?

What do you expect the world to look like 100 years from now, when you consider all the ways your company will create goodness for your customers, your team members, and your expanded community? How will people's lives have changed? Really imagine what the culmination of the aligned and empowered choices you and your team will make might look like, infused with the wisdom of your Inception Story and Core Purpose.

The combined answers to these questions inform your Company Vision, the picture of a brighter, better world made possible through the intentional impact of your business. Your Company Vision describes what is possible when everyone in your company infuses your organization's values and purpose into everything they do, and they do it for 100 years.

As we have now established together, your Inception Story and Core Purpose are the timeless, grounding aspects of your company. Your Company Vision, along with your 10-Year Impact Goal (which we'll discuss later in this chapter) is about looking ahead and planting a brilliant seed for the future.

A COMPANY VISION STORY AND HOW IT HELPED

When, after nine long years of frequent trips to the hospital, Frank and I realized that Amelia qualified for unlimited nursing coverage under our insurance plan, we were flooded with relief. With the written orders from her doctor in our hand, we thought we were days away from finally getting the support she desperately needed. In reality, it would take months of us reaching out and being let down before we found a home health agency that provided the at-home complex continuous nursing care Amelia required. And then, even when we did find such a provider, we were put on a waiting list. It was several more months still before our first nurse, Karen, became available and started services with Amelia. Access to nursing care and a founding source for all who need it has always been my vision.

When I founded Allumé, my vision was crystal clear. I wanted to provide families like ours who wanted their medically fragile loved one to be with them, safe at home, with the appropriate nursing services and a funding source that would serve them.

I know firsthand that parents of medically fragile children experience a long litany of struggles: the heartbreak of being told again and again that your child won't make it to important life milestones we take for granted; arguing with an ambulance driver who is trying to take your child to the small local hospital that won't know how to care for her rather than the specialty hospital where her doctors are; your boss saying, "I'm sorry about your kid, but we cannot have you absent from so many days of work"; the conflict of deciding to pay for a special medication not covered by insurance instead of the mortgage.

These parents live through difficult decisions and life-or-death moments every day. Many of them have other children, sometimes also with special needs. It is not unusual for them to lose jobs, file bankruptcy, and often divorce.

Our Company Vision at Allumé was a world where anyone could safely care for their medically fragile loved one at home, through an available team of caring nurses and a funding source.

Our Company Vision gave every single member of our team a purpose larger than themselves. Whether it was Jennifer in finance trying to figure out how to get insurance approved, or it was Christine insisting on finding more nurses, or it was Elaine who would eagerly work extra shifts to make sure the mother of her patient had the support she needed: this is and was our Company Vision.

It is impossible to have a truly great company without having a clear Company Vision.

Consider those significant, universally known brands. Apple changed the world with its vision of beautiful products with elegant, simple designs. Habitat for Humanity holds in focus every day on its vision of a world where everyone lives in a safe, suitable dwelling. And TED, who believe passionately in the power of ideas to change attitudes, lives, and ultimately, the world.

WHY YOUR COMPANY NEEDS A COMPANY VISION

An inspiring, heartfelt Company Vision puts the wind in your sails. *Knowing where you're headed creates indelible alignment.* This benefit is critical. To survive and prosper, more than anything else, your company needs the bright minds of your organization all moving in the same direction. This is what creates the essential breakthroughs that companies need to scale, generate prosperity, and deliver impact.

When your team is united in a Company Vision, meaningful breakthroughs become possible, and you will deliver the impact you long to create.

ELEMENTS OF A POWERFUL COMPANY VISION

Here are the attributes of a Company Vision that moves others to move mountains:

1. **Inspiring.** A Company Vision will evoke emotion and create momentum. It will cause a visceral response in both your customers and your team. It will engage the deeper hopes and wishes of what they believe could be possible.

2. **Specific.** It contains specific outcomes, goals, or manifestations that evoke absolute clarity about how your company will transform others, society, the industry, environment, or some other beneficiary.

3. **Future-oriented.** A strong Company Vision provides a clear picture of where your company will be in 100 years or more, giving everyone a sense of where to look for their true north.

4. **Grounded in Core Purpose.** It demonstrates what your company would look like after 100 or more years of everyone in your organization living and breathing the Core Purpose every day.

5. **Transformative.** Feeling like a stretch to get there, but grounded in reality, your Company Vision will require everyone in your organization—especially you—to grow, transform, and bring out their best.

6. **Prosperous.** It needs to be connected to your business, creating impact and value for others while also ensuring it can survive, thrive, and prosper. The impact made through the Company Vision must also enrich the bottom line, or ultimately you will set yourself up for misalignment. Think win-win.

7. **Force for Good.** It demonstrates how your company is a Force for Good. It is the picture of the impact you long to create amplified.

CREATE YOUR COMPANY VISION

Company Vision Expander

It is time to create your Company Vision. Building a company from scratch or growing from surviving to thriving can happen easier and faster when everyone on your team is committed. All aspects of your purpose—Inception Story, Core Values, Core Purpose, and Company Vision—give rise to heartfelt commitment. When hard times come, and they will, commitment is what keeps you and your team moving forward. At times when you feel like giving up, commitment will carry you through another day.

Access the Company Vision Expander in the FFG ToolKit: *www.aforceforgood.biz/book-bonuses*

YOUR 10-YEAR IMPACT GOAL

The next piece that any company planning to survive, thrive, and better society needs to have as part of its consolidated purpose is a long-term, big-picture Impact Goal.

What is a 10-Year Impact Goal? It is the primary and specific outcome your company intends to actualize over the coming *10 years. A 10-Year Impact Goal is the intersection between the good you long to create in society—and with your constituents—and what you define as financial success in a decade.* It's grounded in your Core Purpose and Company Vision, and is an extension of all the stories you tell about your company. It is the pinnacle of what you stand for, what you want to create in the world, and what simultaneously brings financial harvest to the business.

Why 10 years? 10 years might seem like a long time, but the 10-year horizon is intentional. My friend, Carolyn Buck-Luce, often says we often overestimate what we can achieve as a team in 12 or 24 months yet underestimate what is possible in a decade. By thinking in 10-year increments, we can envision and achieve far more for both the long-term and the short-term. This expansive view allows us to set clear, inspiring goals that drive meaningful progress. In Chapters 14 and 15, we will establish shorter-term goals that align with our long-term vision, ensuring a cohesive and ambitious trajectory.

Founded by the innovative Christie Lagally, Rebellyous Foods is a pioneering company committed to producing delicious, affordable plant-based nuggets, patties, and tenders. Their mission extends beyond creating great food; they aim to revolutionize the manufacturing process to make it more efficient and safer for employees, with the goal of addressing health and environmental issues on a global scale. The company's ambitious Impact Goal, termed the "Next-Gen Meat Machine," focuses on reducing costs, lowering energy consumption, and improving worker safety. Detailed on their website, this goal drives team motivation, spurs innovation, and contributes to the company's scalable impact and financial success.

CONFLICT AND ALIGNMENT

Contradiction and conflict are present throughout our businesses, and we often must attempt to achieve opposing goals at the same time:

- Conflict lives between our desire for perfect product quality and the desire to create an affordable product.

- Conflict lives between our desire to provide a service quickly to meet the demanding timelines that our constituents want and the needs of our team to deliver the results successfully, without giving up time with family or otherwise compromising their well-being.

- Conflict lives between our hopes to make a dramatic, meaningful impact on community and society, and our desire to generate abundance for both our teams and our shareholders.

This means that our team members, too, live in a sea of conflicting priorities and often struggle to know what to do. Without clarity about what is most important and where the ship is headed, our employees cannot possibly know exactly which decisions are best from moment to moment. They cannot know how best to prioritize their time and resources. They won't know their highest and best use because different ideals are tugging them in opposing directions.

Without clarity:

- Team members might decide for themselves what is important, which may or may not be aligned with what others believe is most valuable, leading to everyone paddling the boat in different directions, which results in everyone going nowhere.

- Team members may stop trying to prioritize and simply respond to the squeakiest of wheels, which is almost never what is truly most important.

Your 10-Year Impact Goal embraces and aligns your purpose to do good with your need for sustainable profits, crossing the chasm between the seemingly opposing forces and showing your team how they can powerfully coexist.

DECLARE YOUR 10-YEAR IMPACT GOAL

10-Year Impact Goal Distiller

It's time to create your 10-Year Impact Goal! Use the 10-Year Impact Goal Distiller to capture your thoughts and responses as you:

1. Explore the Impact You Crave
2. Select an Inspiring Impact Goal
3. Test and Edit for Key Attributes
4. Commit to Your Goal

Access the 10-Year Impact Goal Distiller in the FFG ToolKit: *www.aforceforgood.biz/book-bonuses*

THE POWER OF LEVERAGE

When you build a purpose with all the attributes we've already discussed—your Inception Story, Core Purpose, and Company Vision—and you top it off with a crystal clear, genuinely inspiring and achievable goal sitting about 10 years out on the horizon, you arm yourself and your team with the opportunity for leverage.

Leverage is one of the most important elements you need to systematically cultivate in your company as an entrepreneur. It's your key to breakthrough. It moves everything forward. It's about being able to very lightly, and with very little energy, tap the first domino and watch as all the other dominos effortlessly fall into place.

Your team is your greatest leverage—if their hearts and souls are motivated, if they know where to direct their efforts, and if they know how to prioritize the actions of their day.

Your team, united by a clear goal that has evolved from the conceptual to the specific, can be that domino at the front of the line. As you will see, your Core Purpose, and by virtue of its specificity, the Impact Goal, is the starting place for the Force for Good System™.

PURPOSE TAKING YOU BEYOND

The same purpose that launched Allumé has led me to other advocacy and leadership roles. When you have a purpose that's larger than yourself, it's probably also larger than your single business. Your company can create a connection with your industry and with a larger community, so you support something that transcends your own needs. To get what I needed for the business—a rate increase—it took years. But one of the first steps was partnering with our competitors to convince the state we'd save them money if they would facilitate the change we were looking for.

Through our combined efforts, we got just that, and those other healthcare providers who were solely my competitors are also now my collaborators. I never would have been invited to be the Chair of the Connecticut Association of Healthcare at Home if I wasn't looking at more than just my own business. Now I have the chance to be an advocate, and I am able to push for legislative change on the state and national level.

The power of purpose has held true for me time and time again, all the way through my journey, to what I'm immersed in now. Despite feeling a deep sense of commitment right from the start, I didn't feel entirely connected to A Force for Good until I discerned my purpose. Once I realized it was *women* founders who I wanted to serve, with increasing the equity of their access to networks, knowledge, and funding being at the forefront, everything fell into true alignment.

CHAPTER 4
CORE VALUES—*HOW* YOU WILL SUCCEED

"Core values act as your internal compass
in manifesting your desires."

—Esther and Jerry Hicks

Money, and the Law of Attraction: Learning to Attract
Wealth, Health, and Happiness

"Your core values are your north star. They
guide every decision, every relationship,
and how you navigate challenges."

—Rosalind Brewer

CEO, Walgreens Boots Alliance

"Values go beyond ethics. It's about your place in the
community, your place in the world. Your core values
should help you make your world a better place."

—Ursula Burns

Where You Are Is Not Who You Are: A Memoir
Former CEO, Xerox

Sitting at my dining table with Christine and Stephanie, one of the first important conversations we had was on the topic of Core Values. Your company's Core Values are those ideals that are of the greatest importance to you. They answer the question, *"How will each person in your organization ideally behave in every likely situation? What qualities will everyone need to bring to work every day to achieve our purpose, vision, and impact goal?"*

Core Values are important because they help set the stage for every decision your team makes, providing the attributes and qualities used to help determine what to do next. Core Values tell you HOW you will succeed by choosing the most critical qualities, characteristics, and guiding principles that will make it possible for your company to live its purpose, fulfill its vision, and deliver the full-scale impact and profits you aim to achieve.

Core Values also act as a critical filter for selecting each new person you choose to bring on-board. It is important to grow a team of hires who align with the values that underpin your entire operation. It's largely your Core Values that help set the culture of your organization, as they articulate HOW we choose to behave individually and collectively as a company.

Core Values don't change. They become the taproot of your business from which every branch extends. Along with your Core Purpose, your Core Values stand as the evergreen aspects of your company that give it fortitude, timelessness, and endurance.

In the spring of 2016, I led Christine, Stefanie, and myself through a workshop that I had developed years before in my work as a coach and consultant for entrepreneurs. We sat around the table and shared our heartfelt ideals for the kind of company we longed to build, and a kind of magic erupted. The act of articulating these words together infused a creative energy into the company that I can still feel today. A strong clarity and deep commitment surged between us. The torch we lit has ignited every other person who joined the company thereafter. Creating

Core Values builds a palpable bond between you and everyone in your company and calls forth the best from each individual.

Out of that workshop, we chose six Core Values for Allumé:

- **Remarkable Care™**. We are impeccable in how we care for others, ourselves, and our community.

- **Meeting Unspoken Needs**. Beyond what is asked for, we seek to understand and respectfully honor others' wants, needs, and preferences. We convey through our actions that "Allumé cares about you."

- **Highest Standards**. We are collectively and personally compelled to do the best and right thing, all the time. No exceptions. No excuses. Just a commitment to find a way and to do it right.

- **Learning and Growing**. We are passionately engaged in doing, and investing in, new things that will continuously produce better outcomes for others and ourselves.

- **Worthy of Trust**. Our gold standard is to earn and deserve trust. By being honest, dependable, and respectful, we communicate that it is safe to rely on and believe in us.

- **Enduring Strength and Sustainability**. By always finding a way to overcome challenges and being wise stewards of our precious resources, we provide steady, caring service to our patients, families, employees, communities, and shareholders.

PROGRESS, NOT PERFECTION

In concept, the Core Values you select will be a foundational, unchanging aspect of your business. However, the idea of selecting something *now* that will never change can be overwhelming. I invite you to release that sense of overwhelm. Instead, I encourage you, as I will throughout all of the lessons and exercises in this book, to not fritter and fret, not overanalyze or overthink. Just write down whatever comes to you. Trust what emerges.

I like to think of the journey of crafting your Core Values as a try-it-on-and-see-how-it-feels process. Give yourself permission to make progress. Perfection is neither required nor helpful at this stage.

Give yourself a limited period of time to freewrite something on paper. There will be plenty of opportunities to make revisions. I promise you, as we move through the Force for Good System™, you'll have opportunities to refine, and in some cases, change your Core Values. But right now, the key is to take a first pass at what your Core Values could be.

If you already have a list of Core Values at your company, brava! This means one of the key elements of being ready for a breakthrough is already in place. If not, go ahead now and use the process below to craft your Core Values.

LESS THAN FIVE

I am a strong advocate for having five or fewer Core Values to best support your company. When you have more than five, you and your teammates may not be able to remember what they are. Because you cannot focus enough attention on each of them, you won't be able to stand by them, and they lose their potency.

While five is the maximum, three is even better. At Allumé, we initially had six, but, at times, that felt unwieldy. I'm certain my teammates could not recite all of them at any given time, and incorporating six into our systems was challenging. Additionally, assessing every new hire for all six Core Values was a tall order.

Each Core Value takes commitment, nourishment, creativity, and care to implement comprehensively. And like most things, focused attention produces the most remarkable results. At Allumé, after some time had passed, I discovered there were some Core Values that were more true, more accurate, and more indelible in our culture than others. Some were a more accurate reflection of who we were, the decisions we made, and what we prioritized.

After almost five years, I saw there were only three of our six Core Values that came up again and again in everything we did:

- Remarkable Care™

- Learning and Growing

- Enduring Strength and Sustainability

The other three were simply subsets of the first three. (Meeting Unspoken Needs, Highest Standards, and Worthy of Trust were all subsets of Remarkable Care™.)

Of those remaining three, just one—Remarkable Care™—was the cornerstone of absolutely everything we did, and it became our company mantra. We developed incredibly rich content, and delivered it during our monthly Town Hall Meetings and in all of our marketing materials, that described and defined what Remarkable Care™ is and how to embody it, personally and professionally. We included Remarkable Care™ in hundreds of our practices and processes. It was ultimately our highest priority value.

Remarkable Care™, more than any plan or strategy, directed us in what to do and how to do it.

Remarkable Care™ will live and breathe in me for the rest of my life. It shaped and changed me for the better, as every true Core Value will do. This is the ultimate test of whether a Core Value is present and alive in your company: *it is actively making everyone better.* Again, I invite you to trust that the refinement of your Core Values will come with time. For now, it's about generating your starting list.

BUILD AND IMPLEMENT YOUR CORE VALUES

Core Values Revealer

In the pages ahead, I will guide you step by step through a process to craft your Core Values, following the Core Values Revealer provided at the link below. If you are reading this book for the first time, I encourage you to follow the process on your own. Later, in Chapter 17, I will provide a specific way for you to utilize this tool with your leadership team. But for now, it is good for you, the founder, to have contemplated what you feel the values of your company are before discussing with your larger team. While the input they provide later may change what you originally drafted, the exercise of articulating what is most important to you will deepen your awareness of the fundamental beliefs and priorities you choose to drive your business.

Access the Core Values Revealer here:
www.aforceforgood.biz/book-bonuses

Having Core Values written down is not enough to ensure they are actively alive in the systems and processes of your company, however. In this four-step process, you will unlock, establish, implement, and measure your company's Core Values:

1. **Unlock**—Bring to surface what lives at the heart of your Core Values.

2. **Establish**—Craft three to five Core Values that can hold up over time.

3. **Implement**—Integrate each Core Value into key functional systems so that they become built into daily operations.

4. **Measure**—Establish ways to assess that your Core Values are alive and well in your company on an ongoing basis.

If you already have company Core Values, great! Use the process below to reconnect, perhaps adjust, and reaffirm your commitment to them. Even if you don't change their essence, I promise you will find something fresh and invigorating about them that enhances your commitment to this amazing company you have created.

1—Unlock Core Beliefs

Core Values help companies determine if they are on the right path to fulfilling their goals by creating a clear philosophy about how they behave, individually and collectively. To start, record your responses in part one of the Core Values Revealer.

2—Establish Your Core Values

Now that you have done the preparation work necessary to unlock the beliefs living within your organization and found the words that best convey the attributes and behaviors most valued, it is time to craft your Core Values.

Go ahead and brainstorm a list of three to five Core Values. They are often phrases, single sentences, or words organized into a bulleted list. Some companies choose to expand upon their Company Values by describing them in more detail. To support you, I've listed a few examples below.

Bumble (Founded by Whitney Wolfe Herd)

- Empowerment: Encouraging women to make the first move and take control of their connections.

- Kindness: Fostering a respectful and positive community.

- Accountability: Upholding high standards of behavior for users and employees alike.

- Inclusivity: Creating a safe, welcoming space for people of all genders and orientations.

Cora (Founded by Molly Hayward)

- Empathy: Supporting menstrual health and hygiene with dignity and respect.

- Sustainability: Offering organic, eco-friendly menstrual products.

- Social Impact: Donating menstrual products to girls in need around the world.

- Transparency: Being open about ingredients and ethical sourcing practices.

Go ahead and list your Core Values in the second section of the Core Values Revealer.

3—Seven Core Value Tenets Test

Now that you have drafted three to five Core Values, it is time to make sure they pass the Seven Core Values Tenets test:

1. **Required.** Does it describe a value or belief that is required to build this company? Is it essential for delivering your Core Purpose, moving toward your Company Vision, and achieving your 10-Year Impact Goal? This is not a "nice to have." It is absolutely necessary. Without this value, would the company be unable to meet its goals and fill its purpose?

2. **Hiring decisions.** Even if someone is a strong individual performer, would you choose not to hire them if they don't embody this Core Value? At every level of the organization, will you hire only people who possess this value?

3. **Employee decisions.** Would you immediately counsel an employee who is not living according to this value? Would you terminate employment with an employee whose behaviors or actions did not move into alignment with this value after aforementioned conversations?

4. **Decisions.** Does this Core Value impact what you will and will not do as a company? Rather than providing general direction, does it contain the specificity and clarity that informs strategic and operational choices that will steer your business into the future?

5. **Behavior.** Is it possible to clearly define and articulate to your team the behaviors that are aligned—and misaligned—with this Core Value? Can you think of specific ways your functional systems (marketing, sales, customer service, product/service delivery, finance) would change if you fully committed to this Core Value?

6. **Long-term commitment.** Is this a value you will stick with long-term, rather than being part of your short-term strategy? Do you see this value being essential to your company long into the future? Will it still be relevant 100 years from now?

7. **No matter what.** Are you willing to uphold this value even if it becomes unpopular? Even if it becomes temporarily unprofitable at some point in the future?

If each Core Value passes all 7 tests, take a moment to ensure they also fulfill the purpose of Core Values in describing the essential **traits or qualities, deeply held beliefs, and fundamental driving forces** of the business.

Once you have drafted your Core Values, it is time to move them into action!

4: Implement Values-Infused Systems

Here is where it gets really exciting. Having Core Values is good, but having systems infused with the spirit and intention behind them will bring them to life. It's about getting these guiding principles off the paper and into practice.

Values-Infused Systems Shaper

Once you have selected three to five Core Values, use the Values-Infused Systems Shaper to reflect on how you can imbue every area of your business with the characteristics and qualities you deem most essential.

Access the Values-Infused Systems Shaper in the FFG ToolKit:
www.aforceforgood.biz/book-bonuses

Here, it is important to ensure that ***each function completes its goals and breakthroughs while also embodying the company values***. It's a worthwhile investment. Taking the time to infuse each Core Value into every function of your company will amplify and hasten the achievement of your goals, and generally boost your organization's readiness for breakthroughs.

Later, in Chapter 8, we will discuss the Customer Experience and, specifically, the Three Customer Experience Improvements. The Values-Infused Systems Shaper helps you identify how you can improve company operations to be in better alignment with what is most important.

5: Measure Values Ongoing

Implementing Core Values into each function of your business is one important, game-changing way to ensure your company is set up to be its very best. Another essential step to ensuring everyone in your organization is living, breathing, and embodying your Core Values is to measure and track each Core Value.

The truth is, what gets measured gets done; what you focus on expands.

Most companies track revenue, expenses, and profit. You might also track service volume, marketing leads, and closed sales. You track things that are important to you, the things you want to make sure happen perpetually.

To get started, I invite you to select one metric to track for each Core Value, something that would strengthen your commitment to said Value. Over time, add other key indicators.

At Allumé, Remarkable Care™ was at the center of everything. One aspect of it that was incredibly important to me was making sure each nurse in the field felt remarkably cared for. This is why sending handwritten thank-you cards was so important to us. All members of the leadership team and members of our scheduling team were asked to send out at least five handwritten thank-you cards every week. And during our Weekly Dashboard (more on this in Part Four), everyone would report their metrics, including the number of thank-you notes sent.

Values-Infused Metric Maker

Discovering a few key metrics that demonstrate you and your team are living up to the standards of your Core Values will set your team up for remarkable success. Coming up with these simple indicators of your Core Values can be super fun once you get the hang of it, but when you start out, you might be scratching your head and thinking, "How do I measure integrity?" (or Remarkable Care™, or Commitment to Learning and Growing, or whatever your Core Values happen to be). Use the Values-Infused Metric Maker to help you explore and choose ways to measure the level at which your company is embodying each Core Value.

Access the Values-Infused Metric Maker in the FFG ToolKit: *www.aforceforgood.biz/book-bonuses*

Here are examples of ways you might measure various Core Values:

- Thank-you cards sent weekly/monthly

- Town Hall Meetings monthly

- Trainings on "Core Value" monthly

- People who read the "book of the month"—aimed at learning more about a Core Value

- Calls to customers to thank them for their service

- Company newsletters sent featuring something about a Core Value

- Social-media posts about a Core Value sent weekly

- Text messages sent to team members weekly to inspire a Core Value

- Employees participating in weekly company luncheon

- Employees participating in monthly community-service day

- Nominations submitted monthly by employees for stories that demonstrate a specific Core Value

The ways you measure your Core Values will depend on what they are at your organization. The more specific you are with your Core Values—*What do "High Integrity" behaviors look like? How can employees express "Commitment to Excellence?"*—the better. The deeper you embed clear, measurable actions that demonstrate each Core Value, the more your company culture will be enriched and transformed by it.

THE POWER OF CLARITY

After intentionally articulating and implementing your Core Values, the process becomes about engaging your employees in working and living in true alignment with the ideals and values co-created by you and your team. Going the distance to define what you value creates a whole new level of understanding within your organization about what is expected, valued, appreciated, and prioritized.

Think of it like this: When you give a value like "integrity" a meaning in your organization, and you match it up to certain behaviors and activities each person is doing—like ensuring every nurse arrives to her shift on time, or always delivering a project to a customer on budget, or confirming the safety of all staff who leave after the 3 p.m. to 11 p.m. shift—and those activities are measured as what matters, it starts to become a key thread in the fabric of every team member's daily life.

Implemented this way, your team knows integrity is important, not because you have "integrity" written on the wall, but because integrity is called out and demonstrated again and again in multiple ways throughout your company. Soon, the Core Value of "integrity" will show up more prominently in your team members' other life roles: as a partner, spouse, parent, daughter, sister, friend, and community member.

Set your values high, nurture them with love, and let them be the wind beneath the wings of your team and your company.

IT'S TIME TO SERVE

Now that you have completed Part One of the Force for Good journey and defined your Inception Story, Core Purpose, Vision, 10-Year Impact Goal, and Core Values, it's time to refocus attention on those you serve.

PART 2
KNOW WHO YOU SERVE

"The best way to find yourself is to lose
yourself in the service of others."

—MAHATMA GANDHI

"When we serve others, we find our true purpose."

—DEBBIE FORD

Your Holiness: Discover the Light Within

"It's not just about selling a product or service; it's about
enriching lives. That deeper emotional connection
is what transforms a customer relationship."

—MINDY GROSSMAN, CEO, WEIGHT WATCHERS

There are two primary audiences that every entrepreneur has to keep at the forefront of her mind: her team members and her customers. Part 2 of *A Force for Good* is dedicated to the latter, those you serve.

I'm very intentional with the language I use here; it's not about who you're selling to. They're not just customers. They're constituents. They're partners. Providing them true value and earning their trust require that you build your company's processes mindfully. It requires you to get in their shoes and consider: What is the gift you're offering to them, and what is the gift that you're receiving in turn? It's about service.

My perspective on service in business began to take shape in 2002, when I founded my consultancy firm, WorldChangingBusiness. There I was trying, as every founder does, to get my business off the ground and gain traction. There were all kinds of marketing programs out there about how to write the perfect pitch, how to put together the perfect sales letter, how to do this and that to get your funnel right. I was doing everything I could, everything that everybody told me to do, but it just wasn't working. Sound familiar?

At the same time, I was doing a lot of internal work in my personal life and utilizing guided meditations to help me to tune into and trust my inner voice. I had grown my daily practice of listening to my wisdom, but I hadn't integrated it into my business process yet. All of a sudden, that struck me as so silly—*of course*, it should be part of my business approach! It was then I decided to write a meditation for myself around my customer: *Who are they? What do they want? What do they need? How can I give to them what they most crave?* There was no specific outcome I had in mind. The goal wasn't to figure out what to say in a particular pitch or meeting. I was simply pursuing a more-intimate level of understanding of my customer.

I transformed what is often a very mechanical, analytical exercise of trying to define one's demographics for their market into deep questioning—an inquiry of the soul. I leaned on the internal place that I'd cultivated over the years, from which I can call forth wisdom, and tried something new. This was the first time I had given myself permission to integrate that part of myself into my methodology for work. It made a difference.

I came out of that first meditation with a clear picture of who I was called to serve with my unique contributions, and how meeting their needs would bring out the best in myself. That radically shifted the voice that I used with WorldChangingBusiness. I held the idea of that specific person in my head while I was doing everything—and it transformed my results. I was speaking out of meaningful truth. I was coming from an earnest place of abundance and wholeness.

My work at WorldChangingBusiness became about taking necessary concepts such as marketing and connecting them to the higher self, inviting meaning into even the seemingly mundane. When we talk about being of service, it's not so much an exercise of the mind as an exercise of the spirit. In the years since, I have realized I can always be sure of when I'm really drawing from my core while speaking to my audience, because, in those moments, it brings about true and meaningful results.

Through that experience, I developed a guided meditation called the Authentic Customer Avatar Experience. I've turned to this guided-visualization exercise many times over my years of working with founders and teams. We'll explore that meditation in the chapters to come, but it's about bringing dimension and clarity to your understanding of those you serve. It's about shifting that customer from a concept in your head to a person in your heart. It's a very important piece of the Force for Good System™ because it stems from a place of authentic generosity, whereas so much of the sales and marketing out there comes from a place of scarcity. It's about "I have gifts to give" rather than "I need something from you."

Part 2 kicks off with Chapter 5, which will help you answer the incredibly important question, *"Who is your customer?"* through an exercise designed to guide you toward a succinct and clear definition of who your company's primary customer is.

Chapters 6, 7, and 8 will explore the question, *"What do you do for your customers?"* What specific benefit, desire, or outcome does your company deliver to those you serve? How is the customer experience of interacting with your company and utilizing your solutions? Which products or services drive the most profit into your company?

Chapter 9 encourages you to put your "*Who*" and "*What*" together to build a remarkable system for engaging, enrolling, and connecting with your most desired customers.

Taken altogether, the purpose of the next five chapters is to shift your relationship with customers from transactional to transformational. Once you embed the deeper meaning of how you serve them into your process, the value you will bring to their journey—and the enrichment they will bring to yours—will elevate every aspect of your business.

CHAPTER 5
YOUR AUTHENTIC CUSTOMER

"You have to feel love to harness its power."

—RHONDA BYRNE

The Power

"When we focus on what matters, we can build something truly remarkable."

—MELINDA GATES

The Moment of Lift: How Empowering Women Changes the World
Co-Founder, Bill & Melinda Gates Foundation

"Engagement comes from feeling heard. Our customers must know that we are not just *selling* to them—we are *listening* to them."

—BOZOMA SAINT JOHN

Chief Marketing Officer, Netflix

Your business exists to be of service. When you accept what an inspiring gift that is, you and your team are empowered to serve not just with the mind but also with the depths and power of the heart.

Homing in on a particular type of customer and dedicating ourselves wholeheartedly to serving them enables us to enter into an even-deeper and, dare I say, soul-connected relationship with them.

I call this specific type of customer an Authentic Customer. They are the perfect match for your company, with its specific purpose, values, and strengths. They make up the audience who long for what you offer and derive the greatest value from what your company delivers and will, in turn, provide you with the assurance that the work you do matters.

Society tells us that bigger is better and that more is preferred. As purpose-led entrepreneurs, we must rise above that message. Trying to be all things to all people is a desperate and shortsighted pursuit grounded in the belief that customers are scarce. Try to speak to everyone, and no one will hear you. However, if you instead focus on one customer—your Authentic Customer—your message will resonate in the hearts of those who hear it, and your business will prosper. This is why crafting your Authentic Customer Avatar is essential. You must know who they are and trust that they're out there, which will allow you to get down to the important business of being truly great at what your company uniquely provides to the world.

YOUR AUTHENTIC CUSTOMER AVATAR

Your Authentic Customer Avatar is the vivid picture and story behind a single person your company is best suited to serve. Developing an Avatar helps you define the specific market you are meant to inhabit by having the courage to drill it down to just one individual persona.

When your company shifts from speaking to the masses with a generalized and impersonal voice to having every communication feel like it was written to a singular persona, your company has the power to create intimacy and a much-deeper connection with the market.

You are here to serve a very specific audience. If you allow it, the relationship you create with this specific type of customer will open you, and your company, to new levels of greatness. The Authentic Customer Avatar guided visualization outlined in this chapter is one I have been using for 20 years. It has served me and the others I've shared it with well, and it can be used in many ways.

The guided visualization and the corresponding tool will allow you to discover the following:

1. The image and personal attributes of the single person you are meant to serve

2. Their primary challenges and complaints that your business can address

3. The hopes and fears they have about your journey with them

4. The transformational journey your company is meant to lead them through—the deeper need that lives hidden within

5. The feelings they want to feel (and the ones they want to avoid)

6. The life changes they want to make

7. What they are here to teach you and your company, provided you are willing to listen, evolve, and grow

8. Where they most need your company's greatness to shine through

THE GIFTS OF AN AUTHENTIC CUSTOMER AVATAR

Having an Authentic Customer Avatar at the heart of what you do helps foster a more-meaningful commitment to your audience and allows you to discover their deeper needs, which, otherwise, would remain hidden. This will help you:

1. **Hone Your Voice.** Understanding your Authentic Customer Avatar enables your company to determine the most effective tone, messaging, and personality for communicating with your audience.

2. **Find the Best Fit.** Some prospective customers will not appreciate your approach, not resonate with your values, and not care about your purpose—and that's okay. A clear, thoughtful voice will attract your most desired customers, the ones you're meant to serve, allowing your team to do its best work for those who derive the greatest value from what you offer.

3. **Cultivate Real Engagement.** Being able to speak directly to what your customer is looking for, thinking about, and interested in transforms your marketing and communications, leading to a more-effective, powerful, and dynamic conversation with those you serve.

4. **Grow External Trust.** When your customer feels like you genuinely understand their motivations and care about them, you build the important bridge of trust needed for them to consider implementing your product or service into their lives.

5. **Develop Internal Integrity and Alignment.** Because your company is deeply focused on delivering solutions that customers truly need, marketing and selling your products and services

will feel more like a mission than a transaction. This removes all fear and conflict from making the sale, emboldening your team to become evangelists for your brand and to do so with conviction.

6. **Loyalty.** All of this works together to organically establish and further the loyalty of your customers and your team.

7. **Be Preceded by Your Reputation.** Once you have loyal fans as both customers and team members, the positive reputation of your company will grow and spread, creating a virtuous cycle that draws in more customers and attracts great hires.

MEET YOUR AUTHENTIC CUSTOMER AVATAR

It is now time for you to create your Authentic Customer Avatar. Even if you have done an exercise like this in the past, I invite you to take the opportunity to do it again. This process tends to bring forth something new and profound every time you do it. I encourage you to embrace your imagination as you move forward through this process. Avoid the urge to think about an actual person who exists, and do your best not to get hung up on the specifics. Instead, allow your mind to answer the questions posed effortlessly, without worrying about getting it "right." Take liberties, and trust whatever answers come, even if they don't make immediate sense. This process is not intended to be the end-all, be-all of the market research you might ultimately conduct. In Chapter 6, we will dive deeper into a more analytical approach to understanding who you serve. The primary purpose here is to humanize your prospects and customers, to help you see and feel what it is like to be them. As you move into this space, your understanding of their true desires, needs, and fears will evolve and create a deeper sense of meaning and purpose as your heart connects to theirs.

Authentic Customer Avatar

There are two tools available to you at this juncture.

First, there is a guided-visualization exercise called the Authentic Customer Avatar Experience. I invite you to take a deep breath, still your mind, and, with a spirit of gratitude, discover who it is your company is authentically meant to serve.

In the visualization exercise, you will imagine that you are having tea with someone you are authentically meant to serve in the future. The idea is simply to allow yourself to connect at a heart level with one such customer, knowing that there will be thousands of others who might be similar to this person. As you pose your questions to this imaginary companion, let their answers come to you simply and effortlessly, writing down the first thing that comes to mind.

The second tool, the Authentic Customer Avatar Designer, will help you craft a company-wide persona to help you align and serve a focused market.

The object today is not to try to define your target market, per se. We will do that in Chapter Six. Free yourself from trying to think strategically about how you answer the questions or which person you choose to invite to visit you. Rather, gently allow your inner wisdom to carry you, and you will find exactly what you need from this journey.

- Authentic Customer Avatar Experience
- Authentic Customer Avatar Designer

Access Authentic Customer Tools in the FFG ToolKit here:
www.aforceforgood.biz/book-bonuses

THE POWER OF GRATITUDE

Being in touch with the humanity of your Authentic Customer opens the door to feeling "of service," which is a powerful force in business. The sense of purpose it brings elevates the work we do and cultivates teamwide positivity. In this framework, your employees will be happy to go to work every day, which has a palpable trickle-down effect on the level of service your company is able to provide. The gold standard of creating remarkable culture is when your team feels grateful to be of service.

In previous chapters, we discussed the importance of creating clarity, alignment, and commitment, and then leveraging each throughout the constructs of your business. Gratitude is another important ingredient in building a purpose-led company capable of experiencing tremendous breakthroughs. Think of it like this: Your customer-service representative can answer the phone feeling bored or feeling eager to help. Your bookkeeper can code transactions as quickly as possible just to get it done, or she can do it with care, knowing the numbers are connected to real people. Your service team can rush through their tasks while thinking about their lunch break, or they can find pleasure in the faces of those whom they will serve today. Gratitude truly has a transformative effect at every level.

Now that you know your Authentic Customer intimately, you can home in on creating and improving your products and services to be exactly what they need.

CHAPTER 6
PURPOSE-LED SOLUTIONS

"When we serve others, we are contributing
to the healing of the world."

—CAROLYN MYSS

Invisible Acts of Power: Channeling Grace in Your Everyday Life

"Creating an authentic connection with your customers isn't
just about delivering what they bought; it's about creating
community and belonging around your service."

—JULIA HARTZ

Co-Founder and CEO, Eventbrite

"We must strive to humanize every interaction with
our customers, creating trust through each touchpoint."

—RASHMI SINHA

Co-Founder and CEO, SlideShare

As entrepreneurs, our deepest hope is that our products and services will enrich the lives of customers in unique and palpable ways. A Purpose-Led Solution is a product or service you offer that will create this effect. In this chapter, you will articulate what that deeper value you aim to provide to customers is.

Purpose-Led Solutions live at the intersection of these four ideals:

1. Your Company Purpose

2. What your Authentic Customer yearns to receive

3. The specific products and services you offer

4. What drives company growth and profit

PURPOSE-LED SOLUTIONS

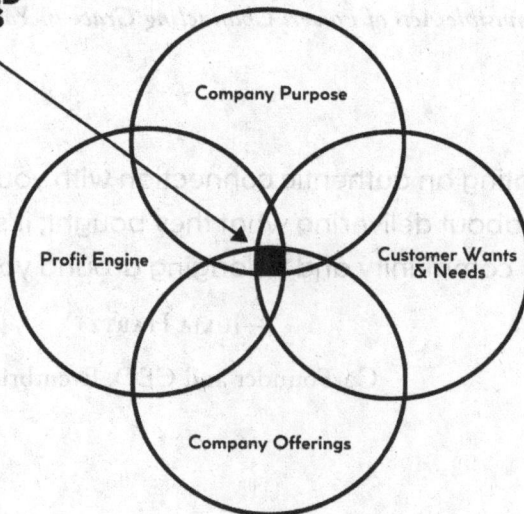

Company Purpose

Profit Engine

Customer Wants & Needs

Company Offerings

All four elements need to be in place for your products and services to provide the momentum needed to align company purpose, customer needs, the solutions you provide, and the financial engine that fuels profit. Brought together, these four elements bring about more interested prospects, more satisfied customers, and more committed employees, all of which automatically translates into growth and prosperity.

Since you already know your Company Purpose from Part One (Inception Story, Core Purpose, Vision, 10-Year Impact Goal, and Core Values), the key to this section is to drill down into the other five areas:

1. Who your customer is

2. What your customer needs

3. How you are positioned to serve

4. What you offer

5. What generates profit

Together, these topics will help you extract what is most important to your customer and how to align customer needs with company profits.

WHO YOUR CUSTOMER IS

The goal is to shift our focus from our own experiences and into the experiences of others. My dear friend John Grady often says, *"I know I'm not much, but I'm all I think about."* This always makes me chuckle, mostly because of just how true it is. We are all very consumed with seeing the world from our own perspective.

The pages ahead invite you to move into the mind of your customer. Remember, the goal is to go from relating to customers in a transactional way to providing them a transformational experience. So often, as business owners or employees, we focus on the product we offer rather than the person who will use that product. We think about how great our product is, what it does, and how we make it. All of this is about ourselves. To create, deliver, and sell something remarkable, this must change.

Say, for example, you're in the business of selling shoelaces that help kids learn to tie their shoes. Your Authentic Customer is a 34-year-old mother named Julie, who works part-time as a bookkeeper, attends business school at night, and is married to 38-year-old Martha, who travels three days a week as an architect. They have a five-year-old daughter, Pearl, who is enrolled in public school in Park Slope, Brooklyn.

This is *who your customer is*.

WHAT YOUR CUSTOMER NEEDS

The next step is to determine *what your customer needs*.

Julie desperately wants to help her five-year-old little girl, Pearl, learn how to tie her shoes, because Julie hates to see her child struggle and not succeed where other children in her preschool class are achieving. Thus, while teaching Pearl how to tie her shoelaces might not be able to fill *all* of Julie's needs—her desire to finish her MBA, balance a part-time job, and manage the home while her partner travels—it can help her feel like she's supporting her little girl in feeling confident about herself.

Julie's Many Wants and Needs

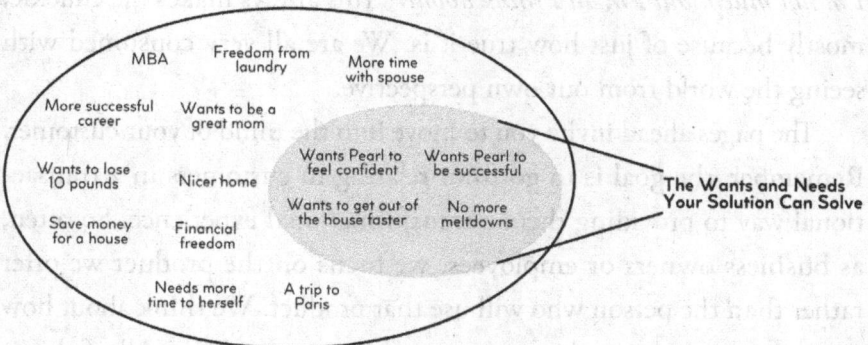

68

If you didn't really think about Julie and instead think only from the perspective of your product, you might not get to the heart of why Pearl knowing how to tie her own shoelaces could be so impactful for Julie and mothers like her everywhere. You might think the greatness of Pearl's shoelaces lies in the special fiber you use, or the cool colors, or in the unusually wide width. It's only when you take the time to understand Julie as a person that you see how you might help her fulfill her desire to be a great mom, get out the door in the morning without losing her mind, and continue to keep things running while her partner travels. You might miss that Pearl's shoelaces are about building confidence, one preschooler at a time. You might overlook the beautiful moments of mother-child connection that can be bridged through something as simple as shoelaces.

The WHO + WHAT Builder

Here you return to the mind of your Authentic Customer from Chapter Five. Again, without over-thinking, this Tool encourages you to list all the possible needs and desires your Authentic Customer might have. It then leads you step by step to distill who your customer is, what they need, and a single "WHO + WHAT" statement that articulates your company value proposition.

Access the WHO + WHAT Builder in the FFG ToolKit:
www.aforceforgood.biz/book-bonuses

HOW YOU ARE POSITIONED TO SERVE

Once you have clarity and alignment on who your customer is and what they need, next comes how you are positioned to be of service. We will look at positioning through these lenses:

- Market Size

- Macro Trends

- Buying Triggers

- Competitive Analysis

- Market Positioning

Market Size

First, examine the size and scope of your market. How big is your total worldwide market? How big is the market you want to serve? Who are the customers you would like to target and serve now? This examination helps you understand the bigger picture. It helps you learn from a larger aperture of customer need.

There are three common ways to size a market:

1. Total Available Market (TAM)—The total worldwide demand for a product or service in a given market. It encompasses all potential customers or revenue opportunity for a particular product or service, without considering any constraints.

Example: If you're in the business of selling smartphones, the TAM would include every potential buyer of smartphones worldwide, regardless of brand preference or affordability.

2. Serviceable Addressable Market (SAM)—The segment of the total available market (TAM) that your business can effectively serve or target, based on its resources, capabilities, and constraints.

Example: Using the smartphone-business example, if your company sells only high-end smartphones, your SAM would be the portion of the TAM that consists of customers willing and able to afford high-end smartphones.

3. Serviceable Obtainable Market (SOM)—The portion of the serviceable addressable market (SAM) that a business realistically expects to capture or obtain within a specific timeframe, considering competition, marketing efforts, and other factors.

Example: Continuing with the smartphone business, if your company forecasts that it can capture 15% of the SAM within the next year, then that 15% represents the SOM.

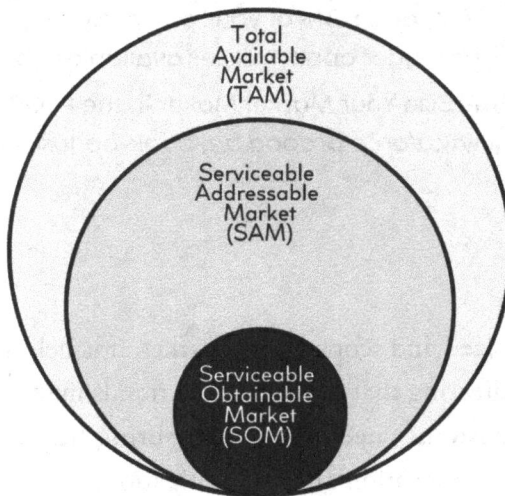

Understanding TAM, SAM, and SOM enables you to differentiate your company from other alternative solutions (competitors) and carve out a unique position in the market. By focusing on underserved or niche-market segments, companies can tailor their offerings to meet specific customer needs and differentiate themselves based on value proposition, customer experience, or other consumer-perceivable factors.

Drawing from the shoelaces example above, the TAM might be children's teaching toys, tools, and accessories. The SAM might be children's learning wearables. And the SOM might be kids' shoelaces in North America.

Knowing the broader view of your market also keeps you open to future possibilities. It is a reminder of future markets your business could one day serve. It is a reminder of what is possible as your company delivers its purpose at scale.

The Size Your Market Maker

Step by step, you are guided, as you define the TAM, SAM, and SOM of your company, helping you see the bigger opportunities available to be of service.

Access the Size Your Market Maker in the FFG ToolKit: *www.aforceforgood.biz/book-bonuses*

Macro Trends

Once you have sized and scoped your market, it is helpful to know the Macro Trends affecting that market. Some trends may bring tailwinds, creating more customer need. Some may bring headwinds, creating opportunities for innovation and risk mitigation.

Macro Trends are overarching patterns or changes in the broader environment that impact multiple industries and markets, shaping consumer preferences, market dynamics, and business opportunities.

Understanding Macro Trends will allow you not only to anticipate and adapt to changes in the market landscape but also to align products, services, and marketing strategies with prevailing Macro Trends. This allows you to better meet the evolving needs and preferences of Authentic Customers, resulting in increased relevance, resonance, and sales potential.

Macro Trends help articulate *why* the market needs your company.

Using the shoelaces example from above, a 2019 study[1] showed 46% of parents of children in kindergarten thought that being able to tie one's own laces was an important life skill, yet 62% of parents admitted to tying their children's laces for them to save time and stress every morning. The study also showed that 76% of parents said they taught their children to tie laces at home, with only 14% relying on school to teach their child. Notice how these statistics validate the need for special shoelaces.

Here are other illustrative examples:

- The COVID pandemic led to a shift to remote work, and several companies pivoted successfully. Modern Fertility thrived with at-home fertility-testing kits, meeting the demand for remote healthcare. Eventbrite supported virtual events and online ticketing, allowing continued event hosting. Guild Education offered online education and upskilling, essential for workers enhancing their skills from home.

- The rise in demand for sustainable products has led to the success of women-led companies. Thinx produces reusable period underwear, reducing disposable waste. The Honest Company offers eco-friendly baby care, personal care, and home products. Eileen Fisher's fashion brand prioritizes sustainability with organic, recycled materials and a clothing take-back program.

- AI has transformed every industry. Zebra Medical Vision enhances diagnostic accuracy with AI-analyzed medical imaging. X2AI uses AI chatbots for accessible mental-health support and therapy. Stitch Fix employs AI and machine learning for personalized fashion recommendations and improved online styling services. Narratize

---

1 https://www.lifestyledaily.co.uk/article/2019/09/20/3–10-children-cant-tie-their-shoelaces#:~:text=Of%20the%20500%20surveyed%2C%2046,time%20and%20stress%20every%20morning.

uses AI to create scientific, technical, and medical insights, and distill them into impactful content that scales.

Macro Trend Explorer

Investigate and explore all the external forces affecting your market. Home in on specific trends that present risk and other trends that present opportunities. Identify the larger market conditions that validate the need for your solution.

Access the Macro Trend Explorer in the FFG ToolKit: *www.aforceforgood.biz/book-bonuses*

Buying Triggers

Next, consider your company's position in the market by looking at customer-buying triggers. Buying triggers are the cues—psychological, emotional, or practical—that compel consumers to make a purchase. These triggers could be driven by the need to solve a problem, seize an opportunity, or satisfy an emotional or aspirational goal. Understanding these triggers helps you create a more seamless and satisfying customer experience. It also helps you create a more intentional, impactful experience for those you serve.

Think of Julie and her five-year-old, Pearl. Here are some possible triggers that would lead to Julie recognizing her need for special shoelaces:

- Kindergarten is coming soon. Helping Pearl know how to tie her shoes will help her feel confident.

- Another morning of tears! Pearl tried again and again and could not make the bunny ears tie into perfect loops.

- Pearl looks crushed! She noticed two other friends able to tie their own shoes when leaving today's playdate.

- Pearl's sixth birthday is coming! Our little girl is growing up! Let's support her in taking the next steps as a big girl.

- Here are some other examples of triggers in other industries:

- A software engineer realizes they need a new laptop because their old one is slow and unreliable, hindering their productivity. They recognize the need for a faster, more efficient device to meet their work demands, giving a computer-hardware company a perfect opportunity to serve.

- A couple discovers they are expecting a baby and realize they need to purchase baby essentials such as a crib, stroller, and baby clothes to prepare for the arrival of their newborn, offering the perfect introduction to a baby-equipment company.

- Mom just took a new job and needs to move her family—husband, four children, and a golden retriever—to NYC and needs to find a new home fast. Given the very limited supply of 3+ bedroom apartments, they know they will need to choose quickly, opening door for NYC realtors.

- A month before spring break, and, somehow, a family from Minnesota hasn't yet made plans! A travel agency promotes limited-time discounts on spring-break-vacation packages designed for a family reprieve in the sun.

Buying Triggers Mapper

Use the Buying Triggers Mapper to help you identify a list of core moments when your customer will have a heightened sense of need for what your company offers.

Access the Buying Triggers Mapper in the FFG ToolKit: *www.aforceforgood.biz/book-bonuses*

Competitive Analysis

While focusing on your Core Purpose, Vision, 10-Year Impact, Goal, and Values must *always* be the most important driver of your business, studying your competition can also provide great context on your market and help you see how your business can be uniquely great and deeply satisfying to Authentic Customers.

As humans, we are creatures of contrast. We find clarity and definition by seeing what resonates and what doesn't, what we like and what we don't like, what soothes and what repels. Reflecting on your competition will help you home in on what makes your company distinct, desirable, and different.

A competitive analysis is a strategic evaluation in which a business identifies key competitors and researches their products, sales, and marketing strategies to understand their strengths and weaknesses relative to its own. In the FFG system, we do this in service of discovering the underlying, unique value we can offer as a company.

For example, a quick look at the shoelace market reveals several other companies that offer shoelaces for kids. From Catery, whose laces promise to stay tied, to U-lase, who offers "no tie" laces, to Xpan, who offers extra-wide rainbow-colored laces that claim to be easier to tie— knowing the other options available to Julie and Pearl help inspire your shoelace company on how to be unique.

Have no fear of competitors. Every company has competitors. It is valuable for you to know the alternatives your Authentic Customer has in meeting their needs. Additionally, the presence of other successful players in your market demonstrates there is a real need. It demonstrates customers already exist who will pay for a product or service that solves the specific need your company addresses.

Also, the success (and mishaps) of others in your market will help you navigate a journey that requires sure footing. Learn from the brilliance of others who have traveled before you, and you you'll be able to avoid potholes and discover shortcuts.

Competitive Analysis Framework

In this worksheet, you will follow this simple step-by-step process:

1. Identify Your Competitors
2. Build Comprehensive Criteria
3. Draft Your Competitive Matrix

Access the Competitive Analysis Framework in the FFG ToolKit: *www.aforceforgood.biz/book-bonuses*

Market Positioning

Market Positioning is the image or identity of a brand or product in the target consumer's mind relative to the other providers in your market.

Positioning differentiates your offering from alternative solutions in a way that builds resonance within the hearts and minds of your Authentic Customers. The ultimate goal of market positioning is to occupy a distinct and valued place in the target-customers' minds, leading to increased customer loyalty, brand equity, and brand preference.

Position Through Contrast

Positioning can relate to a variety of factors:

- Perceived quality being low or high.

- Pricing can be inexpensive, value, or luxury.

- Your company might focus on selling directly to consumers or only to businesses.

- The size of the companies you serve might be solo entrepreneurs, micro-businesses, mid-sized companies, or enterprise-sized companies.

Consider how your brand contrasts with the other options available to customers in your market.

Position Through Brand Identity

In addition to contrast, brand identity is crucial for market positioning. It's the visual and emotional impression your brand makes on consumers. The personality and emotions your brand evokes greatly influence how potential and current customers view your company. By intentionally choosing a brand identity that deeply resonates with Authentic Customers, you build connection, trust, and understanding with your target market.

Other important aspects of your brand identity include how you communicate visually through brand colors, fonts, typography, images, and symbols. We also communicate through our core messages, tone, and the words we use when speaking to customers.

Your Position Statement

Your Position Statement is a declaration that summarizes a brand's unique value and its promise to the market.

Use this fill-in-the-blank mad-lib format to help you craft your Position Statement:

For [Target Audience], [Company]
is the
[Single Most Important Claim]
because
[Evidence that Supports the Claim].

For example, for our shoelace company, the Position Statement might be . . . "For active moms and bright kids, Savvy Kids offers simple-to-learn shoelaces that encourage children to develop independence, because confidence nurtures lifelong enthusiastic learners."

Here are a few other Position Statement examples:

- Thrive Market—for health-focused shoppers. Thrive Market is the premier online retailer of organic and non-GMO products, delivering sustainable shopping at wholesale prices. Thrive Market offers carbon-neutral shipping and zero-waste warehouses, and has donated millions of dollars in healthy groceries to families in need.

- Grameen Bank—for the underserved and unbanked populations. Grameen Bank is a pioneering microfinance institution, offering small loans to empower and promote entrepreneurship without requiring collateral. Grameen distributed more than $24 billion in loans to impoverished individuals, boasting a repayment rate higher than traditional banks.

- Zipline—for remote and underserved communities. Zipline delivers life-saving medical supplies via the fastest autonomous aircraft, revolutionizing access to urgent healthcare. Zipline has completed more than 200,000 commercial deliveries, including vaccines, blood, and medical supplies across multiple countries.

Market Positioning Analyzer

You will be easily guided to do the following:

1. Build Your Positioning Matrix
2. Explore Your Brand Identity
3. Articulate Market Differentiation
4. Declare Your Company Promise
5. Craft Your Position Statement

Access the Market Positioning Analyzer in the FFG ToolKit:
www.aforceforgood.biz/book-bonuses

WHAT YOU OFFER

Now that you know your customer, their needs, market size, trends, triggers, competition, and positioning, it's time to articulate how your company is of service. What you offer includes far more than your products and services, though, certainly, they are among the important items to consider. What you offer includes all the following:

1. Your talent-attraction, -engagement, and -retention process (human resources)

2. Your engagement process (marketing)

3. Your enrolling process (selling)

4. The specific products you sell

5. The way you build or create what you sell

6. Your customer-support systems and approach

7. Your customer-retention and -loyalty process.

8. Your customer-complaint-and-resolution process

9. Your quality-assurance process

10. Your research-and-development process

11. The way you bill your customers and receive payments

12. The technology you use in all aspects of your business

13. Anything else you do to satisfy the needs, wants, and desires of a customer.

Your company, how it operates, and the myriad of ways you support and serve customers is what you offer. Often, we are shortsighted, limiting ourselves to just what we sell. This leaves out all the other ways your company is already delivering value. And with focused awareness, you can create even more all-encompassing, wholehearted, and transformative ways to serve customers.

Once you start to think about your customer wants, needs, problems, and preferences, you and your team will likely come up with all sorts of ways you could elevate the way you serve—again, so that your connection with your customer transcends from transactional to transformational.

What You Offer Developer
Here you will map out the wants, needs, and desires of your customer, and all the ways your company offers specific solutions.

Access the What You Offer Developer in the FFG ToolKit:
www.aforcegood.biz/book-bonuses

WHAT GENERATES PROFIT

After using the What You Offer Developer to help create a comprehensive list of the ways your company satisfies the desires of your Authentic Customer, it is time to think about the specific products and services you sell, what is selling best, and what is generating the most profit.

What Generates Profit Clarifier

You will use the **What Generates Profit Clarifier** to help you explore your many product and service offerings, and identify which solutions amplify profit. This information will be helpful both now and in Part Three, where you'll choose a strategy and create a big-picture plan for your company.

You will create a list of all your products and services and identify the following:

1. Which products and services you're most successful selling
2. Which products and services have the highest profit per unit
3. Which products and services are generating the most profit to your company overall

Access the What Generates Profit Clarifier in the FFG ToolKit: *www.aforceforgood.biz/book-bonuses*

Why is this information valuable? As you will notice, it helps you see which solutions you sell that are both most popular with your customers *and* driving profitability. It will help you consider on which solutions to focus more marketing effort, which products to drop, which services might need improvements, and which ones need lower costs. Very quickly, you will be able to identify which solutions are driving value to customers *and* profits to your bottom line.

From here forward, you will start to see more metrics incorporated into our journey. Metrics give you the power to know what to do. Much of the work we have done thus far has been based in intuition or qualitative analysis. We will now start layering in hard data, which will help your mental clarity about where you are today and how you will arrive at wherever you want to go.

We covered a lot of ground in this chapter, delving into (1) who your customer is, (2) what your customer needs, (3) how you are positioned to serve, (4) what you offer, and (5) what areas of your business generate profit. Having spent time examining and articulating these facets of your company, you are now able to see what you might like to adjust in your approach or what improvements could be made. These tools can also serve as a communication and discussion tool to use with your team to help everyone become aligned.

Remember, a Purpose-Led Solution is a product or service you sell that truly enriches the lives of your customers. Now that we've explored the intersection of the four ideals that inform such a purpose, it is time to move into the next important topic related to Knowing Who You Serve: your company's Area of Chosen Greatness.

CHAPTER 7
AREA OF CHOSEN GREATNESS

"The universe buries strange jewels deep within us all,
and then stands back to see if we can find them."

—Elizabeth Gilbert

Big Magic: Creative Living Beyond Fear

"Owning your greatness means being unapologetically
you and shining your light without fear."

—Danielle LaPorte

*The Fire Starter Sessions: A Soulful + Practical Guide
to Creating Success on Your Own Terms*

One of the greatest challenges as a leader lies in declaring where you want to be great. It is the novice leader who thinks that all parts of the business are critically important. They give into the temptation to try to be excellent in every area. Unfortunately, being super at everything essentially means being great at nothing. It takes a wise and, dare I say, *brave* leader to select the area where you feel your team or organization can truly shine. An even-wiser leader knows where *not* to be great, where to lessen your commitment to resources in order to instead go all-in on one or two things where you aim to be truly remarkable.

Greatness requires commitment, determination, innovation, and investment. Your Area of Chosen Greatness is where you and your team opt to prioritize additional time and resources—even at the expense of other areas—to be remarkably great at meeting the needs of your Authentic Customer. It is that group alone, those you serve, who can report that your company is great; you cannot self-evaluate on your Area of Chosen Greatness. You should be getting positive feedback consistently and passionately from those who really count.

Rather than being a jack-of-all-trades and master of none, I invite you to chase greatness. Choosing where to be great requires evaluating three factors:

1. Where you are uniquely suited to be great

2. Where your audience longs for you to be great

3. Where being great will drive the economics of your business

THE TENETS OF GREATNESS

Let your deliberation of where you are suited to shine be guided by the following Tenets of Chosen Greatness:

1. **It is one thing.** It's not about being good at everything; it's about identifying the single area where you want to excel and dedicating ten times the energy and attention. Focus on what truly matters, and pour your resources into that area, knowing it will make a significant impact and is worth the investment.

2. **It is already in your company's DNA.** It is unlikely to be something completely new that you aren't already aware of or doing to some degree. Much like your Core Values, it is something you already are, but when you name it, choose it, and elevate it, it can make your company more than it is today.

3. **It can be informed by your purpose.** No doubt, where you should prioritize and invest in lies somewhere within the crux of your purpose. As you try to feel out what that is, consider your Inception Story, Core Purpose, Company Vision, 10-Year Impact Goal, and Core Values.

4. **It matters to your customer. A lot.** It should fill a deep, core need within those you serve, and the thought of receiving it should be something that creates a surge of positive energy within them.

5. **It separates you from the pack.** It needs to be unique and something that sets your company apart from the other players in your market.

6. **It makes everything else better.** You don't have to worry about investing so much of your resources into this one thing, because, as you become truly great at it, it naturally elevates everything else that your company is doing.

7. **It fuels profit.** Because this one thing solves a big problem or satisfies the desires of your customers, it also fuels your profit engine and adds to the overall success of your company.

8. **It is measurable.** What you measure you can improve, and that is crucial for attaining greatness. Without having some way to quantify what you're doing and how it's working, it is near impossible to know if you're achieving greatness or how to continue moving in the right direction.

EXAMPLES OF CHOSEN GREATNESS

Let me give you an example of choosing where to be great.

From the moment I founded Allumé, I was searching for that one clear way we should choose to be great. I thought about it constantly with my team, but it wasn't until we went through the amazing process of mapping out the journey of our customer (which I will invite you to do later on) that the mystery was revealed. In this case, we studied the many needs and challenges of our Authentic Customer, Judy, the mother of a child patient receiving around-the-clock nursing care.

From this exploration, we discovered **two outcomes we wanted to create:**

1. selecting nurses who genuinely loved caring for others

2. consistently filled nursing schedules

We could see that by hiring and keeping the right nurses, and by having a consistently filled nursing schedule, we could create the most acute relief for the patients and families we served. This led us to ask the important question: *"What specific area of greatness would help us produce these two outcomes?"* After some deliberation, the answer was clear: **We needed to be great at hiring and retaining reliable nurses who genuinely love caring for others.**

Pause for a moment, and consider this choice. Allumé was a nursing agency. Yet, our Area of Chosen Greatness was not about nursing or clinical operations. It was about being remarkable at recruiting and retaining the right nurses. I offer this for your consideration: sometimes a company's area of greatness is the less-obvious path of focusing on something other than the product or service itself.

Consistency was most important to the families and patients we serve, even over having a full schedule. We knew that a mother dealt better with a schedule that was not full but was entirely reliable, versus a full schedule on paper, but with lots of last-minute nurse call-outs. Hiring people who would show up and provide top-notch care with no exceptions is what mattered most. The parents of our patients could handle knowing certain shifts were not going to be filled in advance, with time to prepare, whereas last minute call-outs were extremely upsetting.

Our one thing was clear. And choosing to be great at hiring and retaining the right nurses was not only good for our patients and their parents, but it also fueled our company's growth. The more hours that were filled by consistent nurses, the fewer complaints we would receive, which reduced the workload of our schedulers. The more hours filled, the easier it was to oversee the patient care, which meant fewer needed RN Case Managers. After figuring out our Area of Chosen Greatness, our primary constraint to growth was not needing more patients but not being able to hire enough of these high-quality nurses quickly enough to fill all the schedules.

Our Area of Chosen Greatness drove everything.

In the most obvious, targeted way, it affected who we would hire and whether we deemed them to be, first, someone who genuinely loved caring for others, and, second, someone who was competent, reliable, consistent, and would rarely call out. But it also informed the processes and resources we put in place in order to accomplish that driving goal, such as:

- Choosing to see nurses and team members alike as our primary customer and orienting our entire marketing engine around nurses

- Building a recruiting playbook to ensure every single nurse we interviewed would feel valued, appreciated, and deeply cared for

- Creating a series of programs designed to attract, train, engage, and retain our team

- Cultivating our "employee-first philosophy," which radically differs from the typical approach of "customers first."

- Launching a monthly Town Hall to engage and empower our nurses.

As you consider what your areas of greatness might be, ensure that it passes the litmus of all eight tenets. To help you imagine where you might be great, let's look at some examples of where other companies have chosen to be great.

Southwest Airlines focuses on friendly service to frequent point-to-point locations. Thus, their aim is not to be in every airport going to every location. Rather, they home in on specific hub locations and go back and forth between those locations constantly. This lets them master the art of getting in and out fast, which means each plane makes more profit per minute. They have also held true to their identity as a "friendly" airline and haven't tried to be a "luxury" provider. This enables them to focus on a specific market who values a lower price in exchange for some of the perks and luxuries of other airlines. All of this allows Southwest to sell lots of tickets at the lowest possible price to the customer they long to serve.

Ikea and its founder, Ingvar Kamprad, unapologetically and proudly declare to their customers that their furniture will come in a box—that customers have to locate and pull from the warehouse shelves themselves—and requires at-home assembly. In exchange for this, customers are assured a wide selection of appealing, modern design at the lowest possible price point. This model set Ikea apart from the competition, making it the most valuable furniture retail brand in the world, valued today at more than $21 billion.

BRINGING PATIENCE TO THE PROCESS

Some might call your Area of Chosen Greatness your "unique selling proposition," but I am incredibly focused on the benefits of being intentional with language. To me, a "unique selling proposition" sounds misguided. It seems centered around success being defined by selling alone, and being influenced by external factors, rather than internal.

That's not the energy we're looking to channel here. Instead, claiming your greatness calls for patience, because what often happens during the journey to getting it right is attempting several things that don't quite get you there. It can be tempting to try to expedite the process. You're a business owner, and you need sales. You want to do the thing your customers want, so that they'll buy from you. And you end up looking in the wrong places. You might check out what your competition is doing; look to see what the headlines are talking about; pull from what's trending on social media.

However, finding what your company is designed to be great at is a self-reflective process, not merely an analytical exercise. It's not about studying the quadrant of different things you could be great at by mapping out speed and precision and cost. It is found through plumbing the DNA already present in what you're building. It comes from purpose.

I have a timely example of what I'm talking about. While writing this book, my team and I worked on the messaging around it, trying to figure out what was truly authentic, in terms of supportive materials and, also, what would stick. I really wanted the answer to be self-service tools created to accompany a *Force for Good*. That would be most convenient for me because it's scalable. It's economical. But there was no traction. It was a bit too forced, a touch too calculated. However, as soon as I started talking about my passion for supporting women founders, aha! I started to get more traction. It was coming straight from my heart. My excitement was driven by getting my authentic customers excited, and the cycle went on and on. I got to dwell in my deeper sense of truth. As I watched the engagement on socials start to climb, what I had been envisioning morphed. I began to talk about it not as just self-service tools but as an ecosystem—as a community, because that's what it is.

When I really reflect on what makes me a great leader, it's that I build communities of elevated prosperity. I try to make sure everybody else is at the heart of it—not me. Before, I tried to strongarm an Area of Chosen Greatness that didn't have my customers at the core. I didn't capitalize on what was uniquely made possible through a Force for Good, when it was obvious that the overlap between what this business does and my ardent love for women founders was the sweet spot. Again, part of being an early-stage company is holding the willingness to play those things out while also making sure you have the right analytics in place to measure what is and isn't working to meaningfully attract people. There, you find the perfect coalescence of your Core Purpose, what you really do well, and what somebody is going to pay for.

THE 17-STEP CUSTOMER JOURNEY

About a year after Allumé was launched, one of our board members offered to lead us through an exercise to help us imagine the journey of our customer, which we found to be an incredibly valuable practice. In this section, I will guide you through a modified version of this process, the "Journey of Your Authentic Customer." This will help you choose where your company should elect to be great by seeing where your customer needs your greatness.

In Chapter 5, through a guided-visualization and journaling exercise, you created your Authentic Customer and began to study the complexities of who they are as a person. In this section, you will imagine that fleshed-out Authentic Customer interacting with your company through the lens of their thoughts, feelings, and experiences.

As we slice it, the customer journey has at least 17 steps. That may sound like a lot, but understanding the journey a customer goes through deserves that level of attention. So often, we miss the nuances of what they are experiencing and, as a result, miss all the ways we could serve them. Realizing that each stage presents opportunities to shine, create connection, and develop a win for your customer is key in figuring out where to be great.

Journey of Your Authentic Customer

As you complete the Journey of Your Authentic Customer, remain mindful that your Area of Chosen Greatness may be something that transcends just one stage and is the base that needs to be present throughout, or it may be something that happens at one specific moment in the journey when you want to indelibly rise above the pack.

Walking through the Customer Journey can help clarify where you should choose to be great, serve as an effective way to identify areas to improve, and be used as a training exercise to help deepen the connection of every team member with your customer. That said, I recommend that you first take the Authentic Customer Journey now, on your own, and then again, later, with your team. When you're done with the Journey of Your Authentic Customer, you're ready to move on to the next section.

Access the Journey of Your Authentic Customer
in the FFG ToolKit:
www.aforceforgood.biz/book-bonuses

CHOOSE YOUR AREA OF GREATNESS

Congratulations on completing the Authentic Customer Journey! Now you have everything you need for you and your team to decide where to be great.

Area of Chosen Greatness Identifier

It's time! Use the Area of Chosen Greatness Identifier to help you make a powerful choice to make your company remarkable. Be sure to have the following at hand to help you make your choice:

- Journey of Your Authentic Customer (from earlier in this chapter)
- The WHO + WHAT Builder (from Chapter Seven)
- What You Offer Developer (from Chapter Seven)
- Authentic Customer Avatar Designer (from Chapter Six)

Access the Area of Chosen Greatness Identifier
in the FFG ToolKit
www.aforceforgood.biz/book-bonuses/

Well done! Choosing your area of greatness is a very important step in the operation of your company. Whatever it is, acknowledge that pursuing your area of greatness can only make you better. It can only lead you forward. Should you decide to change it later on, so be it. But for now, let this one thing shape you and your company into something remarkable.

CHAPTER 8
CRAFT YOUR CUSTOMER EXPERIENCE

"People will forget what you said, people will forget what you did, but people will never forget how you made them feel."

—Maya Angelou

"Make the customer the hero of your story."

—Ann Handley

Everybody Writes: Your Go-To Guide to Creating Ridiculously Good Content

"Leadership is not about being in charge. It's about taking care of those in your charge."

—Ursula Burns

Where You Are Is Not Who You Are: A Memoir
Former CEO, Xerox

The next step of Part Two, Know Who You Serve, is crafting your customer experience. Every interaction a person has with your company—your team, your product, your communications, your marketing, your billing process—creates an experience for the customer.

Those interactions will either serve them, or they won't. The aim is to craft every experience to elevate the moment and move your relationship from transactional to transformational.

Pause for a moment to reflect upon what goes into a great customer experience. What creates remarkable customer moments? What elicits a palpable positive feeling? What forges satisfying customer memory? Oftentimes, these questions lead into discussions about our marketing and sales funnels or our customer-services systems. These are both important elements to consider, but building a unique, impactful customer experience comes from more than just what you do. It comes from more than the language you use on your website, social-media posts, and email newsletters. You have to take a step back and consider the necessary base from which those things rise.

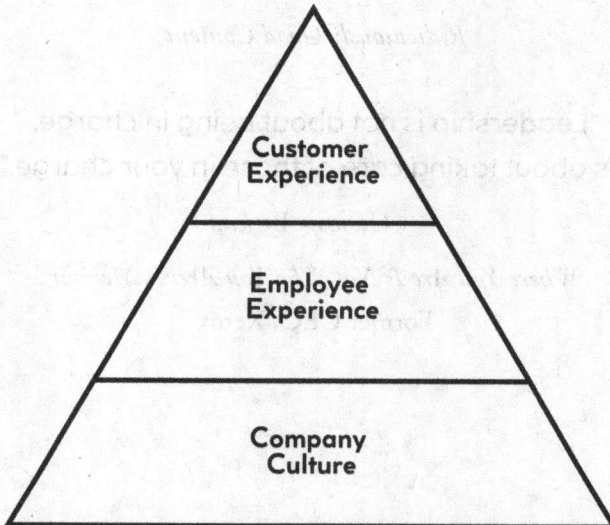

Customer
Experience

Employee
Experience

Company
Culture

Creating the best possible customer experience, then, relies upon a company's culture. A powerful, effective company culture can exist only when a business's employees are passionate about and devoted to what it stands for. Your team needs to be individually and collectively empowered to serve, interacting with customers in authentic ways that are consistent, while individualized. In other words, a profound customer experience is born out of a remarkable employee experience, and the interplay between those two depends upon a healthy, carefully constructed company culture.

THE ELEMENTS THAT CREATE REMARKABLE COMPANY CULTURE

Over the course of this chapter, you will figure out:

1. **Three Feelings to Cultivate**—The specific feelings you want to create for your customers (and your team) through every interaction you have.

2. **Your Impact Mantras**—These are three to five guiding phrases that remind you and your team of the impact you are longing to create.

3. **Three Improvements**—How you will boost your company culture, which elevates both the employee and customer experience. Even as you resolve outstanding areas that need work, keep three improvements on this list so that the experience of customers (and team members) is always being bettered.

THREE FEELINGS TO CULTIVATE

"Knowing how you actually want to feel is the most
potent form of clarity that you can have."

—Danielle LaPorte

The Desire Map: A Guide to Creating Goals with Soul

At the heart of every customer journey lives a set of needs and desires. How do your customers feel before these are met by your company? How do you hope they will feel after? Here is where you select Three Feelings to Cultivate, consciously chosen, that will help you internally, consistently connect with the hearts and minds of those you serve. The aim is to move the emotional experience of customers:

- from a problem to the solution

- from pain to relief

- from overwhelm to calm

- from happy to fulfilled

What are your customers feeling that they want to transform? What are the feelings they want to elevate? Where do you want them to end up?

Why Is Feeling Important?

Recall, from Chapter 6, when we tracked the Seventeen Steps of the Authentic Customer Journey, one of the lenses we looked through was the lens of feeling. Perhaps you noticed the highs and lows your customer experienced along the way. At certain moments, your customer might feel more excited and hopeful, while at others they may feel more frustrated or even angry. It is important to understand the overall tone of their experience. Some businesses, like a clothing retailer or an amusement park, might experience customers in a generally light, happy state, while other businesses, like hospitals or funeral homes, have customers who are generally in a more somber mood.

Ideally, the many messages, images, and experiences your company provides will meet your customer where they are and then aim to elevate them. Taking someone from devastated to ecstatic is probably too big of a stretch, but devastated to composed might be just what a person needs. Sense what your customers might be feeling, and try to understand what would soothe, heal, elevate, or transform them.

Once you select the three distinct feeling transformations you want to bring to your customer's journey, they are to be brought to every message, interaction, web page, phone call, social-media post, etc.

As I mentioned in Chapter 8, Allumé selected our Area of Chosen Greatness to be recruiting, engaging, and retaining nurses. With that, our team became our primary area of focus for everything. Thus, when we considered our nurses and what they most longed to feel, we surveyed them on their desires and expectations of an employer, and we assessed their core motivations. We discovered that what they long for is to feel *valued, appreciated,* and *deeply cared for.* As we dug deeper into the needs of our patients and families, we found their longings were similar. Thus, these feelings—value, appreciation, and deep care—became the intended feelings we wanted to cultivate for the company. We aimed to ensure these feelings were embedded into every system, process, and communication we made.

Feelings Empower Your Team

Articulating the specific feelings you're aiming to create in simple, clear terms can also prove incredibly empowering to every single member of your team. If they understand the specific feelings your company is looking to bring to every situation, and you give them the power to implement that on their own terms, in their own way, and with an authenticity that only truly held feelings can convey, then powerful change will occur. Further, bringing those good feelings into your meetings, conversations, internal communications, and SOPs is what makes your brand feel genuine, authentic, and real.

Select Three Feelings to Cultivate

Three Feelings to Cultivate Finder

Getting the needed feeling into your company is a game-changer. Using the Three Feelings to Cultivate Finder, we will walk through the steps to help you choose the three feelings to cultivate again and again in your business:

1. Meet Them Where They Are
2. Uncover What They Want to Feel
3. Commit to Three Feelings to Cultivate

Access the Three Feelings to Cultivate Finder in the FFG ToolKit: *www.aforceforgood.biz/book-bonuses*

Meet Them Where They Are

In order to support your customer on their journey to transformation, you must know and feel where they are when they arrive at your door (or website, or your ad in a magazine).

It is important to be laser specific. If they are feeling hopeful, what components are playing into that? If they are feeling discouraged, which word precisely characterizes their annoyance? It is also helpful to remember that how your customer is feeling while searching for the solution you offer varies dramatically, depending on what you offer. If your customers come to you shopping for bridal shoes, they will feel very different from someone planning a funeral and needing a casket for a loved one.

Below is a link to a list of feelings. Feel free to go deeper or use a thesaurus to help you uncover words that most express how your customers feel when they come to you.

Identify the top-three feelings your customers are experiencing when they first come to your company, before their problems are solved and desires are met. Use the Three Customer Improvements Selector to write down your answer. These feelings depict where you, as a company, must always meet your customers.

Here are some examples:

- A bride-to-be looking for bridal shoes might feel **hopeful, elated, and nervou**s when she arrives at Beatific Bridal Shoes.

- A mother looking to enroll her third-grade daughter who has just been diagnosed with dyslexia into an online reading program is feeling **overwhelmed, worried, and fragile**.

- A CFO struggling each week to provide the data her CEO and Board of Directors want to receive because the information lives in several disparate systems, visits ABC Data Integration website feeling **defeated, frustrated, and stressed**.

Feelings Words List

To help you find specific words you would like to cultivate, review the list of possibilities on the Feelings Words List.

Access the Feelings Words List in the FFG ToolKit:
www.aforceforgood.biz/book-bonuses

Uncover What They Want to Feel

Having defined how the customer is feeling as they approach you, and knowing what you can offer, it is time to determine the leap in feelings you are looking to cultivate.

Draw on the examples above to see what each prospective customer wants to feel:

- The bride-to-be looking for bridal shoes arrives feeling hopeful, elated, and nervous. She longs to leave with a pair of perfect bridal shoes—ones that make her feel like royalty. She wants to feel **beautiful, celebrated, and 100% certain** she is leaving with the pair of her dreams.

- The mother looking to enroll her third-grade daughter with dyslexia into an online reading program longs for a program that will help her daughter experience success in reading. This will help transform her experience from feeling overwhelmed, worried, and emotionally fragile to **empowered, relieved, and grateful**.

- The CFO who felt defeated, frustrated, and stressed from not being able to quench the CEO's desire for information will feel **triumphant, resilient, and self-assured** when she rolls out the new integrated-data dashboard.

Notice how the journey of the customer led them to new, desired feelings. After you brainstorm the list of the emotional states you'd like to deliver for your customers, review the feelings you wrote down. Notice how some might be very similar, like *excited* and *elated*, while other feelings are uniquely different, like *triumphant* and *self-assured*. Ultimately, your three feelings will be truly unique from one another and express a three-dimensional experience.

Now it is time to choose the three specific feelings you want to incorporate into every aspect of your company brand, communications, images, and experiences, using the Three Feelings to Cultivate Finder.

YOUR IMPACT MANTRAS

Impact Mantras inspire the best in ourselves and allow our teams to be set free. As entrepreneurs, we are given the privilege of building a community—composed of both the people we work with and our customers—whose lives can be bettered through our companies, should we allow it. I have observed that Impact Mantras can transcend the workplace and get to the very heart of why I believe purpose-led businesses are a Force for Good. They foster intentional living and positivity that can spread to our homes and larger communities, shifting the way we agree to interact with one another. Personally, I believe this is how we move mountains.

Impact Implies Action

The word "impact" was carefully selected and refers not only to big, wide-reaching ways we hope to impact our communities and the world but also to how we can make a difference through our small, everyday choices. Impact implies action. It is not only about what we do, but the intention underpinning it. That's something that can be felt every time a receptionist answers the phone, each detail when a retail sales-clerk arranges merchandise, in the way a server sets a table, or how a programmer keys her code. A customer-service rep answering a phone call who is deeply committed to "surrounding every person she meets with Remarkable Care™" changes the texture and tone of how she says, "Good morning. Thank you for calling Allumé Home Care. How can I serve you?"

Examples in Action

Impact Mantras not only inspire your team to be and do better but also help create consistent experiences inside the walls of your company and out in the world. Like the feelings we choose to cultivate, these words empower the company to know how to serve each other and the customer.

The athletic-wear brand for women Title Nine embodies this wonderfully. "Our philosophy at Title Nine can be summed up with one of my favorite sayings: 'Not all things that count can be counted,'" says founder Missy Park. Another important mantra at Title Nine is "Our 'models' have day jobs." Rather than hiring runway beauties to feature their wares, Title Nine chooses "ordinary women doing extraordinary things," which aligns and reflects the Core Values of the company. "They are the carpool organizer, the woman leading the meeting, and the one making her case . . . They are athletes and moms, with careers and causes."

How Women Lead, founded by my dear friend Julie Castro Abrams, is a community of twenty thousand C-suite executives, board directors, and experienced entrepreneurs. All women. Every meeting or event begins with the community credo: (1) be fierce advocates for each other, (2) say yes to helping each other, (3) be unabashedly visible, and (4) reinforce her voice. These mantras elevate the community and how we interact with one another, and establish a new standard for how women can support each other in the world at large.

Here are a few examples from Allumé:

- **Surround every person you meet with Remarkable Care™.** This Impact Mantra means we will go the extra mile to provide those we interact with whatever they might need. It is meant for patients, their family members, and our team members alike. Whether it is a patient returning home from the hospital, a mother struggling with a personal challenge, a team member frustrated by a project that's behind schedule, or a field nurse who made a mistake and was beating herself up about it, our mantra of "surround them with Remarkable Care™" results in everyone thinking outside the box, going the extra mile, and giving their all to help.

- **How can I support you?** This simple phrase is perhaps the most powerful of our Impact Mantras. Whenever anyone is upset, confused, angry, or frustrated, we ask them, "How can I support you?" These words ring through our hallways. Rather than responding with defensiveness, or immediately supplying a fix, or looking for someone else to blame, we model and coach the use of this question in an acknowledgment that struggling humans need a moment of pause to be heard and to feel cared for.

- **Listen for unspoken wants, needs, and preferences.** Most (maybe all) of our patients are non-verbal. This means their bodies cannot tell us what they want, need, or prefer. It is entirely up to us to bridge that gap. In training, we discuss Maslow's Hierarchy of Needs and how even a person who is hospital-bed bound has a need for belonging, contribution, self-actualization, and transcendence. We invite our team members to deeply contemplate more than just the physical needs of their patients and realize how they are serving a purpose on the planet. We encourage our nurses to reflect that back to their patients so that our patients will know that their beauty, light, and significance had been witnessed. While this impact statement was initially directed at our patients, we came to use this with everyone. It applies to the families we serve, our teammates, and our referral partners in the community; it helps us all focus on being of effective service to others.

■ **Catch people doing the right thing!** This is a statement we use to cultivate appreciation, encouragement, and gratitude with our team. So often, we in the office find reasons to reach out to field-team members only when they have "done something wrong." We encourage our office team to "catch people doing the right thing" and use that as a reason to send them a text, write them a nice email, or even drop a handwritten thank-you card into the mail with a lottery ticket inside. Being in the mindset of looking for what is right instead of what is wrong is at the heart of our culture. This Impact Mantra allows us to breed this intention across the company.

Impact Mantras Developer

Use the Impact Mantras Developer to build your list of positive, inspiring, guiding statements to activate within the walls of your company. As you build Your Impact Mantras, take a moment to breathe and digest. Dwell on the deep hopes you have about how your team is meant to interact with each other—and the world—through your company. Own that your ongoing commitment to bring these intentions to fruition is what separates your company from the masses. It's what makes your company a Force for Good.

How to Use Them

There are a myriad of ways to infuse Impact Mantras into your company culture. Here is a short list of ideas to get your creative juices started:

1. Lead an internal training event to discuss each one.

2. Post them on the walls of your office, both individually and collectively.

3. Include them repetitively in social media.

4. Sprinkle them throughout your company website.

5. Include a different one each week in your email signature.

6. Blog about them.

7. Host a roundtable discussion with your team about what each of them means.

8. Put them on company notecards.

9. Print them on the back of your business card.

10. Send them to your team via a postcard through the mail.

11. Ask members of your company to contribute new Impact Mantras. Vote on them, and add the winners to your list.

12. Collect 12 and put them on a company calendar that you give to your team and customers.

13. Dedicate a month to each Impact Mantra. Every day, send out examples, tips, videos, and fun ways to inspire its use.

A Company Mantra

You may find that one particular Impact Mantra is especially reflective of your purpose and culture. Should this be the case, allow it to become your Company Mantra. At Allumé, Remarkable Care™ is ours. It can take a bit of time, but if and when a Company Mantra emerges for your organization, go deep and far with it. A Company Mantra has the power to build tremendous clarity within your team about who you are and what you stand for. The word "remarkable" became sacred to us at Allumé. It entered our conversations daily and organically grew into the corners of our culture. When members of our team wore their "remarkable" T-shirts, drank from their "remarkable" water bottles, and carried their "remarkable" backpacks, it meant something. We even had a nurse who asked for an extra-small "remarkable" T-shirt so that she could make a shirt for her dog. Every Monday, when the two of them came into the office sporting their matching T-shirts, I got the sense that this nurse truly felt "remarkable." This makes my whole heart smile.

THREE IMPROVEMENTS

Building your company culture to bolster both employee and customer experience is a constant pursuit. Your company is a living, breathing organism. It requires attention and oxygen to prosper. Always having three areas of improvement you're actively working on ensures that your culture will continue to grow and evolve. Especially for high-growth companies, what worked to create culture for a team of four likely needs to evolve when the team is made up of fifty. And while having certain traditions in place fosters continuity and an unshakable base, introducing new mechanisms reminds yourself and the team of what you stand for and wards off stagnation.

It is valuable to have a running list of ways you would like to improve your customer experiences, employee experiences, and overall company culture. Returning to the list on a quarterly basis and choosing three to implement or improve is a great way to keep attention on being of service and is also incredibly rewarding and fun for everyone involved. This process is a virtuous cycle that feeds the fire of customer and employee loyalty.

Brainstorm Possible Improvements

Over the last three chapters, you have contemplated who you serve and crafted the following:

- Your Authentic Service Avatar

- Your Authentic Customer Wants, Needs, and Problems

- Map of Customer Desires to Your Company Solutions

- How You're Positioned to Serve

- Purpose-Led Solutions List and Profitability

- Your Chosen Area of Greatness

- Three Feelings to Cultivate

- Your Impact Mantras

Three Customer Improvements Selector

Now it is time to translate these concepts into ideas to implement at your company. In the Three Customer Improvements Selector, you will find questions to help you brainstorm a list of ways you would like to improve your customer and employee experiences. Don't worry about when or how you will implement these ideas. Let your creativity flow. Reflect upon the work you've already done. Recall who your customer is and what they're looking for from you. Remember how your company offers the solution they long to receive, how you've chosen to be great, and how you want to make them feel. Allow all of this to direct your brainstorming. Now, use the Three Customer Improvements Selector to capture your ideas.

Access the Three Customer Improvements Selector
in the FFG ToolKit:
www.aforceforgood.biz/book-bonuses

Congratulations—you now have a map of possible improvements! Before you move on, allow yourself to imagine how good it would feel for your company to embody all of these ideas.

Prioritize Your List

Now it is time to bring some order to your list, so you can determine where best to begin. Turn again to the Three Customer Improvements Selector as you consider your list of improvements along the two scales provided.

Having completed the exercise, selecting the three improvements you want to focus on first should feel easier. Over the next quarter, make it your mission to implement those you've chosen. To get started, set a meeting right now with at least two other people in your company to discuss the launch of these improvements. Ideally, schedule it for a time in the next week; you want to capture the momentum of this moment to move your company forward in your commitment to be of service!

CHAPTER 9
CUSTOMER ENROLLMENT AND RETENTION SYSTEM

"Every connection is a new opportunity for impact."

—BECKY ROBINSON

*Reach: Create the Biggest Possible Audience
for Your Message, Book, or Cause*

"Understanding the broader context of our customers'
goals and challenges is fundamental. Only then can we truly
add value and foster a transformative relationship."

—ADENA FRIEDMAN

CEO, Nasdaq

"When we create strong connections with our customers,
we move from merely a brand to becoming part
of their lives."

—JANE WURWAND

Founder, Dermalogica

In this chapter, we will discuss the mechanics of how to build a system that enrolls a flood of authentic customers into your business, as well as the metrics by which to track its effectiveness. When building measurable systems, it can be tempting to keep it purely intellectual. Resist this! Include your heart in the process of crafting your customer-enrollment system, and keep service firmly at the center.

At its healthiest and most effective, enrolling customers is about *being of service* rather than *making a sale.* This framing infuses the act with grave importance as you look to build connection and trust with the people you serve—and to do so at a deep, genuine level. The goal is to bring inspiration, transformation, relief, and hope to those who engage with your company; building the right customer-enrollment system helps accomplish this aim by acting as a bridge to authentic solutions.

Moving away from the "trying to make a sale" mindset matters. When that's your focus, you are acting from a place of scarcity and desperation. That feels bad internally in and of itself, but it is palpable also to potential customers, getting in the way of cultivating the desired connection that leads to long, mutually beneficial relationships. Instead, adopting a position of generosity and gratitude is elemental to the success of your business.

THE PURPOSE OF A CUSTOMER-ENROLLMENT SYSTEM

A customer-enrollment system is the mechanism that moves those you're looking to serve along the journey from initially discovering that your business exists, to the moment they choose to become your customer, and through to the ongoing process of providing value and deepening existing relationships. The Customer-Enrollment System attracts, engages, educates, enrolls, and re-enrolls the ideal people who could receive value from your company and solutions.

The levels of relationship with those you serve—now and into the future—can be broken down into six categories:

1	**Suspects**	Suspects fit the profile of your authentic customers; you would like to create connection with these people but haven't yet.
2	**Prospects**	Prospects are those who have, in some way, learned about your business, products, or services but have not yet made a purchase.
3	**Qualified Prospects**	These are prospects who have taken clear steps to get to know your business and the offerings you provide. A Qualified Prospect demonstrates a match for your products and services and has the budget to pay for them.
4	**Customers**	Customers are individuals or companies who have purchased something from you, exchanging dollars for a product or service.
5	**Satisfied Customers**	A customer is elevated to this status if they have purchased from you repeatedly and/or if they have expressed explicit satisfaction through a survey or a written testimonial.
6	**Loyal Ambassadors**	Satisfied customers level up when they 1) start referring friends and colleagues to your company, 2) speak publicly about your company in a positive light, 3) participate in a case study, or 4) make some other significant show of appreciation and value for your brand.

CUSTOMER ENROLLMENT AND LOYALTY FUNNEL

There are five stages in the Customer Enrollment and Loyalty Funnel. Each stage further down the funnel represents a deeper level of connection and commitment to your products and services. The funnel is an intentionally designed method of helping build transformational relationships with every customer you serve. The funnel converts suspects into prospects, and prospects into customers, moving them all the way along into ultimately transforming into loyal brand ambassadors:

1. **Shine Your Light**—Make it possible for your ideal people to first learn that your company exists. Much like a lighthouse, you employ marketing channels that attract future customers to you at a rate and frequency needed to support the vision, growth, and prosperity of your company. *This funnel stage attracts suspects to the top of your funnel.*

2. **Deliver Profound Experiences**—Once someone discovers that your company exists, provide intentionally designed experiences that help suspects learn more about how your company can serve their wishes and needs. This could be a free report, assessment, free trial, personalized meeting, or some other specific way that delivers value to them before they spend a dime on your products and services. In this process, a suspect provides more information about who they are (e.g., name, email, phone) so that your company can connect directly with them and see how you can deliver value. *This funnel stage moves suspects into being prospects.*

3. **Make Invitations That Build Trust**—These are additional intentionally designed experiences that allow a prospect to get to know your company, learn about products and services, meet the important members of your team who can support them,

and use the opportunity to get questions answered. This stage satisfies the emotional and rational needs of a prospect, so that they can feel ready to make a purchase. *This funnel stage moves prospects into being qualified prospects.*

4. **Invite Them to Be Your Customer**—This is the moment you invite someone to be your customer. The three stages leading to this moment foster trust and give prospects the opportunity to say what they need to say: "Yes, I'd love to be your customer!" *This funnel stage moves qualified prospects into being customers! (Whoohoo!)*

5. **Connect and Nurture**—Beginning with customer onboarding, this is a (hopefully) long and fruitful stage, where your company serves customers for years to come. *This funnel stage moves customers into satisfied customers and later into loyal ambassadors.*

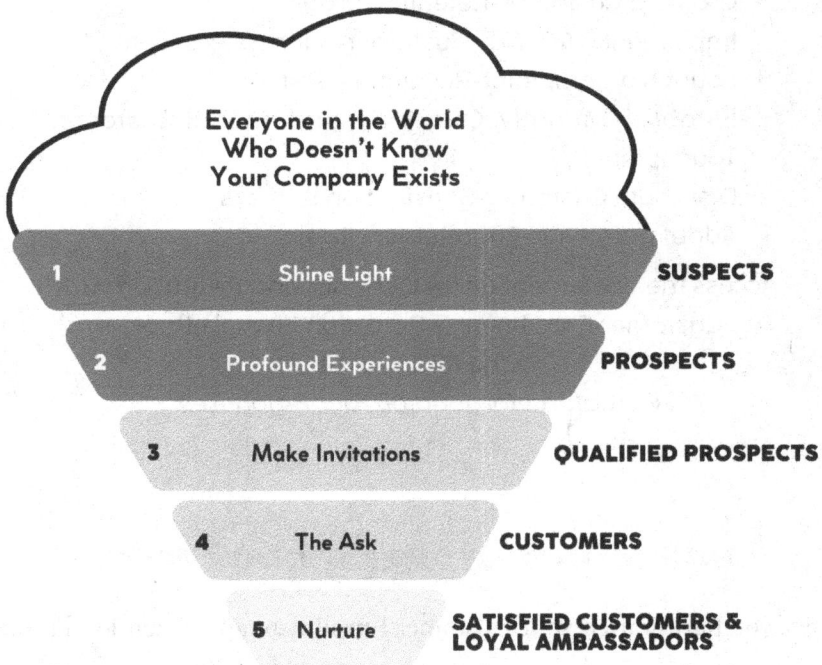

Everyone in the World
Who Doesn't Know
Your Company Exists

1	Shine Light	**SUSPECTS**
2	Profound Experiences	**PROSPECTS**
3	Make Invitations	**QUALIFIED PROSPECTS**
4	The Ask	**CUSTOMERS**
5	Nurture	**SATISFIED CUSTOMERS & LOYAL AMBASSADORS**

Customer Enrollment and Loyalty Funnel Tools

Now is the time to build the Customer Enrollment and Loyalty Funnel for your company. Use the Customer Funnel Designer to craft all five stages.

If you want to dive even deeper, there is a Customer Enrollment & Retention eBook included with the FFG ToolKit. This resource details every aspect of building a system for enrolling and retaining customers, moving step by step through the process of how to:

- Build a Complete Customer-Enrollment Engine
- Create Channels to Develop Suspects
- Generate Profound Experiences to Convert Suspects to Prospects
- Develop Invitations that Convert Prospects to Customers
- Create a Customer-Retention Program
- Implement a 90-Day Customer-Success Program
- Launch a Complaint-Resolution System
- Establish Monthly, Quarterly, and Annual Customer Touchpoints
- Distribute Customer-Satisfaction Surveys
- Adopt Customer-Engagement Tools

Access the Customer Funnel Designer and the Build Your Customer Enrollment & Retention Funnel eBook in the FFG ToolKit:
www.aforceforgood.biz/book-bonuses

HOW MANY CUSTOMERS DO YOU NEED?

Once you have crafted your Customer Enrollment and Retention Funnel, the next question is: *how many customers would you like to move through your funnel?* In order to meet your profitability needs, how many sales would you need to create on a monthly and annual basis?

But before we set about determining those answers, let's take a step back so we can frame things in terms of your specific Growth Model.

What Is Your Growth Model?

Now, we will look at how many customers you would need to generate $10M in revenue annually, based on five different Growth Models. How you approach marketing and selling varies among the frameworks we'll talk about in the coming pages. As you read through the list, consider which model most closely resembles your company. The statistics included are based on averages across many industries, so it will not give you a truly accurate read on the figures for your company, of course, but it will give you some round numbers to work with as you begin to predict how many suspects, prospects, and offers you need, monthly and annually.

The Whale Model

When your average revenue per customer (ARPC) per year is $100K+ and you need ~100 customers for every $10M in annual revenue, you will need a Whale Growth Model.

Typically, companies serving customers who spend $100K+ per year will have a more personalized marketing and selling experience, as well as a sales process that could take months or even years to convert. Because the enrollment experience is more focused and highly tailored to each individual prospect, the conversion rates will likely be higher than with other Growth Models where the level of personalization is simply not achievable, given the larger volume of prospects. Also, the cost a company is willing to incur to attract and enroll each customer could be fairly significant, especially in the likelihood a new customer will be a customer for many years.

The key to executing a Whale Growth Model is providing finely tuned personalized experiences that are contingent on knowing customers impeccably well. Having a team of experienced salespeople who already have deep relationships within the market you serve is critical.

The Deer Model

When your average revenue per customer (ARPC) per year is $10K+ and you need ~1,000 customers for every $10M in annual revenue, you will need a Deer Growth Model.

In the Deer Model, there is likely a fair amount of personalization in the marketing and selling experience, and the timeline to convert a suspect to a new customer might take months. Again, a company will be able to afford a somewhat higher cost per prospect and cost per customer, given that, each year, customers generate at least $10K in revenue.

The key to the Deer Model is having both a strong marketing team capable of generating an abundance of prospects *and* a team of excellent sales professionals. Most likely the sales professionals working within the Deer Model will either conduct sales virtually via phone or online platforms, or have a concentrated territory of prospects within driving distance. Deer Model sales professionals may not need the same level of industry experience as the Whale Model sales executives; instead, they are good at connecting and selling quickly and probably have experience selling a multitude of products.

The Rabbit Model

When your average revenue per customer (ARPC) per year is $1K+ and you need ~10,000 customers for every $10M in annual revenue, you will need a Rabbit Growth Model.

With the Rabbit Model, volume is critical. Thus, you need an experienced and highly skilled marketing leader and team who have demonstrated success building, measuring, and tuning marketing systems. The goal is to generate consistent suspects and prospects at an adequate volume. You may have a few sales professionals who reach out to prospects and help them say "Yes" to offers, but the large majority of your enrollment engine is in automated marketing systems that build well-established customer pipelines.

The Mouse Model

When your average revenue per customer (ARPC) per year is $100 and you need ~100,000 customers for every $10M in annual revenue, you will need a Mouse Growth Model.

Even more than the Rabbit Model, the Mouse Model is dependent on mass outreach and conversion to huge volumes of people. Leveraging lower cost and highly targeted marketing methods like social-media placements, affiliate marketing campaigns, and free virtual experiences are critical. Rabbit Model businesses have to work hard to keep customers. Making sure that their $5.99/mo subscription remains active for months and years is critical to long-term success.

MEASURING AND TUNING YOUR SYSTEM

Now that you have reviewed the Whale, Deer, Rabbit, and Mouse Models, consider which most emulates your business. This will help you have a general theory in place to support the specific tracking and measurement of conversion rates within your own Customer Enrollment System.

Conversion Rates

There are five basic conversion rates every business would be wise to track, although there are almost certainly additional conversion metrics that will help you diagnose and tune your system as you dig deeper into your Customer Engagement and Retention Funnel.

1. **Suspect-to-Prospect Conversion**—The percentage of suspects who convert to a prospect.

2. **Prospects-to-Offer Conversion**—The percentage of prospects who participate in experiences and stick around for an offer.

3. **Offers-to-Customer Conversion**—The percentage of those who receive an offer to be a customer who say "Yes" and officially pay for a solution.

4. **Customer-to-Satisfied-Customer Conversion**—The percentage of customers who hit your threshold for being a satisfied customer (for example, they make a certain purchase more than three times *and* give your company a Net Promoter score of four or more).

5. **Satisfied-Customer-to-Loyal-Ambassador Conversion**—The percentage of satisfied customers who hit your threshold for being a Loyal Ambassador (for example, provide a business case you can use in your marketing, refer four-plus other customers, and/or speak regularly as a reference to your prospects).

Once you start tracking these statistics, you can compare your conversion rates to industry averages to get a sense of the health of your processes. Tracking your conversions will help you see where the bottlenecks are in your current system and what kind of changes are needed to tune your Customer Engagement Funnel to reap better results. *What gets measured gets transformed.*

Cost-Per Metrics

Another important metric you will want to track is your "Cost-Per" Metrics. There are lots of ways to approach this, but the simplest way to begin is to start by calculating the total cost of your Customer Enrollment and Retention System in a month or year. Consider: What is the cost for your company to attract and enroll a new customer? What are your costs to engage and retain them on an ongoing basis?

Using the total cost of enrolling a customer, you can now calculate these averages:

1. **Cost per prospect**—Take the total cost of enrolling a new customer, and divide it by the number of prospects you generate in a month or year (the number who give you their contact information in Step Two of the Customer Enrollment and Retention Funnel).

2. **Cost per new customer**—Take the total cost of enrolling a new customer, and divide it by the number of new customers who say "Yes" and buy a solution in a month or year (the number who say "Yes" in Step Three of the Customer Enrollment and Retention Funnel).

3. **Cost per retained customer**—Take the total cost of retaining customers, including all engagement and satisfaction tools and operations, and divide it by the number of customers you keep for a specified period of time (say, 6 months, 12 months, 24 months, and 36 months).

Track these metrics both monthly and over the course of a year. As you improve your conversion rates, you will see the costs per prospect, cost per new customer, and cost per retained customer go down (assuming you don't add more costs to the system to generate those improvements). This is key. The goal here is to tune your Customer Enrollment and Retention Funnel to always be improving conversion rates and reducing costs per prospect and customer.

Customer Lifetime Value

Customer Lifetime Value (CLV) is another crucial metric that estimates the total revenue a business can expect from a single customer over the duration of their relationship. By considering the revenue generated and the predicted customer lifespan, CLV provides a comprehensive view of a customer's long-term value to the business.

For founders, understanding CLV is vital, as it informs marketing strategies, highlighting the importance of targeting and retaining high-value customers. It aids in business valuation, helps in accurate revenue forecasting, and guides product development to better meet customer needs. Ultimately, optimizing CLV leads to sustainable growth and increased profitability.

BUILD AND TUNE YOUR GROWTH MODEL

Growth Model Builder

If this feels overwhelming or complicated, it may be time to turn to the Growth Model Builder, which will help you begin this important process. This tool is delivered to you in both PDF and Microsoft Excel formats.

Access the Growth Model Builder in both the Excel and PDF versions in the FFG ToolKit:

www.aforceforgood.biz/book-bonuses

There is nearly limitless data that can be mined within each Customer Enrollment and Loyalty Funnel, and having someone on your team who is a dataphile, committed to helping track and improve your systems, will be revolutionary. Mastering this competency in your business is one of the critical factors that distinguishes prosperous businesses from struggling ones by fueling growth, mitigating costs, and making you unstoppable.

KNOWING WHOM YOU SERVE

Over the last five chapters, you have made sure that you know whom your business serves, inside and out. You've defined your Authentic Customer and made sure you can articulate and understand what they want, what you offer, how you are positioned, and how those things work together to generate profit. You selected an Area of Chosen Greatness to invest 10 times the focus, energy, and resources into, in order to set your company apart. You've considered the role your company culture plays in cultivating positive customer feelings, and you have mapped out a system designed to attract, enroll, and keep the people you want to serve around.

Now, it is time to move onto the next important topic every founder should know and keep top of mind at all times: What Is Your Impact Plan?

PART 3
KNOW YOUR IMPACT PLAN

"With a clear plan, you become the master of your destiny."

—ELEANOR ROOSEVELT

"Clarity, conviction, and action equal success. The three most important ingredients to your success are the clarity you have about your vision, the conviction that you can make a difference, and the action steps you take to get there."

—LISA NICHOL

Abundance Now: Amplify Your Life & Achieve Prosperity Today and *No Matter What!: 9 Steps to Living the Life You Love*

At this point, it should come as no surprise that the language I'm using here has been carefully selected to provide you with the proper orientation. For everybody else who does business, this section is simply about strategy: the business plan. And I'm not saying that piece isn't important; I'm just saying that, if this is residing *in your head alone*, there's only so far you can go.

Conversely, an Impact Plan—and here I define *impact* as your purpose fully manifested to the audience that you hope it reaches, at scale—ties your purpose and the service you provide through that into reality. It is only through that one door that you can effectively then move through to the very analytical side of things, always framing what you're doing through the elevated narrative of impact, rather than business strategy alone. We're not just talking about making money here; we're talking about changing people's lives.

I'm analytical by nature. I have written many personal business plans and worked with many other founders on writing their business plans. That isn't a step that can be skipped. But it is very clear to me that what made Allumé so successful in its planning, in its operations, and in its execution was its consistent connection to, and focus on, *impact*. Certainly, one component of that is scale, and another is profit, but those things become even more important when they're connected to the good they can do and when the focus of daily activity is in service of those goals—not just more for the sake of more.

I was in a private-equity meeting some months ago, speaking to two male founders (also in the healthcare space) who were extremely analytical and very financially minded. We were talking about how they just can't quite understand why their team isn't responding to their prodding to chart higher figures. I asked, "How are you talking to your nurses about it?" They said, "Well, we tell them we need to grow our revenues." I thought to myself, "You really think that nurses give two hoots about your revenue? You serve nurses. How do you not know the language they speak in terms of impact? This is your audience!" If they were instead talking about growth in terms of how much value their team is bringing to the people they serve or how many patients are being brought home from the hospital, it would have been a whole different story.

Impact stands at odds with pure self-interest. "We're starting this business to create an exit." "I want to be featured in this magazine." "I want to ring the bell with my IPO." All of those are self-referential. It smells like manipulation, right?

The thing is, a lot of businesses do it and get away with it. But what I observe is that, when you truly, genuinely—not just for optics—focus on impact, that is a generator of your profits; that's good for your people, good for your teams, good for your community, good for your customer; it creates an energy and a momentum that feels very different. It opens so many doors beyond, *"How do I get more customers? How do I get them to pay more? How do I get my costs down?"* which is the equation otherwise.

This orientation fuels innovation. It fuels collaboration. It fuels personal growth. It's more sustainable. Again, *impact is purpose in action.*

During Covid, I had to dig deeper than ever into purpose, to lead and to create impact, in order to move my people to go out and do the things they needed to do: to show up, deliver more hours, take on more shifts, all to take remarkable care of our patients in their homes. If, in those terrible times when people are exhausted and there's burnout, the language you're using to ask for more is analytical, it's not going to work. Properly refueling my team came down to reminding them of the good they were creating in the world with their efforts and their energy.

Additionally, something that has become so clear to me over the last year is that venture investors and angel investors are really looking to invest in leaders with vision—vision that can be executed and measured. They crave a founder who shows up with purpose and clarity—and we're not talking about pie-in-the-sky stuff here, but with a clear goal and an Impact Plan that has got the scaffolding of how you're going to achieve that future—*and* with a team they've trained to be on the same page behind them. Investors know what they're searching for: unstoppable founders. And that is what I want for all women founders.

CHAPTER 10
YOUR PERSONAL DEFINITION OF "PROSPERITY"

"Desire is the interface between you
and that which is greater than you."

—REGINA THOMASHAUER

Pussy: A Reclamation
Founder, The School of Womanly Arts

"You have to participate relentlessly
in the manifestation of your own blessings."

—ELIZABETH GILBERT

Eat, Pray, Love

"The basis of life is freedom; the purpose of
life is joy; the result of life is growth."

Esther & Jerry Hicks
*The Vortex: Where the Law of Attraction Assembles
All Cooperative Relationships*

The journey that culminates in a complete Impact Plan begins with you. Your business must feed not just your customers and team members, but it must also nurture *you*. The Force for Good System™ is meant to help you survive and prosper not only as an entrepreneur but also as an holistic person. The needs of you and your family are an essential inclusion in the plan you are about to create.

YOUR RELATIONSHIP WITH YOUR COMPANY

The trajectory of your company can be likened to that of a human being. When it was first founded—born, if you will—it needed certain things from you: time, energy, grit, capital, perseverance. While providing those things tends to bring about some sense of fulfillment or purpose, early-stage businesses likely won't offer you more than you're putting into them until later in their life. As it gains strength, however, it will take off at a crawl; then it will walk, and finally, it will run. At that point, it has achieved independence and can exist freely and successfully without your vigilant involvement. Now, things have shifted, and it is your business that should be giving abundantly to you.

This transition doesn't necessarily happen organically. We are creatures of habit, and, without clear intentions, the businesses we built in the pursuit of profit and freedom can instead become a lifelong ball and chain. That's why the exchange of giving and receiving is important to contemplate. As with any relationship, it needs balance, boundaries, clear expectations, and evolution to thrive and prosper. In this chapter, I invite you to think intentionally about your relationship with your company: the effort and sacrifice that was necessary to get it going and, later, what is called for to allow it to thrive more independently. Making space for your freedom and your company's independence to take form lays the groundwork to then plot the course to your 10-Year Impact Goal.

WHAT WILL CHANGE FOR YOU?

Sometimes, it can be easier to start at the optimal end and reverse-engineer this transition. Start by visualizing a future where your company has already accomplished its 10-Year Impact Goal, is delivering its purpose and impact, and is generating healthy returns. In this future place, where the impact and success *you* desire is already made manifest, ask yourself:

1. **What do you envision to be different about you?** Looking ahead, what have you learned? How have you grown? How has the journey to this future place given you confidence, determination, grit, endurance, balance, and strength? What do you see is different about your livelihood, your place in the world, your influence in the community?

2. **How has the company changed?** What new team members have you brought on-board? Are there experts in marketing, sales, service, technology, and finance? How have these new team members enriched the company? Notice how their expertise has taken the pressure off you.

3. **How has the relationship between you and your company changed?** Which activities that you currently lead will be handed off to others? Which new, strategic activities have you taken on? What have you done to be able to focus on the areas for which you are best suited and most needed?

4. **How has the prosperity of the company affected you?** How has your lifestyle changed? What are you able to experience, enjoy, and do as a result of having these profits?

5. **How has your level of freedom evolved now that your company has found its stride?** Allow yourself to see the choices

you can make with your schedule, travel, family commitments, and beyond.

6. **What has changed to alleviate your stress regarding security, risk, and reward**? Consider how the worries around sourcing customers, generating profit, finding funding, building the right systems, and hiring the best people have dissolved in this future state. How has your personal risk, financial risk, and overall company-sustainability risk decreased? Allow yourself to see how the level of anxiety you might be experiencing with your business now will, in time, soften.

7. **Is your company giving you the prosperity and freedom you envisioned**? Many of us start businesses with dreams of a beautiful, enriching life—freedom to travel, share experiences with loved ones, give generously, and live a fulfilling lifestyle. We aspire to secure retirement, fund our children's education, and support our parents. Do you have the funds you need to fulfill your desires, live the lifestyle you want, and give to others? Are you able to attend your children's soccer games, go on those magical trips you planned, and spend time learning other interests?

Exploring the answers to these questions will help you both in shaping your day-to-day operations and in laying out the larger plan they're forming. Having a clear vision of your best and most balanced future allows you—and those around you—to make decisions, make mistakes, and make progress in the direction that you want to go.

THE FOUR LENSES OF PROSPERITY

In this chapter, we will use the Four Lenses of Prosperity—profit, freedom, impact, and security—to examine your relationship with your company.

Articulate your definition of prosperity in clear terms, visualizing what it looks like when your business is at scale and producing the impact and profits for which you're aiming.

Assess your current level of operating as compared to that outlined in your prosperity definition.

Next, imagine how you need to evolve your relationship with your company (and your team) to arrive at the place where you are thriving and prospering.

Create Your Definition of Prosperity

Personal Prosperity Expander
As we move through the Four Lenses of Prosperity, defining what success looks like in each area, you'll want to have the Personal Prosperity Expander on hand.

Access the Personal Prosperity Expander in the FFG ToolKit:
www.aforceforgood.biz/book-bonuses

Profit

While profit isn't everything, it is absolutely necessary to your company's ability to thrive and prosper. For you to thrive personally as well, your company will need to produce enough profit to both (a) ensure the business has what it needs to continue robust operations and (b) ensure that you have what you and your family need to be happy and healthy.

One of the great challenges for an entrepreneur is that there is *always* somewhere company profits can be reinvested to great effect: the hiring of additional team members, buying new equipment, upgrading technology, increasing compensation for employees, or outside investments, to name just a few. Without mindfulness, your company can easily soak up any margin, leaving you and your family without what you need.

As discussed elsewhere in this chapter, different stages of business need different levels of investment to grow and thrive as they should. In general, your company needs more from you early on. As time passes, particularly if you're using the Force for Good System™, your company will shift from *needing* you to *giving* to you. Cast your mind to this future state, where your company is fully scaled and generating healthy returns for both company sustainability and your personal abundance, and, from this place, define what you hope to one day receive from your company. Now, turn to section one of the Personal Prosperity Expander (www.aforceforgood.biz/book-bonuses).

As you move through the prompts, I ask that you don't overthink your answers. Breathe through whatever you're feeling, be it excitement, confusion, empowerment, or anxiety. Write down what comes to mind. This exercise is inviting you to do the important work of bringing your ethereal life vision into material reality. Making your desires clear is the first step to making your desires real.

You have given—and will continue to give—your business a great deal, and you deserve rich rewards. It is important to know now what your company needs to one day give back to you. This will ensure that you build it big enough and smart enough from the start to bring your life vision to fruition.

Freedom

One of the greatest riches of owning a company is the opportunity for freedom. The desire for autonomy is inherent in the life vision of most entrepreneurs, as is having full flexibility and ownership over your own creativity, schedule, philanthropy, travel, etc. As you turn to section two of the Personal Prosperity Expander, imagine the freedoms you will have in the future when your 10-Year Impact Goal has been achieved, you have a brilliant team capable of working independently, and you have the systems in place to allow you to work from anywhere.

Thinking about your definition of freedom could bring up unexpected feelings. You might find these questions exhilarating, expanding, and elevating, or you may find these questions frustrating, annoying, or overwhelming. Don't let anxiety pin you down; places where you feel stuck are usually areas that need our attention and love, rather than judgment and resistance.

With Allumé, I made sure to emphasize in our Inception Story that the business was founded by someone who'd had direct experience with what the families we served were going through as a way of fostering trust and connection, but I was also careful to create a company where it wasn't about me. I wasn't special; all the people I employed who were providing the care were special. Our team and our operations were what was special. From the start, it was also my intention never to overstep or undermine my leadership team or any of the case managers involved in keeping things going. It can be hard for founders to do this, to position themselves in this way, and I get it. At its best, the desire to be and remain crucially involved at the core of your business is tied to a deep desire to be of service and to be a model of putting the customer first. It's just shortsighted.

If you always want to be the hero, if you always want to be the one to climb in there and fix things, that undermines the team around you. It means you're going to have a very hard time going on vacation or having a life. It means you can never exit the business, because, now the brand and the people you serve think you're the special sauce. You can't get sucked into that approach thoughtlessly; instead, when every single person in the business has their own connection to their own Authentic Customer, as we discussed earlier in the book, that creates the holistic, beautiful experience that ultimately also allows you more freedom.

Keep in mind that what freedom looks like also morphs over your company's lifespan. At the start, you get to build a culture and purpose that matters to you from scratch, and then, one day, you might exchange certain freedoms to "do what you like" and "make all the decisions" for the freedom to step aside and have a profitable, sustainable business that runs without your hands-on involvement. Like the teenager who finally finds footing on her own, so, too, can your company.

Impact

For purpose-led entrepreneurs like you and me, impact drives us more than anything. We long to build a business that fosters good. We want to create quality products and services we know are great, elevate the way business is done, and improve the lives of our customers in a meaningful and lasting way. We also long to cultivate a company culture in which people say, "This is the best place I have ever worked." We want our teams to feel empowered to climb soaring mountains together.

The great thing about this dimension of your relationship with the company you founded is that you get to experience these make-a-difference moments from the very beginning. We get to feel the excitement of delivering our purpose to our very first customers and teammates. Thus, impact is something we can start experiencing from day one. As your company forges ahead toward your 10-Year Impact Goal, imagine reaching and exceeding this important milestone as you move into the next section of the Personal Prosperity Expander.

As you fill in your answers, remember that the company you are building is quite remarkable. Allow yourself to soak in how special what you are doing is and the goodness it is destined to bring to the world. Feel in your bones the deep fulfillment that comes from creating a business built for good.

Security

Like the other three lenses we've already covered, security is an important component of your relationship with the company you founded. There is inherent risk in entrepreneurship, and the amount of risk you take on will affect how safe and secure you feel. The higher risk associated with a newly launched business might make it hard for you to feel like you're thriving and prosperous. Over time, however, as you build your business using the Force for Good System™, you will have the mental clarity to design a path that begins to strip the risk out of your relationship with your company, replacing it with more and more security. Drawing again from the future state of already having a fully scaled business that you should be growing increasingly familiar with, turn to section four of the Personal Prosperity Expander.

AN INTENTIONAL RELATIONSHIP WITH YOUR COMPANY

Without considering your personal objectives and desires in these four essential categories, you might build a business misaligned with the actual future you want for yourself. Let's turn now to three examples of entrepreneurs who are, according to their own definition, prosperous. As you read their stories, notice how the four different lenses through which to define success flex and interact with one another differently in each scenario.

Sabrina's Story

Sabrina is the 32-year-old founder of a new software startup. Single and living in a small apartment in Menlo Park, California, she spends all of her time launching SoftwareCo. With $50K in savings from her prior corporate career and a $100K line of credit, she and her co-founder, Niko, are working night and day to complete the coding of the product and launch their new software in six months. Sabrina is all in. She is 100%

willing to invest all of her savings, put herself into debt, work 70+ hours/week, take no vacations, and forfeit a social life for this venture—even knowing she could lose it all.

She and her partner plan to launch their product to market in six months, demonstrate a proof of concept with 50+ customers, acquire investors to help them further market their product to 200+ customers and hire additional team members, and scale the company to $20–30M in annual revenues before selling the company to a larger player for $50+ million. The goal is to do all of this within 5–8 years.

Sabrina is willing to invest the funds and time now, with a plan to deposit $10–20M each into her and her partner's personal bank accounts in the near future. She knows this will give her the freedom to decide what her next venture might be and, if she chooses to start a family, she knows it will give her the freedom to be very active in her children's lives.

Layola's Story

Layola is 46 years old and owns a virtual-assistant business she founded 18 years ago. When she started, she invested $20K through credit cards to get it off the ground. In the early days, she did almost everything herself: marketing, outreach, talent acquisition, and all aspects of billing and administration. At times, she even performed some of the client work herself if she was short on staff. She worked 60+ hours/week and took a very small salary, reinvesting every dime she could into marketing, so she could grow her customer base as quickly as possible.

As time went on and Layola developed scale, she hired team members to fulfill all the marketing and administrative functions. Today, she is still the Chief Executive Officer, but she works only about 15 hours/week. Her activities include reviewing weekly data to see how the company is doing, coaching the Chief Operating Officer she hired to run the day-to-day, and speaking at conferences and on podcasts to entrepreneurs on the benefits of leveraging an experienced virtual assistant. Layola loves supporting entrepreneurs, and, through her business, she now serves 500+ clients annually, and, through speaking and interviews, she connects with 10K+ entrepreneurs annually.

With a profitable company that performs when she's not actively onsite working, she can direct more time to her two children, who will soon leave for college, and she enjoys taking four or five international trips each year with her husband.

While she doesn't plan to exit soon, Layola has established an Employee Stock Ownership Plan (ESOP), where trusted members of her team share in the ownership of her company. Her exit strategy is to eventually transition the company leadership fully over to a group of trusted employees who will lead the company and, together with her and her heirs, continue to own the business.

Josaphine's Story

Twelve years ago, Josaphine founded a chain of hair salons aimed at bringing ethnic and non-conforming gender styles to the center stage of fashion. Starting off in South Beach, she invested $750K in the build-out of her first salon and in a massive marketing and PR campaign. She leveraged relationships from her past career in fashion to have runway models wearing her hairstyles. In its first year of operation, her salon received attention from *Vogue, Elle, Vanity Fair*, and *Bazaar* as it developed a reputation for putting out fashion-forward, multicultural, and edgy styles.

Josaphine used this attention to attract nine new investors over the next three years. Each investor funded the opening of a salon in a new city. With each new investment, she strategically maintained 51+% ownership to ensure she always had control of the business. Today, Josaphine's attention is on keeping the culture and brand fresh, creating opportunities for great PR, hosting events that feature salon stylists, and finding investors to fund the opening of the next location. She hired an excellent COO and CFO to ensure operations and financials are impeccable, integrated, and consistent between locations. In the next 18 months, Josaphine's company is rolling out a multicultural hair-and-makeup product line, which can be sold in-salon, online, or at limited department stores.

Josaphine has always put in long hours and has many times chosen to reinvest profit into marketing and talent, but today her company generates $5M in net income and is valued at $50M, and she takes home $1M annually—and growing. Her company offers her the opportunity to focus on what she loves: fashion, PR, and adding new locations. With this comes the opportunity to travel to new places, meet new people, and be a part of the fashion scene. And nothing is more satisfying than seeing traditionally "different" hair and style now being viewed as high fashion. This is how she knows she's making an impact.

At this point, Josaphine does not have plans to exit the company, as she enjoys the work she's doing, but she meets regularly with an investment banker to discuss trends in mergers and acquisitions in her industry, so that she's always aware of the options available to her. Josaphine imagines that one day she will sell the company to the right buyer, ensuring the longevity of what she and her team have built.

All three founders have a unique journey—behind *and* ahead of them—based on each founder's personal definition of prosperity. They have interacted with profit, freedom, security, and impact in distinctly personal ways along their respective paths, each with different ratios and scales, and each with a different exit plan.

EIGHT EXIT STRATEGIES

Every business needs an exit plan. Entrepreneurs often get caught up in the excitement of their creation, forgetting to plan for their future departure or role evolution. Visualizing your ideal ending allows you to design your business so that you have all the options you want when it's time to exit.

There are eight primary exit strategies:

1. **Sell to a Third Party.** You could sell your company to another individual or company.

2. **Sell to Partner(s).** If you have partners, you could sell all or part of your shares of the company to them. If you don't have partners, one strategy is to merge with another similar or complementary company and then later sell your shares to your partner. (Or they could sell their shares to you.)

3. **Sell to Management.** You could also sell your business to one or more members of your leadership team.

4. **Sell to a Family Member.** You could sell your business to someone in your family.

5. **Sell to Employees (ESOP).** Similar to selling your company to one or a few members of your leadership team, another option is to sell to all of your employees through an Employee Stock Ownership Plan (ESOP). This strategy is uncommon, complicated, and expensive to implement, but for the right businesses and founders, it can be a wonderful option.

6. **Hire a CEO.** You could choose to continue owning your business but step away from the day-to-day. With a new CEO in place, you could protect your investment by serving on the board. Hiring a CEO or Executive Director could also be a great interim step before selling the company to another owner or entity. It could also precede selling your company over time to the CEO herself.

7. **Go Public.** Through an initial public offering (IPO), you could make the shares of your company available on the stock market.

8. **Liquidate and Close.** While this is not usually the preferred way to go, it is always an option. Liquidation is where you sell off whatever assets you can (hopefully have the funds to) pay off your debts and walk away with whatever cash is left.

WHAT IS YOUR EXIT STRATEGY?

To shape a basic exit strategy, consider these questions:

1. Which of the eight strategies appeal to you?

2. Which don't?

3. What do you hope to achieve through an exit?

4. When is the soonest you would want to exit?

5. When is the latest you would want to exit?

6. Who (an individual, company, or asset manager) might be a potential exit partner or buyer?

7. Is there anyone in your family or on your team who might be a good fit to run and own the company someday?

8. What would you need to do now and in the years to come to set yourself up for a desirable exit? What will you need to do to ensure that the highest value is paid for your company? What will you need to do to ensure that your company is able to easily transition to new owners when the time comes?

WHAT ARE YOUR PROSPERITY GOALS?

Now that you have defined what prosperity looks like through the lenses of profit, freedom, impact, and security, and you have considered your exit strategy, you can move to the final section of the Personal Prosperity Expander. When answering each question, make sure to be specific, and set actual dates by which you'd like to have each of these goals achieved.

Align Your 10-Year Goals

As you will see in the next chapter, the 4-Page Growth Plan™ focuses on a 10-year growth horizon. Take this moment now to make sure your Prosperity Goals are aligned with your 10-Year Impact, Scale, and Profit Goals. We will discuss these further in later chapters, but now is a good time to ensure that your business is aimed to feed your personal prosperity.

Congratulations are due upon finishing! You have just completed the important step of defining what prosperity is for you. Thank yourself for doing the hard work of creating clarity for yourself, even when it might have been challenging or confronting.

With your personal needs now deeply considered, you are ready to focus again on the exciting work of building your purpose-inspired business. The work you did in this chapter will slingshot you forward, making the remainder of this section, aimed at building your big-picture plan, a cinch.

CHAPTER 11
THE 4-PAGE GROWTH PLAN™ (4PGP™)

"One can never consent to creep when
one feels an impulse to soar."

—Helen Keller

The Story of My Life

"When everyone understands not just the 'what' but the 'why'
behind what we're doing, our collective power is unstoppable."

—Ilene Gordon

Former CEO, Ingredion

"When people are aligned, and they're passionate, and they're
working really hard toward a goal, they can achieve anything."

—Meg Whitman

Former CEO, Hewlett-Packard

Your 4-Page Growth Plan™ (4PGP™) is the living, breathing guide you return to weekly, monthly, and quarterly to chart your progress and realign toward your 10-Year Impact Goal. This plan is critical: to cut through the overwhelm of daily demands and problems, to know where to direct effort, to align your team, to rally your company in a unified direction, and to ensure that you are making progress each day. Because the 4PGP™ is grounded in purpose and service, it also ensures that how you and your team conduct business is aligned with the values and impact you stand for.

A formal and traditional business plan is often needed to obtain funding, but it doesn't necessarily include the most helpful breakdown when it comes to actually running and growing a business. The terms laid out can be big and yawning, and difficult to pin down . . . the whole pie-in-the-sky thing. Most of the time, what people end up doing with a business plan is shoving it into a drawer and never looking at it again. The 4-Page Growth Plan™ combats that. It's a living document, forever relevant, and it doesn't include more than necessary, so you don't have to dread going back to review it. It's mostly summary and numbers, the little pockets of information that keep you going and are easier to update and see progress, flatlining, backsliding, whatever it is. As soon as you see clearly what's going on, you can do something about it.

The 4-Page Growth Plan™ will show you where you should focus your attention. It's about figuring out an approach, trying it, measuring it, and then adjusting so you can do it again. This is a journey of the internal workings, the analytical and thinking part, blended with the wise and knowing part of transformation. This is about how to get from where you are to where you want to go.

The map contained in the 4-Page Growth Plan™ is leading you to one destination: the intersection between your 10-Year Impact Goal set in Chapter 5 and your scale and profitability goals, which we will set using the associated template (www.aforceforgood.biz/book-bonuses).

The 4-Page Growth Plan™ is designed to:

1. Help you capture your entire plan in just four pages.

2. Provide a clear picture of how all the elements of the plan connect with one another.

3. Give you a document you can easily share and update with others—your team, investors, advisors, and other constituents.

PROGRESS OVER PERFECTION

The goal of the Force for Good journey is to (efficiently) draft all the elements of the system—your purpose, who you serve, what you offer, and your plan of impact—into a living, breathing document you fine-tune and revise on an ongoing basis. All the pieces are connected. As you work on one section, something in another might shift. Thus, the goal is not to get the perfect plan in place; the mantra is instead: *"Write something down, and move on."* You will have plenty of opportunities to return and refine down the line.

Within this context, think of your 4PGP™ as a map. It leads you north, south, east, and west; it gives you perspective on where you are in relation to where you are headed. The work of these next chapters is to familiarize yourself with the topography of the landscape you're moving across. This map you're creating does not come with a list of turn-by-turn directions to follow to get you where you need to go. Because your business is unique, the journey to success is still uncharted. The 4PGP™ you craft will instead help you navigate and make powerful, strategic choices about what to focus on this quarter, this month, this week, and today.

HOW WILL THE 4-PAGE GROWTH PLAN™ BE USED?

The 4PGP™ provides a host of benefits, some of which you will immediately see at work in your business:

- It will create clarity, alignment, and excitement for members of your team.

- It will become an ongoing conversation piece that empowers you and your leadership to have thoughtful, creative, and innovative strategic discussions about how to move forward.

- It will ensure everyone understands what they should be doing to make the highest and best use of company time and resources.

- Over time, it will become your ticket to more freedom, as members of your team are able to collaborate in the service of a higher purpose, with or without you.

The 4PGP™ becomes a jumping-off point from which to craft other essential documents you may need to create, including the following:

- Full-fledged business plan
- Investor-pitch deck
- Bank loan or board presentation
- Other conversations and presentations with strategic partners

THE 4-PAGE GROWTH PLAN™ TEMPLATE

The 4-Page Growth Plan™
If you haven't already, now would be a great time to download a copy of the 4-Page Growth Plan™. It will be helpful for you to have it nearby as you move through the upcoming chapters.

The 4-Page Growth Plan™ is part of the FFG ToolKit:
www.aforceforgood.biz/book-bonuses

STAGES AND FACETS OF A BUSINESS

The Force for Good System™ is designed to help you accelerate impact, scale, and profit, and the 4PGP™ is the go-to tool for founders to foster results. Before we jump into building the 4PGP™, I invite you to first assess the stage of your business. While every entrepreneur's business is unique, in the section below, I've provided four stages most companies typically experience on their way to scale, impact, and profits, as well as a list of attributes, challenges, goals, and freedoms generally inherent in each:

Stage 1—Existence
Stage 2—Survival
Stage 3—Scaling
Stage 4—Impact

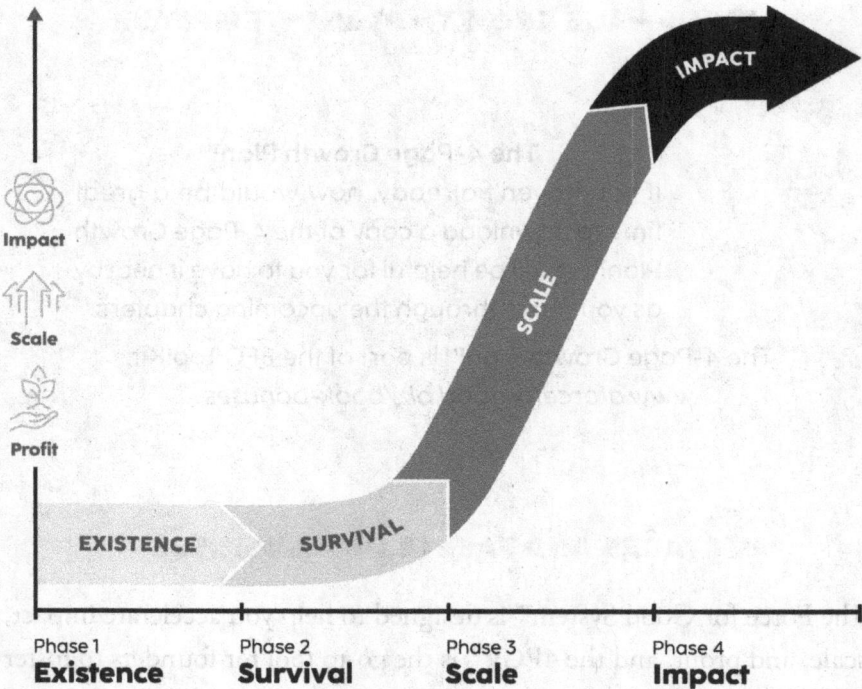

Impact

Scale

Profit

IMPACT

SCALE

EXISTENCE

SURVIVAL

Phase 1	Phase 2	Phase 3	Phase 4
Existence	**Survival**	**Scale**	**Impact**

The Force for Good System™ is designed to help you move through these stages with confidence, success, and personal satisfaction. There are ten facets we will explore in each of the four stages:

1. Common situations

2. Primary goal

3. Team size and complexity

4. Decision-making

5. Systems complexity and efficiency

6. Challenges to solve

7. Rewards

8. Impact Goal progress

9. Exit options

10. Company dependence on founder

Stages and Facets Resources

At this point, I invite you to refer to the additional resources about stages and facets:

- The FFG Stage Assessment allows you to quickly determine which stage your company resides in currently and provides ideas and strategies for moving your company forward. It also functions as a quick-reference table that summarizes the progression and relationship between the stages and facets described above.
- Company Stages and Facets eBook, which contains detailed information about each stage and facet.

Access these tools in the FFG ToolKit:
www.aforceforgood.biz/book-bonuses

Stage 1—Existence

At the "Existence" stage, the company is in its earliest form—the time when there is an idea formulating and starting to get off the ground. This step is about bringing forth a viable product or service and delivering it to an initial group of customers. The owners are likely the only full-time team members, with perhaps a few other helpers lending some time.

Stage 2—Survival

At the "Survival" stage, the company has a handful of customers and is delivering product but is either not yet profitable or is barely profitable.

While it has demonstrated it is a workable business entity, it is barely making it. Many mom-and-pop companies spend years at this stage. To be clear, even companies with significant sales figures count as being in the survival stage if:

- Owner salary is inconsistent, inadequate, or non-existent.

- Company has slow or no growth.

- Company is not consistently profitable on an accrual and cash basis for at least 12 months straight.

- Company cannot afford to invest in scaling or growth.

- Owner still makes all or most of the key decisions.

A company cannot move into the next stage of "scaling" until there are enough profits to both pay the owner a reasonable salary (and do so on an ongoing basis) *and* to invest in the growth of the company, such as marketing, technology systems, and key team members. Moving to "scaling" also requires the company becoming much less founder-dependent, indicating that the company holds value with or without the ongoing presence of the founder.

Stage 3—Scaling

This is a breakthrough stage that few companies ever reach, with so many stalling out in "Surviving." The main attribute of a scaling company is that it has enough profit and/or capital to:

- Break even by covering all operating expenses without any stress.

- Pay the founder both a consistent salary *and* added annual dividends so that she can move toward her prosperity goals.

- Invest in much-needed systems and people capable of efficiently moving the company toward its 10-Year Impact Goal.

- Execute the next level of marketing and sales that unlock big-picture goals.

- Achieve year-over-year double-digit (or more) growth.

During this phase, the founder depends more and more on others to solve the strategic challenges and operational complexities of the business. In this phase, the company is clearly positioned to operate, scale, and achieve ever-higher levels of impact with or without the founder. This ensures both the long-term sustainability of the business and the opportunity for higher levels of personal freedom for the founder.

Stage 4—Impact

Reaching this stage is an amazing feat for any business, as it has nearly reached its 10-Year Impact Goal and is thriving and prosperous on every level. Purpose-focused companies at this size, strength, profit, and impact are no doubt a Force for Good. There is now the freedom to ask the exhilarating question, "What good can we do, given the tremendous strength of our team, products, services, and purpose?"

Summary of Stages and Facets

Below is a table summarizing each of the stages and facets.

	Stage 1: Existence	Stage 2: Survival	Stage 3: Scaling	Stage 4: Impact
Common Situation	Barely exists.	Has revenues but not enough profit to both scale and for owner to thrive.	Profitable, growing company with dollars to invest in people, systems, marketing, and sales.	Hit long-term goal and set new, expanded vision for the company.
Primary Goal	Break even. Don't run out of cash.	Grow profits and cash so that the company can afford great people, systems, and growth.	Exponentially grow the company impact and profits.	Expand vision and goals for greatness, impact, and profit.
Team	Fewer than 5. All report to the Founder.	Still simple and small. Lean administration team. Still wearing multiple hats. A leadership team is forming.	Larger, more complex organization now has functional departments and leaders. Leadership team in place. Talented, experienced people join the team. Founder succession plan in-progress.	Strong CEO reporting to a Board of Directors. leadership team Members report to CEO. Multi-leveled team reports into leadership team. Team fully scaled to meet and expand impact goal. CEO succession plan in place.
Decisions	Founder makes decisions.	Founder still makes most decisions. Companies with a leadership team start to participate in decision-making.	Strong CEO with leadership team makes the key company decisions. A board of directors that meets regularly is in place.	Decisions are made by those closest to the decision; get pushed down to the lowest level. People are empowered to make decisions.

The 4-Page Growth Plan™ (4PGP™)

	Stage 1: Existence	Stage 2: Survival	Stage 3: Scaling	Stage 4: Impact
Systems	Barely exist. Creating systems as you go.	Improving but still inadequate. The proper systems and people needed to fully scale the business efficiently are still not in place.	Best-in-class systems are being implemented during this phase. Data mining and analysis inform smart business decisions.	Elegant systems create consistent results, and feed data needed to stay on track, measure progress, and make constant improvements.
Challenges	Many. Can't afford the smart people and systems. Can't afford marketing needed to scale the company. Not enough customers. Everything inefficient.	Building enough scale to finally afford scaling. Minimal/inconsistent profits. Cash crunches.	Challenges of growth, staying connected to purpose, keeping the culture strong, and replacing team members that aren't suitable for this stage.	Company must re-commit and double-down on purpose, setting a newly expanded Long-Term Impact Goal to keep the company fueled with vision. Team commitment and culture require ongoing focus.
Rewards	Few, other than excitement of launching a purpose-led company.	Maybe some profits, growing team, and excitement of being a part of something with a compelling future.	Profitability, scale, and increased impacts. Pride in a strong, growing business making a difference in the world.	Actualization of a dream. Initial profit goals met. Initial thriving goals met and being expanded. Pride in having built a force for good.
Impact, Scale, Profit Goals	5–10% progress	10–30% progress	30–90% progress	100% and beyond

	Stage 1: Existence	Stage 2: Survival	Stage 3: Scaling	Stage 4: Impact
Exit Options	Liquidate. Possibly sell some hard physical assets. Likely lose most/all invested.	Liquidate. Possible asset sale. Possible sale of customer base or product. Maybe investors can recoup some of their investment.	Plethora of exit strategies becomes available. Founder and investors could exit and receive strong ROI.	Every option for exit is available at this stage.
Founder Dependence	Owner is synonymous with the business.	Owner still working in the daily nuts-and-bolts of the business. Company is still very founder-dependent.	Owner involved at strategic, high level, but dependence on owner shrinks as company proves it can sustain independently.	Company independent of the founder and can thrive without her at this point. Founder participation is her role of choice.

Where You Are Is Perfect

No matter in which stage you currently reside—existence, survival, scaling, or impact—you are in the perfect place to begin the journey of accelerating success. Take a moment to assess your current stage, and start to see what shifts are available in the next stage. Just think: In as little as four to six months of using this system, you could be moving along to the next stage!

What Happens When You Achieve Impact?

As you approach the completion of your first 10-Year Impact Goal, it's time to plan your next stage of growth. Businesses that continuously evolve and grow impact see ongoing cycles of breakthrough impact, as the infographic below illustrates. This perpetual growth, fueled by the desire to create good in the world, is the ultimate marking of a Force for Good business. Companies like Whole Foods, Patagonia, and Cotopaxi are wonderful examples of companies that foster perpetual growth of both impact and profit. They achieve Impact Goal after Impact Goal.

As they do, they become more and more endeared by customers and employees alike, securing their market position and profitability.

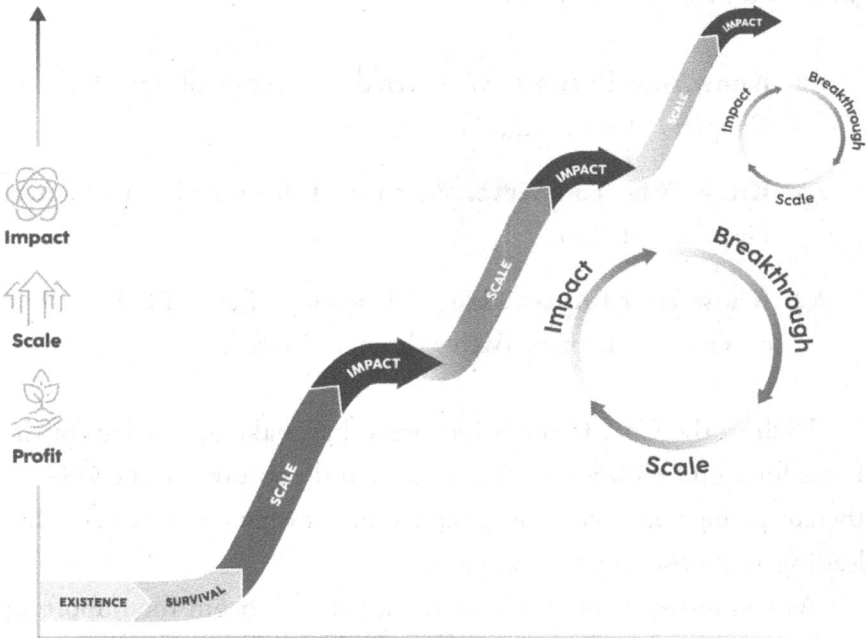

ITERATE THE 4-PAGE GROWTH PLAN™

4-Page Growth Plan™(4PGP™)

If you haven't already, it is officially time to get started on your 4-Page Growth Plan™. Go ahead and fill in the first two sections: know your purpose and know your customer. Also include your current business stage—existence, survival, scaling, or impact.

Access the 4-Page Growth Plan™ in the FFG ToolKit: *www.aforceforgood.biz/book-bonuses*

When you download the 4PGP™, you will see it is divided into three sections that address the first three of the Four Crucial Areas of Alignment (discussed in the Introduction):

1. **Know Your Purpose**. We covered this section of the 4PGP™ in Chapters One through Four.

2. **Know Who You Serve.** We covered this section in Chapters Five through Ten.

3. **Know Your Impact Plan.** This section of the 4PGP™ will be covered in Chapters Twelve through Sixteen.

Each of the Core Growth Elements that make up the legs of the Force for Good Flywheel is summarized in the sections of the 4PGP™, thereby giving you a broad but deep picture of what is most essential in leading and growing your company.

As you move into the next chapter, you will begin the important work of building the third and last section of the 4PGP™, the Impact Plan. The Impact Plan leads you from wherever your business is now to the 10-year results you aim to achieve. In the Force for Good System™, entrepreneurs decide how to define success for themselves and are able to progress to whatever level is desired. This is why, when we talk about measuring success, we do so in terms of your progress on the 10-Year Impact Goal you set for your own company. The goal is for your business to attain its purpose and profitability goals, while you also thrive and prosper personally. That is why it's crucial to take the time to ensure your Impact Goal in business and your Personal Prosperity Goals are aligned.

If your Personal Prosperity Goals require a take-home salary and distributions of $1 million per year, for example, make sure your 10-Year Impact Goal is big enough to meet both your needs and those of the company. Often at this point in the Force for Good journey, a founder may discover that more profit (and thus more impact) will be needed in order to meet the combined set of needs.

With aligned awareness of what you need personally, as well as what your business will achieve over the next ten years, it's time now to get down to the business of making the plan leading to the results you desire.

CHAPTER 12
KNOW WHERE YOU ARE

"Wherever you are is the entry point."

—ALICE WALKER

We Are the Ones We Have Been Waiting For:
Inner Light in a Time of Darkness

"The only time we suffer is when we believe
a thought that argues with what is."

—BYRON KATIE

Loving What Is: Four Questions That Can Change Your Life

"Progress starts with acknowledging where you stand
and then making a decision to move forward."

—NGOZI OKONJO-IWEALA

Director-General, World Trade Organization

The process of building your Impact Plan (the third section of the 4-Page Growth Plan™) starts with collecting key data to help you know where you are today, so that you can design your journey to your impact, scale, and profit goals. The information you start collating today and on an ongoing weekly and monthly basis will empower you to make informed strategic choices about how to navigate into the future of your business. At the same time, I hope it will also remind you to embrace, and even cherish, where you are now. Practice the mindset of feeling grateful and empowered along every step of the way as you look for the opportunities presented by each unique stage. Yes, you are on your way to an incredible 10-Year Impact Goal, but here and now is the only place you can experience celebration, fulfillment, victory, and appreciation. Your purpose is born not out of hitting your goal but out of the many moments when you and your team live out your values and vision.

MEASURE YOUR COORDINATES

In this chapter, I will help you gather Five Critical Reports and choose 12+ Key Metrics to track weekly and/or monthly, in order to give you ongoing clarity about how your business is doing. We will discuss how to collect data, as well as how to implement the ongoing analysis of the numbers and reports delivered.

Consistently measuring where you are now against where you were is one of the most important predictors of long-term success. Companies that follow through on this discipline, on a weekly and monthly basis, are far more likely to cross the chasm of building a high-impact, high-growth, high-profit company.

FIVE CRITICAL REPORTS

What I am about to tell you is not revolutionary. In fact, it is standard best practice. That said, it is absolutely critical, to the point that it feels worth the friendly reminder. Every month, you and your leadership team will benefit from reviewing the standard reports that come out of any basic accounting software, such as:

1. **Profit & Loss (P&L) Statement, by Month, Year-to-Date.** A P&L (aka income statement) summarizes the revenues, costs, and expenses during a specific period of time, allowing you to see your ability to generate profit by increasing revenues and lowering costs and expenses. I find benefit in reviewing monthly, quarterly, and annually.

2. **Balance Sheet.** This important report shows a company's assets, liabilities, and shareholder equity at a specific time. In other words, it outlines what a company owns and owes, along with how much has been invested in the company by owners, revealing company assets at any given moment in time.

3. **Statement of Cash Flows.** This report outlines the movement of cash in and out of the business over time. Similar to the P&L, it helps you see revenues, expenses, and the leftover cash that remains, but it is based on when the cash actually moves through your bank account, whereas the P&L might book revenue today for which you won't actually get paid for 90 or more days. So, a company could have P&L that shows profits, but if you aren't collecting invoices fast enough, or you are paying bills too soon, then you could have negative cash flow. That's why this simple, often neglected, report matters so much.

4. **Accounts Receivable Aging Report.** Unless your company gets paid immediately when (or even before) the product/service is delivered, knowing what is owed to you by your various customers at any given time is critical. Accounts Receivable are debts owed to a company by its customers for products/services already

delivered but not yet paid for. You can configure these reports to cater to your specific business and the typical timeline it takes to be paid by your customers. The data presented here can help you decrease the time it takes to collect payments from customers, which is extremely beneficial to your company.

5. **Accounts Payable Aging Report.** Accounts Payable refers to the money a business owes to its suppliers, vendors, or creditors for goods or services received on credit. When a company purchases goods or services on credit terms, it creates a liability, which is recorded as an account payable in its financial records. This is a short-term liability, since the payments are expected to be made within a relatively brief time period, usually within 30 to 90 days. An Accounts Payable Aging Report provides a detailed breakdown of a company's outstanding Accounts-Payable balances. It is a crucial tool used by businesses to monitor and manage their payable obligations to suppliers, vendors, and

Five Critical Reports

Get yourself acquainted with these essential reports designed to help you track company progress:

1. Profit & Loss (P&L) Statement, by Month, Year-to-Date
2. Balance Sheet
3. Statement of Cash Flows
4. Accounts Receivable Aging Report
5. Accounts Payable Aging Report

Access Excel and PDF templates for each of the Five Reports in the FFG ToolKit: *www.aforceforgood.biz/book-bonuses*

creditors. The report categorizes payables based on their age, showing how long invoices have been outstanding and unpaid.

Now is the time! Call your accountant or bookkeeper, and ask them to send you these reports. Don't sweat it if you can't source everything. You can certainly start with what you do have.

Take a few moments to look at the numbers and digest them. If poring over financial statements is new or feels uncomfortable to you, you're not alone. Most entrepreneurs come from the school of trial by fire, rather than business school. Just start the practice today, and, over time, you will be able to derive more and more knowledge from it.

You will use these reports again in the chapters ahead as you develop your Impact Plan, so keep them at your fingertips.

12+ KEY METRICS DASHBOARD

There are additional aspects of your business it is helpful to quantify. Perhaps you already know this and have key metrics that you track in place—in that case, you're off to a great start. Let's try to bring some more structure to that.

The goal is to find the fewest possible data points needed to understand a business and diagnose where it needs attention. It's good to start with around 12 metrics. More than that will be unwieldy as you're getting started. Fewer than that will mean you miss important areas of discovery. The numbers these metrics reveal, tracked over time, will tell an invaluable story to help you know exactly what to do next to move the needle on your business.

In the remainder of this chapter, we will focus on the four essential measures to mine for key metrics:

1. Metrics that measure *purpose*

2. Metrics that measure *scale*

3. Metrics that measure *profit*

4. Metrics that measure *cash*

We measure purpose, growth, profit, and cash because we wholeheartedly believe in the *value* of generating these four essential outcomes through our business. We measure what matters and, thus, must ensure each of these elements is generated ongoingly by the company. As we explore each element below, the goal will be to start tracking these metrics weekly as a Dashboard. Some might be tracked only monthly, but most will be tracked weekly to create focus and clarity on where you are and what needs to happen next.

12+ KEY METRICS RESOURCES

12+ Key Metrics Resources
Now would be a great time to visit the Key Metrics Resources that will guide you, step by step, in choosing which key measures are most important for your company to track, and in developing a daily, weekly, and monthly dashboard.

- Key Metrics Dashboard Handbook
- Key Metrics Selector

Both resources can be found in the FFG ToolKit: *www.aforceforgood.biz/book-bonuses*

Purpose Metrics

Establishing Purpose Metrics ensures the integrated presence of the five elements of your purpose: Inception Story, Core Purpose, Company

Vision, 10-Year Impact Goal, and Core Values. The critical marking of a Force for Good business is its commitment to both positive impact and healthy profit. Companies painstakingly find ways to measure and improve profits. We must apply the same focus when measuring and elevating our purpose.

Consider the question below to help you choose three to five Purpose Metrics to start regularly tracking to ensure that your purpose is active and integrated into the operations of your company:

What are three specific ways your company could demonstrate that your systems and team are actively fulfilling the promises embedded in each of the following?

- Inception Story

- Core Purpose

- Core Values

- Company Vision

- 10-Year Impact Goal

For detailed instructions to help you choose three Purpose Metrics, refer to the Key Metrics Dashboard Handbook, included with the linked resources available above.

Scale Metrics

"Scale" refers to growing your number of customers, units sold, and their corresponding revenue. Scale is a measure of the positive impact your company intends to deliver to the world and will move you closer to fulfilling your Core Purpose and Company Vision. Scale is also a measure of prosperity. There is a certain scale you need to break even (cover all your costs) and another scale you need to achieve the level of profit needed for you and all of your constituents to thrive and prosper.

Like purpose, scale can be measured in many ways. Here are just a few:

- **Customers**—The number of new customers, retained customers, and loyal customers

- **Units Sold**—The number of widgets sold, be it a service or a product. This includes units sold per product, per customer, and overall.

- **Revenue**—The amount of sales overall, sales per customer, and sales per product

- **Prospects**—The number of suspects, prospects, offers, and closed sales

- **Marketing**—The number of email subscribers, social-media followers, lead conversions, and inbound requests

Of course, there are overt metrics that demonstrate growth, like units sold, number of customers, total invoiced, and service hours delivered. These definitely need to make their way onto your Key Metrics Dashboard as well. It is also important to measure what drives and constricts growth.

For most companies, what drives growth is marketing and sales-related activities. If this is true for your business, then the number of prospects, meetings, offers, and customers generated each week might be among the important growth metrics you track. Consider your marketing funnel. What are the steps to bringing in new customers? How might you measure these steps?

Growth could also be about increasing the products or services sold to existing customers. How does that take place? Are phone calls made?

Service trips delivered? Email marketing that cross-sells and up-sells? Each of these could be measured.

Then, consider: What constricts your growth? What elements stop you from adding customers or volume? What is in short supply? What is hard to get? Where is there friction, frustration, or disorganization? Where are balls dropped? Measuring your constraints is critical to unlocking growth. At Allumé, our primary growth constraint was hiring enough nurses. Thus, we measured every aspect of the recruitment-and-retention process, including number of social-media followers on our career pages, participation in online career events, applicants, interviews, offers, and the number of people who made it through orientation and ultimately out into the field.

It is also important to measure growth-related costs, though those are often tracked monthly rather than weekly. Marketing spent, cost per click, cost per lead, and cost per customer conversion, to name a few, all fall within this category. It is also helpful for you to also track average revenue and units per customer, especially if you are focused on increasing this amount.

Measuring growth data over time allows you to deconstruct and diagnose what is working and not working so you can fine-tune a sustainable growth model. Take a moment, and come up with a list of the three to five key measures of your growth.

Profit Metrics

Most Profit Metrics can be found in the P&L, including revenue, cost of goods sold (COGs), gross profit, operating expenses, operating profit, and net profit. These may be difficult to acquire on a weekly basis; usually monthly is fine, but there are likely key drivers of profit that, when tracked weekly and even daily, can dramatically impact your bottom line in a short time.

In addition to these, consider ways to measure either heightened throughput or efficiency. Examples of these include production time, average cycle time, labor costs, overtime, number of days/hours to do "X," number of units unfinished, downtime, % downtime, etc.

Take a moment to contemplate what drives and depletes profit in your business. Write down three to five ways you could measure profit in your company.

Cash Flow Metrics

Becoming intimate with your company's cash flow will make your whole organization stronger. "Cash flow" refers to the movement of money in and out of a business over a specific period. It represents the inflow and outflow of funds resulting from various activities, including operating, investing, and financing activities. Increasing the speed at which you can collect and looking for ways you can be more efficient in all the systems and processes that enable money to come in are crucial, all while simultaneously slowing down the timing of when dollars need to flow out.

Especially for companies that are Existing or Surviving, tracking your cash balance—the inflow and outflow—each week is incredibly important. These three numbers, tracked over time, are extremely telling.

Where does cash get stuck? What holds up the completion of your product? What delays shipping of your product? What is the process for getting paid, and are there steps along the way where you need to focus attention?

For your business, think about the three to five key measures that would help you track activities that lead to increased cash flow. Use the resources linked above to learn more about cash-flow drivers and metrics.

Create Dashboards

Once you have considered the Four Essential Measures—purpose, growth, profit, and cash—the next step is to create dashboards to be reviewed monthly, weekly, and daily. Using the Dashboard Metrics Templates, you will assemble the most important data you and your team will review regularly. Setting up your dashboards includes:

- Deciding the frequency of collecting each metric.

- Determining who is responsible for collecting the data and reporting it in the desired format.

- Setting initial three-month goals for each metric, so you can move toward progress.

Daily, Weekly, and Monthly Metrics-Tracking Templates

Use these templates to help you track metrics, daily, weekly, and monthly.

- Daily Metrics Tracker
- Weekly Metrics Tracker
- Monthly Metrics Tracker

These templates can be found in the FFG ToolKit: *www.aforceforgood.biz/book-bonuses*

IMPLEMENT WEEKLY AND MONTHLY RITUALS

With Critical Reports, Weekly and Monthly Dashboards, and Profitability Goals set, I invite you to open up your calendar and select a time each week to collect and review the Weekly Dashboard. Also, designate a time each month when you will collect the Five Critical Reports, along with the Monthly Dashboard Data. Put it in your calendar, put it on repeat, invite your leadership team, and go for it!

You may find that certain metrics are difficult to collect—that's okay. Keep those desired metrics on the list, and, for now, simply collect what you can. Over time, your systems of data collection will improve. There were certain metrics on the Allumé dashboard that took years to collect consistently (just ask our CFO Jennifer how hard it was to track unbilled clinician hours!). What is most important here is that you meet weekly and monthly to review whatever data you have. This enables you to know clearly where you are and what you and your team need to do next.

UPDATE YOUR 4-PAGE GROWTH PLAN™

Now that we have come to the end of Chapter 12, you can update the "4-Page Growth Plan™. (The template is in the FFG ToolKit.) The "Know Your Purpose" and "Know Whom You Serve" sections should already be completed, and now you can add in:

- Profit & Loss History—Include financial information from this year to date, last year, and two years ago.

- Daily, Weekly, and Monthly Dashboard Metrics—Include the ongoing metrics you plan to track weekly and monthly to measure the health of your business.

Let's move on to Chapter 14 and dive into the Focused SWOT.

CHAPTER 13
THE FOCUSED SWOT

"Nothing in life is to be feared, it is only to be understood.
Now is the time to understand more, so that we may fear less."

—MARIE CURIE

Physicist and Chemist

"The only thing worse than being blind
is having sight but no vision."

—HELEN KELLER

Author and Activist

The collection of data from Chapter 12, along with the in-depth work you completed in Parts 1 and 2, sets you up beautifully to conduct a Focused SWOT (strengths, weaknesses, opportunities, and threats) Analysis.

WHY SWOT?

The purpose of doing a SWOT Analysis is to help you assemble a plan for how best to achieve your goals. There are about a million ways for your company to get from point A, where it is now, to point B, where it wants to be. The route you choose will, ideally, lean on your company's strengths, minimize your company's weaknesses, and avoid as many threats as possible along the way, as you seek out the external opportunities that could help you make progress. A SWOT Analysis will help you see the best way forward, so you can ensure that your company is operating at its highest and best ability.

The way I do the Focused SWOT now, which starts with a customized assessment of your business, came while I was working with Allumé. After using the old-school method a couple of times—the open-ended *"What are our strengths and weaknesses?"*—I kept ending up with long lists from which it was hard to lift truly useful information. I knew there must be a better way, and so I developed a method that made more sense to me.

I recently led a Focused SWOT with an organization where I'm on the board, Worldwide Orphans. It was a "Holy crap!" moment, as it always is. *This is what we do a lot of the time. This is where we're mediocre. These are the really big problems. This is what we're really good at and should drill down on.* Then when the team came together, we were able to really quickly distill the things that were holding us back and jump straight into what can be done about it. In that sense, it makes things simpler, if not easier.

HOW THE FOCUSED SWOT WORKS

The FFG Focused SWOT focuses not only on what our strengths are, in general but also on our strengths in *achieving* the specific goal at hand. Thus, the process in this chapter is designed to help you specifically tease out the key strengths, most detrimental weaknesses, most helpful opportunities, and the most constrictive threats as it relates to:

1. Reaching your 10-Year Impact Goal (set in Chapter Three)

2. Fulfilling 10-Year Scale Goals you long to achieve (set in Chapter Ten)

3. Achieving your 10-Year Profit Goals (set in Chapter Ten)

WHAT THE SWOT!

Very few conversations are as exhilarating, collaborative, and thought-provoking as a well-orchestrated, Focused SWOT. And unlike more-advanced strategic discussions, a SWOT can be done with anyone on your team, making it an inclusive experience that creates alignment and awareness of the business while also building connection and enthusiasm. At the heart of every SWOT lives the question, *"What do we do now?"* The ensuing conversation can help build consensus among team members who might not see why changes or improvements are necessary.

I remember the first time I led the Allumé team through this experience. I began by distributing an assessment of our healthcare business to each member of the leadership team to complete individually. They were asked to rate our performance from one to five (one being poor, and five being excellent) in roughly 100 different customized measures across each functional area of our specific home-health operations without overthinking it. The entire form took about 15 minutes to complete.

Everyone did the assessment on a Google form so that the results would be immediately aggregated for our discussion. It was fascinating to see how perspectives converged and diverged. First, we considered where there were lots of ones and twos, and lots of fours and fives. This helped us quickly identify our overall company strengths and weaknesses. We also looked at areas where there was significant divergence, with some scoring low and others scoring high, and asked members to share why they chose the rating they gave.

The first time we did this, the team discovered that there were many areas where we were doing just fine, with consistent threes and fours. But a golden five was rare. We also realized there were more ones and twos than we wanted to stomach. I remember a team member saying, "I didn't know there were so many areas of our business that needed work."

We then had an important framing conversation about how, right now, despite things not being perfect, we had much to be proud of and plenty to celebrate. We discussed how a company can operate well and also not be perfect. We could still feel tremendous love for the healthy number of patients we were serving and the constantly growing team of nurses.

Standing in the presence of imperfection and accepting that we could not improve everything all at once, we could then focus on our goals—particularly our 10-Year Impact Goal, which was to double the number of patients receiving complex care nursing in Connecticut.

From this place, we were able to dig in and clearly see the strengths that could increase our momentum, as well as the weaknesses most constraining progress, the opportunities accessible to boost success, and the threats that were posing the greatest risk.

CLARIFY 10-YEAR IMPACT, SCALE, AND PROFIT GOALS

Before engaging in the three FFG self-assessments, the Customized Business Assessment, and the Focused SWOT exercise, it is important to first set a clear destination of where you'd like your company to be in terms of impact, scale, and profit 10 years from now. All these goals are SMART goals (specific, measurable, achievable with greatness, resonant with the team, and time-bound).

Focused SWOT Resources

In the remainder of this chapter, I invite you to follow a process similar to the one described above, to help you determine the best approach for moving forward:

- First, assess your business using these tools:
  - FFG Growth-Readiness Assessment
  - FFG Stage Assessment (from Chapter 11)
  - FFG Traction Assessment
- Second, clarify impact, scale, and profit goals, and create a Customized Business Assessment for you and your leadership team to complete.
- Third, have everyone on your team—you included—take the assessment independently.
- Fourth, meet with your leadership team to conduct a Focused SWOT to fine-tune your impact, scale, and profit goals, and discuss, brainstorm, and document the strengths, weaknesses, opportunities, and threats that can help or hinder progress.
- Fifth, identify the most significant data points that could either accelerate progress forward or act as a significant constraint.

You will find all of these tools and resources
in the FFG ToolKit:
www.aforceforgood.biz/book-bonuses/

Work together with your team to clarify the following goals, and add them to your 4-Page Growth Plan™:

10-Year Impact Goal:

- A singular goal that represents your purpose at scale. (See Chapter 3 to help with this.)

10-Year Scale Goals:

- *Customers Per Year (#)*—Ten years from now, how many customers will your company be serving per year? For example, "We will serve 3000+ customers per year by 2034."

- *Unit Volume/Yr. (#)*—Ten years from now, how many units of product or services will you sell? For example, "We will sell 15,000+ units per year by 2034."

- *Revenue Goal ($)*—Ten years from now, what is your goal for annual revenue? For example, "Our annual revenue will be $10M+ by 2034."

- *Average Revenue/Customer ($)*—Ten years from now, what is the average revenue you'd like to generate per customer? For example, "Our average revenue per customer will be $3,333+ by 2034."

10-Year Profit Goals:

- *Gross Profit Margin Goal (%)*—Ten years from now, what will your gross profit margin goal be? For example, "Our gross profit margin will be 60%+ by 2034."

- *Gross Profit Goal ($)*—Ten years from now, what will your annual gross profit goal be? For example, "Our annual gross profit will be $6M+ by 2034."

- *Operations Expenses ($)*—Ten years from now, what do you project the annual costs of operating your business will be, including people, marketing, sales, R&D, rent, systems, technology, consultants? For example, "Our annual operations expenses will be $2.5M by 2034."

- *Net Profit Margin Goal (%)*—Ten years from now, what will your net profit margin goal be? For example, "Our net profit margin will be 40%+ by 2034."

- *Net Income Goal ($)*—Ten years from now, what will your annual net income goal be? For example, "Our annual net income will be $4M+ by 2034."

THREE SELF-ASSESSMENTS

The first step of the Focused SWOT is to use these three quick-and-easy self-assessments that help clarify where you are today and help illuminate the next essential steps for growth.

FFG Growth-Readiness Assessment

This tool helps you answer the question, *"How ready is my company to grow?"* By examining your company's current strengths and weaknesses in the Four Crucial Areas of Alignment, you can discover where focus and attention is needed: (1) Knowing Your Purpose, (2) Knowing Whom You Serve, (3) Knowing Your Impact Plan, and (4) Knowing Your Highest and Best Use. You will discover your overall Growth-Readiness Score, as well as a score in each of the Four Crucial Areas. A score of 80% or higher on all areas leads to exponential growth.

FFG Stage Assessment

This tool helps you answer the question, *"In what stage of growth is my company right now?"* This tool (discussed in Chapter 11) helps you see at which stage your company resides (Existence, Survival, Scaling, or Impact). It helps you quickly see which facets of your business are holding you back and which areas you can leverage to accelerate progress forward.

FFG Traction Assessment

This tool helps you answer the question, *"How well is my company able to attract, enroll, retain, and serve customers?"* This tool (mentioned in Chapter 9) helps you examine where you are along the journey of customer validation, product-market fit, and having a viable go-to market strategy. This awareness helps you see clearly where to focus energy to create breakthrough growth and customer success.

These three assessments will prime the pump before you create and conduct a Customized Business Assessment.

CREATE A CUSTOMIZED BUSINESS ASSESSMENT

The next step is a detailed assessment of all the functions of your company, including R&D; Product and Service Operations; Marketing; Sales; Quality Assurance; Human Resources; Finance; and Technology, Equipment, and Facilities. For each function, there are key systems, outputs, and competencies. These will be measured on a scale of one to five, with one being a level of very low or non-performance, and five being outstanding performance.

Select Assessment Criteria

The listed criteria in the Business Assessment Template are intended to be a starting point that you can then customize for your unique company. Keep the functions that apply, remove what is not relevant, and add specific items that apply to your business. The more detailed your criteria can be, the better.

Utilize a Survey Platform

While you can certainly conduct the business assessment on paper, the process of aggregating the data is much easier using a basic survey system like Google Forms or Survey Monkey. Both will enable you to quickly see the average score for each criterion, as well as the disparity between scores for an individual criterion. This will give you an immediate list of items to bring into the next stage of the process.

THE FOCUSED SWOT MEETING

With the results of the three self-assessments and your Customized Business Assessment in hand, it is time to meet with your leadership team to discuss, brainstorm, and document what will move you closer to your impact and profit goals. Don't show up to the meeting empty-handed. Bring the following documents from your journey thus far:

1. The completed and aggregated self-assessments and Customized Business Assessment

2. Five Critical Reports (or whatever most recent statements you have is great!):

   - Profit & Loss (P&L) Statement, By Month, Year-to-Date

   - Balance Sheet

   - Cash-Flow Statement

   - Accounts Receivable Aging Report

   - Accounts Payable Aging Report

3. Weekly/Monthly Dashboard (with whatever data you have, even if it is minimal)

4. Customer Enrollment Funnel data

5. Area of Chosen Greatness

Next, walk through the Focused SWOT Blueprint (www.aforcefor-good.biz/book-bonuses/) with your leadership team. After completing the Focused SWOT and assessing your business to identify three key levers, three key strengths, three key opportunities, and three key threats, you are ready for the important step of creating a strategy with milestones leading you all the way to 10-Year Impact, Scale, and Profit Goals.

The meeting that followed the Focused SWOT I conducted with Worldwide Orphans, mentioned earlier in this chapter, was incredibly fruitful. The exercise had revealed the most pressing issue at hand: while the organization is serving in a really powerful and measurable way in six countries, the current approach to fundraising was preventing them from expanding to the level needed to grow that impact. Realizing the issue doesn't necessarily make it easy to address, but it's better to clearly understand what the problem is that you need to solve. That's where the making things simpler, if not easier, piece comes into it again.

With Worldwide Orphans, the plan for many years had been to pursue this very linear growth. But after the Focused SWOT, there was a shift. Resources that had been going toward attracting new donors were reallocated to the development of the team and the upgrading of internal technological infrastructure. Without starting there, they wouldn't be able to implement the many things that would help achieve the desired growth: investment in grant writing, AI-driven technology, and corporate sponsorships. So, phase one was acknowledging that it wasn't about growing right now. It was about getting the pieces in place that would make growth possible in a meaningful and sustainable way down the road. Then, stage two can be about attracting new customers—in this case, new donors—in a more strategic and sophisticated way than before. That's when we can expect to really start seeing the anticipated growth. Stage three is entirely focused on leveraging the elevated systems and new relationships developed in stages one and two, leading to the fulfillment of their 10-Year Impact Goal to serve one million children in vulnerable communities around the world.

UPDATE YOUR 4-PAGE GROWTH PLAN™

I invite you to return to your 4PGP™. Go ahead and add the following:

- Make sure your 10-Year Impact Goal is SMART—a specific, measurable, achievable (with greatness), resonant, and time-bound goal driving everything is essential to the remaining planning process.

- Specific 10-Year Scale Goals—Tied directly to your 10-Year Impact Goal, include the number of customers/year you aim to serve, the total units/year you plan to sell, and your annual revenue by year ten.

- Specific 10-Year Profitability Goals—Aligned with your 10-Year Impact Goal, make sure you include a gross profit margin percentage goal, net profit margin goal, and net annual income goal, all of which you expect will happen at the same time your Impact Goal is achieved in year ten.

- 3 Key Strengths—Lever expected to bring momentum to your Impact and Profit goals.

- 3 Key Weaknesses—Constraints holding you back from your Impact and Profit goals.

- 3 Key Opportunities—Priorities which could boost progress to your Impact and Profit goals.

- 3 Key Risks—The things most likely to slow or derail progress outside the company.

Now you're ready to create a strategy and milestones that will lead you to your goals!

CHAPTER 14
STRATEGY AND MILESTONES

"Ours is not the task of fixing the entire world all at once,
but of stretching out to mend the part of
the world that is within our reach."

—Clarissa Pinkola Estés

"We Were Made for These Times," an essay.

"Life is not a matter of holding good cards,
but of playing a poor hand well."

—Lynn Twist

Founder, The Soul of Money Institute

"Part of leadership is having the courage to select a path,
articulate why it matters, and then rally
others around that vision."

—Kamala Harris

Vice President, United States

Everything we've covered thus far along the Force for Good journey is in service of helping you see what to do: today, this week, this month, this year, this decade. Understanding your strategy and the specific milestones that outline the path are incredibly empowering for both you and your team.

The word "strategy" might fill you with excitement and thoughts of potential, or it might strike you as something elusive and foreign. In this chapter, it is my goal to make the idea of strategy accessible and understandable, so that you can dig in.

WHAT IS "STRATEGY"

A strategy simply answers the question "How . . . ?"

- How are you going to reach the Impact Goal?

- How are you going to attract, enroll, and retain more customers?

- How are you going to boost revenues?

- How are you going to build profits?

In its simplest form, strategy can be articulated in two ways: chronologically and by priority:

- **Chronologically: How will you scale your business and achieve your Impact Goal?** This is where you describe "how" you will get to your goal through a time-based framework: "First, we will focus on . . ." "Then, we will focus on. . . ." and "Finally, we will focus on. . . ."

- **By priority: On which strategic priorities will you maintain deliberate focus to reach your Impact and Profit goals?** Priorities tell you where to invest time and resources; importantly, they also reveal where *not* to focus attention, something that is almost as important for making daily decisions.

FORMULATE YOUR STRATEGY

In the Force for Good System™, there are three steps to formulating a strategy:

- **Step 1: Strategic Analysis**—This is where you assimilate all of the information you've collected in order to articulate your key observations about your situation.

- **Step 2: Create a Chronological Strategy**—With observations from your strategic analysis in hand, you build a three-step path leading from today to the future place where you can meet and surpass your 10-Year Impact, Scale and Profit Goals.

- **Step 3: Articulate Strategic Priorities**—Name the priorities you choose to invest in and focus on throughout the chronological journey.

I've seen the benefit of doing this firsthand. Building both a chronological and priority-oriented strategy at Allumé gave us great clarity about what was important and what could take a back seat over time. Let's take a look at how that came about.

Our 10-Year Impact Goal was to double the number of patients who receive complex-care nursing in the state of Connecticut. When we started Allumé, the total number of patients receiving complex nursing services was 250, with a waiting list of more than 300 who wanted the services but could not access them. Our 10-Year Impact Goal was to open the doors of access to 250 more patients and families in need, taking on 100 of those patients ourselves and helping 150 find their way to other home-health agencies. Our goal was always to make care better and more accessible to *all* patients—not just the ones we cared for at Allumé.

Strategic Analysis

We chose to make complex nursing care our top priority, despite higher profit margins available through other areas of home-health services. We made this strategic decision for a variety of reasons, including but not limited to:

- **It was at the heart of our Inception Story.** The complex-care market was where our heart was and is, as it was exactly the type of service provided to Amelia.

- **Very little competition.** Unlike the other areas of traditional home-health services, which had, at the time, 120 providers already vying for business, complex nursing had only three other real competitors.

- **Abundance of customers.** Unlike trying to get the attention of doctors and hospitals to refer traditional home-health patients, meetings with complex-care referral sources were easily attained. We were able to acquire as many patients as we could handle from the start.

- **High lifetime value of customers and recurring revenue.** Each new complex-care patient we brought on-board would receive an average of 12 hours per day of care. This was about $15K/month or $175k/year in revenues. Because most of our patients stay on service for five-plus years, this is a lifetime value of $875K per customer.

- **40 patients to break even.** If we had chosen traditional home health, we would have needed closer to 200, and those patients would come and go every 60 days. We felt infinitely more confident that we could acquire and keep 40 complex-care patients, as opposed to a revolving door of 200 traditional patients needing one or two short visits each week.

That said, we also knew there were **downsides** to focusing on complex nursing care, which needed to be addressed in our longer-term strategy, such as:

- **We would need a *lot* of nurses.** While there was an abundance of complex-care *patients* needing care, the biggest constraint to admitting them was having enough qualified *nurses*. Thus, we traded the crowded field of home health for the challenges of hiring enough nurses. But we felt confident that we could reliably differentiate ourselves by being the best place for nurses to work and, therefore, attract the necessary workforce, more than we could in our ability to convince traditional home-health referral sources that we were unique in some way.

- **All eggs in one basket.** Since 90% of complex-care nursing is funded by Medicaid, we recognized the significant risk involved. Medicaid rates are typically lower than those of Medicare or private insurance, and relying heavily on a single payer could be detrimental. A reduction in Medicaid rates or significant regulatory changes could have devastating consequences. Therefore, we understood the necessity of diversifying over time to mitigate this risk.

- **Limited exit options.** At the time, complex care was not a field of home-health specialty that was understood or desired by many potential buyers. We knew we needed to keep that in mind and start to cultivate relationships with buyers and investment partners who would understand our business and be a good fit for when the time was right—far before the time actually came to exit.

STRATEGY AND MILESTONES DEVELOPER

Strategy and Milestones Developer

As you can see, there are many elements that inform the creation of a strategy. The Strategy and Milestones Developer will help you navigate the process of doing so. Use this tool as you walk through the remaining sections of this chapter.

Access the Strategy and Milestones Developer in the FFG ToolKit:
www.aforceforgood.biz/book-bonuses

Writing down your observations and reflections as you analyze your current situation will prime you for the next piece, developing your Chronological Strategy.

Chronological Strategy

After carrying out our strategic analysis at Allumé, we asked ourselves, *"Chronologically, how will we scale to achieve our 10-Year Impact Goal of providing ongoing, active complex care to 100 patients?"* The initial chronological strategy we developed in 2018 was written as follows:

- **First, in years one to three, focus on surpassing break-even through the complex-nursing-care market.** Add one to two new complex-care patients per month, which requires the enrollment and onboarding of 10 to 15 nurses per month. By the end of year three, this will have us at 50 patients and 200 nurses, helping us achieve an initial level of profitability that will allow us to invest in improved systems and a larger workforce. To this end, the lion's share of our attention will be spent on attracting and retaining nurses, rather than sourcing patients.

- **Second, in years three to six, our strategy will be to focus on building people and systems for scale and growing gross profit.** We will focus on enriching gross profit, rather than net profit, as we intentionally re-invest into systems, people, and growth. During this time, we will grow to 75+ complex-care patients by keeping our recruiting engine and nurse culture strong. We will also implement an improved electronic medical records system, accounting system, quality-measuring system, data-analytics system, CRM, and marketing system, as well as grow the team by hiring on one to two more schedulers, a finance assistant, and a quality-assurance manager. We will also diversify our services, expanding to traditional home-health nursing and home-health-aide visits, which are more profitable per hour but will necessitate investment in new marketing strategies.

- **Third, in years seven to ten, we will hit our Impact Goal of 100 complex-care patients, while also focusing on building overall bottom-line profitability and investing in one to three more areas of traditional home-health specialty.** Achieving our Impact Goal will give us plenty of gross profit and company stability to refocus growth on the more traditional home-health business. We will leverage the relationships built organically over past years with hospitals and doctors to achieve contracts with two to three insurance companies and build one to three new areas of specialty. This will help us manage risk through diversification of services, referral sources, and payers.

Note: While it was not part of the written chronological strategy shared with my leadership team at the time, I was also concerned with ensuring the company was a valuable asset that could, should I ever desire, be sold to another owner or acquired by another company. While transparency is of utmost importance, this is not something I felt the need to share at the time, as it did not contribute to them doing their highest and best work. I mention it now, however, to highlight that there will be areas of strategic importance that you might choose to keep private for good reason.

Formulate Your Chronological Strategy

Now it's time to craft your chronological strategy. A chronological strategy describes how you plan to achieve your company's 10-Year Impact Goal over a timeline of three phases. Imagine the timeline between today and the completion of the Impact Goal. Divide the journey into three phases of three to four years each. Describe what you plan to achieve and, specifically, how you plan to make progress on the Impact Goal. Describe each of the stages, including these kinds of strategic elements:

1. Approach to increasing Impact, Scale, and Profit

2. Strengths and opportunities to leverage

3. Constraints, weaknesses, and risks to overcome

4. Improvements or additions to your product and services

5. Improvements or additions to systems, people, equipment, real estate, infrastructure, and funding

Use the Strategy and Milestones Developer to help you explore and integrate the concepts to design your chronological strategy by yourself or with your team. Don't overthink it. Draw from whatever information you have, and remember that everything can be modified and adjusted over time.

Strategic Priorities

The next and final step in formulating your business strategy is articulating what your top three to five strategic priorities need to be to reach your 10-Year Impact, Scale, and Profit goals.

At Allumé, our strategic priorities were as follows:

1. **Our #1 area of specialty is complex care.** We devote ourselves, our resources, and 95% of our marketing dollars toward this area of care. We will expand beyond complex care only when we have a census of 100 patients.

2. **Our #1 focus is on recruiting and retaining nurses.** We see nurses as our primary customer. Specifically, we must build a system and culture that consistently recruits 10 to 15 nurses/month and retains 80%+ of all hired nurses for 12+ months.

3. **Focus constant attention on billing and collecting within 30 days.** Because compliant billing in healthcare is complex and can result in delayed collecting, we focus our attention on implementing systems and technology to help us bill and collect within 30 days. We track unbilled hours, submission of on-time documentation, and timeliness of processing physician-signed orders to help us measure improvements over time.

4. **Focus immediately on 33%+ gross profits and ultimately on 18%+ net profits.** Attaining gross profit of 33%+ from the

start and, in later years, growing net profits to 18% or more will provide long-term health and stability for the company. We are committed to identifying, tracking, and improving key lead measures, such as overtime, distribution of PTO, mileage, cost per nurse hire, and nurse retention.

You will notice that our priorities are a blend of Purpose, Impact, Growth, and Profit. I also want to draw attention to the fact that this is not an exhaustive list of what we cared about as a company. Remember, what separates good leaders from great ones is the ability to prioritize, the ability to choose what is *not* on the top of the list; this unlocks the ability to actually become great at something, rather than dilute your efforts trying to be great at everything.

Formulate Your Strategic Priorities

Unlike the Chronological Strategy, which presents your plan to achieve Impact, Scale, and Profit goals over time, your Strategic Priorities articulate key areas to focus attention on throughout your journey.

Consider these important questions as you craft three to five strategic priorities most needed to achieve 10-year Impact, Scale, and Profit goals:

- **What Is Your Chosen Area of Greatness?** In the Force for Good model, companies are invited to select a specific strength to devote 10x the time and attention of everything else.

- **What are the promises of your purpose?** What is the core reason your business exists, and what do you need to prioritize to deliver this commitment? Look to your Inception Story, Core Purpose, Company Vision, 10-Year Impact Goal, and Core Values for reminders of what your company stands for, no matter what.

- **What is the key to customer attraction, enrollment, and retention?** While your strategies and tactics might evolve over time, what is the unchanging special ingredient that attracts and retains your authentic customers?

- **What generates profit?** What area of focus must you consistently maintain? What is the ongoing discipline, activity, or area of focus needed to attain the gross-profit and net-profit goals you have for your business?

- **What builds a culture of innovation and transformation?** In order for your company to be successful in actualizing its Core Purpose and Company Vision, your team needs to be dedicated to constant evolution. What must be consistently supplied to your team to create a place safe to take risks, measure progress, change mindsets, and deliver new results?

- **What creates value for *all* your stakeholders simultaneously?** Consider your customers, employees, vendors, suppliers, shareholders, and community at large. What is the common need all your constituents share that, when you deliver it, produces value cherished by all?

For more information and guidance, refer to the Strategy and Milestones Developer available in the FFG ToolKit.

CHART MILESTONES

The logic behind how to scale your business and achieve Impact and Profitability goals is supported through the creation of a series of touchstones used to guide and measure progress.

Milestone Timelines

In the Force for Good System™, we set eight to ten key milestones for each of the following time periods:

1. **10-Year Milestones.** Set a series of 10-Year Milestones aligned with your 10-Year Impact, Scale, and Profit goals. Return to these milestones at least once a year to make any necessary adjustments.

2. **3-Year Milestones.** This timeline provides something that is a bit more tangible. Your 3-Year Milestones should be reviewed quarterly and revised at least annually, so that you always have a three-year horizon pointing you toward your long-term goals.

3. **12-Month Milestones.** Your 12-month Milestones are set annually to help you build a 12-Month Plan (see Chapter 15). These will be reviewed monthly and fine-tuned quarterly, with the goal of helping ensure you achieve your end-of-year goals.

Five Guidelines for Crafting Milestones

When selecting your eight to ten milestones, make sure they are:

1. **SMART.** All of your milestones are goals and, thus, should be Specific, Measurable, Achievable, Resonant, and Timebound.

2. **Cross-Functional.** Try to include metrics that best depict progress in all of the functional areas of your business. You don't necessarily need to have milestones for each and every area of function, but you do want to lay the groundwork for how people in each function will know how to focus their attention and prioritize over time.

3. **A Blend of Metrics and Projects.** Ideally, this blend will demonstrate progress over time (like customers served, products sold,

gross profit, thank-you cards sent, employee retention, customer-satisfaction ratings, etc.) and project implementations or improvements (like new financial software system implemented, CRM system installed, regulatory survey passed, customer newsletter started, new website launched, Chief Financial Officer hired, etc.)

4. **Illustrative.** The culmination of the 8 to 10 milestones you select should paint a clear picture of what your business will look like in 12 months, 3 years, and in 10 years when you surpass Impact, Scale, and Profit goals. These milestones will empower members of your team to understand where you're headed by providing specific outcomes you expect to achieve along the way.

ALLUMÉ MILESTONES EXAMPLE

Allumé Milestones Example
At Allumé, we built our milestones in January of 2018 to help us move toward our goal of doubling the number of patients who receive complex nursing care in the state of Connecticut, by serving 100+ ourselves by December 2028.

As an illustrative example, they are posted in the FFG ToolKit:
www.aforceforgood.biz/book-bonuses

Formulate Your Milestones

Using the Strategy and Milestones Developer, document your company's 10-year, 3-year, and 12-month Milestones. Draft it solo, or bring together your leadership team to commit your company goals to paper. The act of depicting these specific results you plan to make over time will usher in clarity and resolve in building the business you envision.

WHY STRATEGY AND MILESTONES ARE IMPORTANT

As you fill out Part 4 of the Strategy and Milestones Developer, keep in mind the many reasons why writing down your strategy and milestones is important:

1. **Written words are more tangible than spoken words.** The process of moving something from your mind onto a page, from the ethereal to the physical, fosters clarity and follow-through.

2. **A clear plan combats overwhelm.** Overwhelm is the product of not seeing how the thing that needs doing will get done. Building a plan empowers us to break the problem down, understand it, and then build a sequential path forward.

3. **Provides clarity to many audiences.** Versions of your company's strategy and milestones generated through the Force for Good System™ can be tailored for a variety of audiences. You might have the full version you share (and craft) with your leadership team, a version you share with departmental leaders, another version for all your employees, one for your website and customers, and one for lenders or investors, creating a sense of shared understanding and alignment.

4. **Builds tremendous leverage.** The ideas previously stored in your head are now out, directing and involving the actions of everyone on your team. You are no longer the one who has to be everywhere. The brilliant people on your team can now start the process of aligning with your ideas and, in time, contributing their own insights to the discussion.

As you and your team continue to build out cohesive strategies and align milestones over time, the benefits described above will only multiply. In Chapter 15, I will introduce a repeatable process for how to share your strategy and milestones, at the appropriate level of detail, with everyone in your organization. For now, give yourself a pat on the back for having created a chronological strategy, three to five strategic priorities, and a series of milestones leading you to 10-Year Impact, Scale, and Profit goals! These things can now be incorporated into your 4-Page Growth Plan™ before we jump into the next chapter.

CHAPTER 15
12-MONTH
BREAKTHROUGH PLAN

"Growth and comfort do not coexist.
That's why it's essential to focus on challenges
that push you beyond your comfort zone."

—Ginni Rometty

Good Power: Leading Positive Change in Our Lives, Work, and World
Former Chairman, President, and CEO of IBM

"Clear goals are not a luxury but a necessity
for the brave and truehearted, who dare greatly."

—Brené Brown

*Daring Greatly: How the Courage to Be Vulnerable Transforms
the Way We Live, Love, Parent, and Lead*

"You will never find your next best version of you
sitting inside your comfort zone. Having a plan to
step out of your comfort zone is key to growth."

—Lisa Nichol

Abundance Now: Amplify Your Life & Achieve Prosperity Today
and *No Matter What! 9 Steps to Living the Life You Love*

Every year you are in business is an invitation to stage a massive breakthrough. Contemplate this idea for a moment. Every year is a new opportunity to experience unprecedented growth, innovation, and resolution to a problem that has befuddled you until now. If you and your team apply deliberate focus to any single goal, even one that has proved elusive in the past, you can most certainly attain it.

This is true no matter what stage of business you're in. Whether at Existence, Survival, Scaling, or Impact, you and your team have the power to produce a single breakthrough that could elevate your entire company to a new level. Every year. You might be wondering: *If this is true, then why doesn't it happen more often? Why do businesses face the same fundamental challenges year after year, never making significant progress?*

One reason:
Lack of committed focus.

Your business is generating results right now—revenue, gross profits, new customers, products or services delivered, cash flow—based on your current systems and team. If you want to experience a new result, deliberate focus won't just be *important*—it will be *100% necessary*. Change is necessary. Change is what will deliver the Impact, Scale, and Profit you long for—change that is possible only with concerted, consistent effort.

Now, you could simply take the 12-Month Milestones created in the last chapter and build a plan out from there. Most companies do. But if you follow this approach, I assure you that no major breakthroughs will be forthcoming in the year ahead. In this model, of setting a bunch of goals and giving them all the same amount of priority, some get accomplished, while others don't. It won't breed true innovation, and the most critical outcomes will stay stuck.

FOCUS ON LESS TO ACHIEVE MORE

Are you nervous that, if you focus on only one big goal, everything else will fall apart? The real truth is this: *breakthroughs beget breakthroughs.* They create momentum and opportunity everywhere else in your company. Your other goals will almost magically move forward, too.

And as each person in your company begins to make progress on the most important thing for them to deliver, improve, or innovate each week, they will undoubtedly discover immediate and ongoing reasons to celebrate, because success is the love child of focus. When you clarify what is most important, set clear goals with your team, and define what real progress looks like, your organization will transform into a highly productive, innovative, and committed collection of individuals capable of just about anything.

BUILDING YOUR 12-MONTH BREAKTHROUGH PLAN

The performance-breakthrough system I will share with you in the rest of this chapter is grounded in all the work you have done up to this point—knowing your purpose, knowing whom you serve, and knowing what your long-term strategic plan is. This deliberate clarification of all of the elements of the Force for Good System™ allows you and your leadership team to see clearly:

What most needs a profound breakthrough in your business right now?

Six Attributes of a Company-Wide Breakthrough

There are six attributes of a solid Company-Wide Breakthrough:

1. **Everyone in the company can influence its progress.** The ultimate Company-Wide Breakthrough will leverage the intelligence,

participation, and determination of every single person in your company. Some may influence the effort more directly than others, but everyone needs to feel she can contribute on some level.

2. **Company-wide, but *focused*.** It cannot be watered-down word-smithing that's code for "Achieve all 12 Milestones." It must discern one important thing that needs to be improved, implemented, or delivered through the collective innovation and conviction of the team. By contrast, it will tell you which of the other 12-month Milestones are *not* top priority and should be treated accordingly.

3. **Worth 10x the Energy.** Remember how you selected an Area of Chosen Greatness in Chapter 7? This follows the same principle. You choose to give this goal far more resources, time, and attention than the others on your 12-Month Milestones list. Make a clear choice, and then go all-in.

4. **80% likely.** The ultimate Breakthrough Goal is a stretch goal that will not happen simply by doing what everyone already does, but it should also feel like it's within the realm of possibility.

5. **Tangible and understandable.** Every single person in your company should be able to explain the 12-Month Breakthrough Goal in their own words—both what it is and why this particular goal is so critical.

6. **Progress can be easily measured.** Guided by instructions coming later, your breakthrough goal is something that can be easily measured and won't require hours of time fiddling with spreadsheets to assess progress. Measurement must be accessible, easy, and frequent.

7. **Requires change.** In order to actualize a Breakthrough Goal, everyone on the team will be invited, encouraged, and stretched

to grow. The status quo simply won't do. A great Breakthrough Goal will transform your company and team from the inside out.

Let these questions drift through your mind:

- What is one individual outcome at your company that would change everything?

- Which specific problem, when finally solved, will make achieving every other challenge easier?

- What is the primary breakthrough that would catapult your company to the next level?

But before we go forward with picking the Breakthrough Goal, let's first circle around to the ever-important Pareto Principle.

Leverage the Pareto Principle

Commonly known as the 80/20 rule, the Pareto Principle is the notion that roughly 80% of consequences come from 20% of causes.

Here are some common examples:

- 20% of a plant contains 80% of the fruit.

- 20% of customers generate 80% of a company's profits.

- 20% of players account for 80% of points scored.

The Pareto Principle should help inform your breakthrough. Certain goals will have a more profound and reverberating impact than others. The graph below illustrates what I mean. Certain milestones will have a more compounding effect than others.

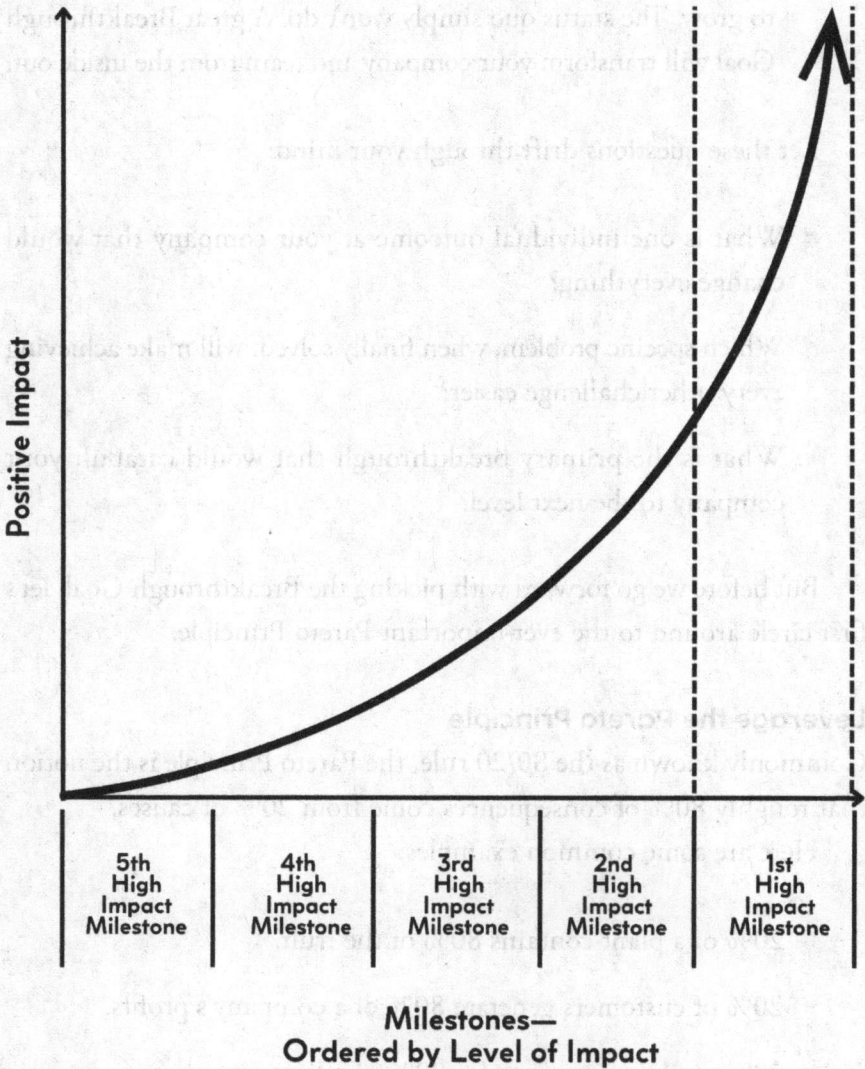

Positive Impact (y-axis)

| 5th High Impact Milestone | 4th High Impact Milestone | 3rd High Impact Milestone | 2nd High Impact Milestone | 1st High Impact Milestone |

**Milestones—
Ordered by Level of Impact**

Try plotting all your 12-Month Milestones (from Chapter 14) on the graph above, with the x-axis being the list of milestones, and y-axis being the level of overall positive impact to company success. Line them up from left to right, from low to high overall impact on the success of your company, as measured by your 10-Year Impact, Scale, and Profit Goals.

Notice how some goals elevate multiple areas of the business and make possible lots of new options and opportunities, while others are more isolated in their benefit. Place the milestones that, when achieved, will have the most prolific and positive effect on the whole company on the far right, and place those milestones that would be good to achieve but whose consequences would have fewer reverberating effects, on the left.

12-MONTH BREAKTHROUGH GUIDEBOOK

12-Month Breakthrough Guidebook

12-Month Breakthrough Guidebook Use the 12-Month Breakthrough Goal and Plan Guidebook to help you brainstorm and clarify the highest-priority result your company needs right now to catapult Impact, Scale, and Profit to the next level. It will also help you develop a quarterly plan to arrive successfully at your goal. Download the Guidebook, and follow along as you read the remainder of this chapter.

Access this resource in the FFG ToolKit: *www.aforceforgood.biz/book-bonuses*

Once you have selected your Company-Wide Breakthrough Goal for the year, it is time to take the next important step of creating a way to measure progress on that front.

ESTABLISH A METHOD OF MEASURING PROGRESS

It is often easier to set a goal than it is to track its progress. Some goals make it easy to collect data—number of service hours delivered or units of product sold. In contrast, goals like customer satisfaction or employee engagement are more difficult to track. This is why this step of building a 12-Month Breakthrough Plan is critical.

The Force for Good System™ introduces a feedback loop, where, on a weekly basis, you and your team look at your data, assess how you're doing, and ask the fundamental question, *"What could we do over the next five to seven days to move the needle on progress?"* If you cannot measure your Breakthrough Goal, you will never be able to manage it, improve it, or even know for certain when it has been accomplished.

Collect Last Week's Data

We will start by determining how you did on your Breakthrough Goal last week. If your Breakthrough concerns the number of products sold, find out how many were sold last week. If your Breakthrough Goal is a certain number of new customers acquired, go find out how many new customers said "Yes!" last week. If your Breakthrough Goal was to increase the percentage of total new-customer sales you were responsible for to be 50% of all sales, go find out how you did last week.

I'm being literal. Go find the data. Come back to this chapter when you have it.

How did you do last week? Are you 10% of the way to your goal? 5%? 12%?

How Difficult Was the Data to Collect?

Now that you have the relevant information in hand, consider how challenging it was for you or someone on your team to collect the data. If it was a slow and cumbersome process, you won't be inclined to follow through on regularly collecting progress data, and then your breakthrough won't happen.

If the data was difficult to extract, there are a few options:

- **Ask yourself if another, similar measurement** would be easier to attain and could be used to measure the same Breakthrough Goal.

- **Build a simple, repeatable system for quick calculations.** Setting up a spreadsheet to effortlessly monitor progress is a great step toward doing this.

- **Establish a data aggregator.** This can be done manually through spreadsheets built out once and then used regularly, or through the data aggregators and dashboard builders now in the market, including Domo, Grow by Epicor, Zoho Analytics, and Cloudera Distribution.

- **Bring in outside help.** You may benefit from working with your technology provider to have them build a custom report or some system enhancement for you to get the data you need.

The key is to find a way to collect this information at least weekly, putting in upfront effort to reduce ongoing effort and friction. With your Breakthrough Metrics in hand, complete the second part of the 12-Month Breakthrough Plan in the Guidebook.

IDENTIFY "MIGs" AND "LEADs" FOR EACH FUNCTIONAL AREA OF YOUR COMPANY

Now that you have a 12-Month Company-Wide Breakthrough Goal—something terrifically important for you to achieve—it is time to align each functional team in your company to focus on an aligned goal that empowers them to move the needle on Breakthrough.

In this step, each functional area of the company will create the following:

1. **12-Month Most Important Goal (MIG)**—Directly aligned with the company-wide Breakthrough Goal, the MIG is where the functional group focuses their highest and best energy throughout the upcoming year.

2. **Three Lead Measures (LEADs)**—These are three metrics that track activities that precede and facilitate the outcome of the MIG. More on this below.

The image below illustrates how the Company-Wide Breakthrough Goal, Functional Team MIGs, and Functional Team LEADs relate to one another. All are working together to create one outcome: *Breakthrough!*

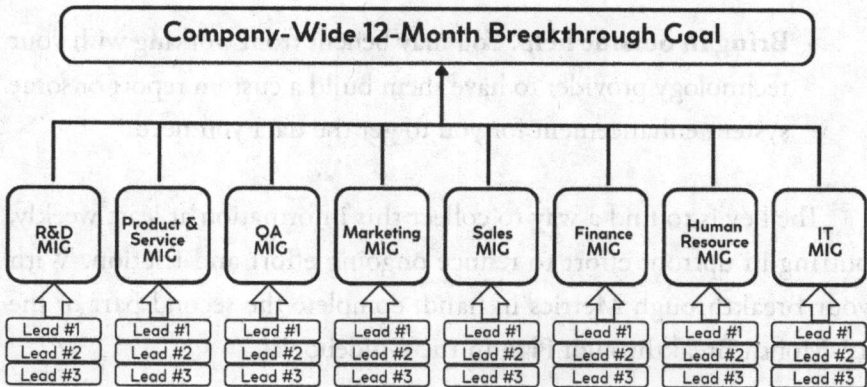

MIGs AND LEADs RESOURCES

MIGs and LEADs Resources

Download the MIGs and LEADs Guidebook and the MIGs and LEADs Template, which will walk you step-by-step through the process of creating weekly functional goals aligned with your 12-Month Breakthrough Goal.

- MIGs and LEADs Handbook
- MIGs and LEADs Tracker

These tools are available in the FFG ToolKit: *www.aforceforgood.biz/book-bonuses*

QUARTERLY GOALS

Establishing quarterly goals is the last piece of the Impact Plan! Clearly defined quarterly objectives make room for a handful of other important projects or outcomes to receive focus—not nearly as much focus as the Breakthrough Goal and MIGs, but some focus.

List out three to five key objectives you and your team would like to achieve in the coming four quarters using the 12-Month Breakthrough Guidebook.

FULL SYSTEM ALIGNMENT

You did it! You crafted the 12-Month Breakthrough Plan with these important elements:

- A 12-Month Company-Wide Breakthrough Goal

- A Most Important Goal (MIG) for each functional team

- A way to measure each MIG weekly

- Three leading measures (LEADs) supporting the MIG of each functional team

- A list of three to five Quarterly Objectives

UPDATE YOUR 4-PAGE GROWTH PLAN™

As we wrap up Chapter 15, be sure to update the following elements in your 4-Page Growth Plan™:

- A Company-Wide 12-Month Breakthrough Goal.

- A Most Important Goal (MIG) for each functional team.

- A way to measure each MIG weekly.

- Three leading measures (LEADs) supporting the MIG of each functional team.

- A list of three to five Quarterly Objectives.

12-Month Breakthrough Plan

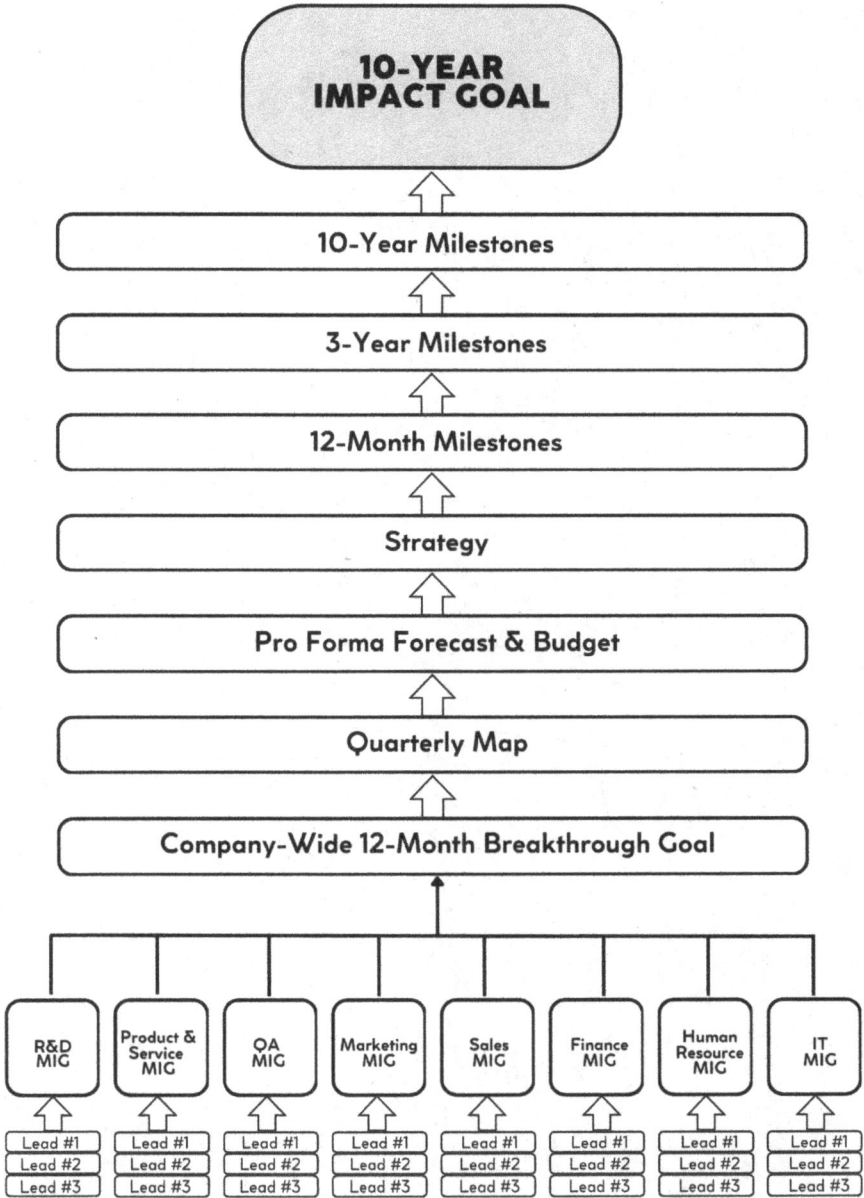

10-YEAR IMPACT GOAL

10-Year Milestones

3-Year Milestones

12-Month Milestones

Strategy

Pro Forma Forecast & Budget

Quarterly Map

Company-Wide 12-Month Breakthrough Goal

R&D MIG	Product & Service MIG	QA MIG	Marketing MIG	Sales MIG	Finance MIG	Human Resource MIG	IT MIG
Lead #1	Lead #1	Lead #1	Lead #1	Lead #1	Lead #1	Lead #1	Lead #1
Lead #2	Lead #2	Lead #2	Lead #2	Lead #2	Lead #2	Lead #2	Lead #2
Lead #3	Lead #3	Lead #3	Lead #3	Lead #3	Lead #3	Lead #3	Lead #3

CHAPTER 16
PRO FORMA BUDGET AND FORECAST

"Sufficiency isn't about the amount of anything.
It's about our relationship to what we already have."

—Lynn Twist

The Soul of Money: Transforming Your Relationship with Money and Life
Founder, The Soul of Money Institute

"The key to abundance is meeting limited circumstances
with unlimited thoughts."

—Marianne Williamson

A Woman's Worth

"A budget isn't just numbers on a spreadsheet;
it's a statement of values and priorities."

—Sallie Krawcheck

CEO, Co-Founder, Ellevest

"A budget tells you what's possible; it's a tool
for empowerment, not limitation."

—Anne-Marie Slaughter

CEO, New America

I studied biology and chemistry in college. I took one business class—not finance, accounting, or even statistics. When I was 22, I launched my first real company—an online art business called The Zoe Collection. I had no idea what a pro forma budget and forecast were. But I had a vision of making beautiful pieces of art available to the masses, freeing up artists to focus on their masterpieces and leaving the work of sales to my new, burgeoning company.

If I had known anything at all about budgeting and forecasting, I would have known we needed a lot more funding to get off the ground. I would have known how many bracelets, paintings, and sculptures I needed to sell just to cover my costs. I would have seen more clearly when I could actually afford to add team members to help scale the company. I would have created a clearer way to communicate to potential investors who could help fund my Company Vision.

But I didn't know any of that then. While I loved creating the Zoe Collection, just like 80% of all businesses, it failed within three years for lack of funding.

That is not what we want for you. In this chapter, I aim to give you the tools to make your 10-Year Impact Plan a reality. Now that you have gone through the process of first, knowing your purpose; second, knowing whom you serve; and third, putting together a 10-Year Impact Plan, it is now time to translate all of that into a financial plan that will bring it to life.

WHAT IS A PRO FORMA BUDGET AND FORECAST?

Your Pro Forma Budget and Forecast will translate your long-term Strategy, 3-Year Milestones, and your 12-Month Breakthrough Plan into numbers, thus helping you fund your purpose and vision.

This chapter will guide you through five sequential steps to create a Pro Forma Forecast and Budget, against which you will be able to test all of your assumptions and predictions moving forward, allowing you to bring a forecasted reality in your business to fruition over time.

WHY CREATE ONE?

I am deeply passionate about financial modeling. Think I'm kidding? I'm not. As I said before, Pro Forma Forecasting was not something I knew about when I launched my first business, but you can be certain that I realized it was the missing link the second time around. Since then, I've come to love the work of financial forecasting and budgeting, because it helps me move ideas into reality in a way I can test and improve.

Over the past 25+ years with clients, teams, and in my own businesses, I have found that the process of forecasting and budgeting serves these essential functions:

1. **It is empowering.** Until you have a well-thought-out forecast and plan, you will always have the lingering suspicion that your approach is a bit of a crapshoot. Once you put your dreams into numbers, you will suddenly see that what you hope to achieve is possible.

2. **It dispels overwhelm.** The process of forecasting and budgeting allows your brain to digest and understand how everything will

come together to achieve what you want to achieve and fund what you need to fund, over time.

3. **It creates clarity.** In the steps outlined in this chapter, we will move through big pockets of information at a time, working through what's important and why. Working together with your leadership team will flush out any misinterpretations and unwarranted assumptions, and bring everyone into clear alignment about where you're going and how you will get there.

4. **It builds ownership.** Building your Pro Forma Forecast and Budget involves all the key players in your organization to participate. Everyone has a voice, and everyone's worries and concerns are addressed. In the end, everyone feels they have a part in building toward the future.

5. **It facilitates accurate decision-making.** This forecasting and budgeting process guides making important choices: How much are you willing to invest in your people? How far are you willing to go to build an impeccable product? How many salespeople will it really take to sell that many widgets? Until this moment, everything is conjecture. Now, it's about putting your money where your ideals are.

6. **It creates reality.** Everything we have done to this point along the Force for Good journey is to bring your Vision into reality. The Pro Forma Forecast and Budget are the closest we can come to reality before you can actualize your Company Vision.

THE MINDSET OF SUFFICIENCY

It is not uncommon for budgeting exercises to be haunted by bad experiences from the past. Scarcity often reigns when it comes to budgeting.

We make it about all the things we can't have, rather than seeing how we can leverage our precious resources for good.

From the get-go, I invite you and your team to enter the process of forecasting and budgeting as *a sacred act of choosing how best to steward the treasures you already have.* There is no scarcity. Instead, adopt the mindset: **You always have exactly what you need to take the next step.** Enough ideas, ingenuity, creativity, and, yes—even funding. So always be looking for the next step.

Second, adjust your mindset to: **Take a leap of faith and make an educated guess.** You won't be able to solve every challenge now, so don't even try. Do your best to make predictions based on truth, but when you aren't sure, don't let uncertainty stop you from moving forward.

Next, know that the process of forecasting and budgeting is iterative. The first time you go through this won't be your last. Holding onto the third mindset—**You can adjust it later**—will help you continue to push forward, even through uncertainty.

The fourth mindset is to **trust that you will get better and better at forecasting and budgeting over time.** But you have to start somewhere. Depending on how long you've been in business and at what stage you're currently in—Existence, Survival, Scaling, or Impact—you will have less or more to work with in building a financial model for your company. If you have been in business for 10 years, you have 10 years of historical experience to help you know how many units you might be able to sell next November. It is much more abstract to make these estimates if your company is only a few months old and hasn't yet sold a thing. Remember that the process of budgeting and forecasting is about mindfully funding your Company Vision, while also gaining ever-increasing clarity about what is realistic and possible.

The goal of the Pro Forma Forecast is *not* to predict exactly what will happen. It's a well-tuned thought experiment that helps you bring your ideas more cogently into reality. The more you allow yourself to experience the gifts of your budgeting and forecasting process, the better you will become at it.

BEGIN WITH THE END IN MIND

Once you have your three-year Pro Forma Forecast and Budget, you will use it to test the accuracy of your assumptions. Every month, you will compare what actually happened with what you projected would happen.

You will want to set up your Pro Forma Forecast and Budget so they align with the systems you already have in place. Use the following guidelines to help you set yourself up for success.

Involve Your CFO

Include your CFO, finance manager, or accountant in this process. S/he will, hopefully, have lots of experience with budgeting and forecasting and can help you sync your business with the process I've outlined below.

Align with Your Existing Chart of Accounts

How you set up your offerings, administrative team, and operations expenses will all need to align if you want to be able to compare your budget versus actuals each month. Involving your finance leader in this effort either will help you connect this process to what is already in place in your accounting system, or it will inform you and your finance team of changes that need to be made within your accounting system. The important takeaway here is that, if your accounting system's chart of accounts isn't aligned with your forecast and budget, you won't be able to accurately test and compare your predictions with what really happens.

Key Comparisons

If it is aligned, however, that will enable you to predict and then compare the actual results by month and by year for these important factors:

- Revenue by Offering and Overall

- COGs by Offering and Overall

- Gross Profit by Offering and Overall

- Administrative Personnel

- Operations Expenses

- Net Profit

PRO FORMA BUDGET AND FORECAST GENERATOR

Pro Forma Budget and Forecast Generator
It is time to dive into the process of creating your Three-Year Pro-Forma Forecast and Budget Generator. Download it now, and use it as you read the remainder of this chapter.

The Pro Forma Budget and Forecast Generator is available in the FFG ToolKit: *www.aforceforgood.biz/book-bonuses*

FIVE SEQUENTIAL STEPS TO BUILDING A PRO FORMA FORECAST AND BUDGET

1: Your Offerings: Price and COGs

First, begin by listing everything you sell, which I refer to as "offerings." For each offering, work with your finance team to determine:

- **Unit Price ($)**—This is what customers pay, on average, per unit for each of your offerings. This will be used to determine revenue in the Pro Forma model, so make sure the price you set here is a realistic reflection of how much you price each unit, on average.

- **COGS per unit ($)**—What is your Cost of Goods Sold on a per-unit basis? Depending what you sell, it could be the ingredients, materials, or supplies to build a product, along with any commissions automatically included with each sale. Alternatively, if you are selling services, it would include the cost of the people who deliver the services provided and any fringe benefits you pay for them. Again, your CFO is the best person to consult on building COGS per unit.

- **Gross Profit Per Unit ($)**—This measures the profitability of each unit of a product or service sold by a business. It helps assess how much profit is generated from the sale of each individual item or unit. Gross Profit Per Unit = Sales Price Per Unit minus COGS Per Unit.

How will this be used? In the next section, you will predict how many units of each offering will be sold. The price per unit and COGS per unit will drive the total revenue and gross profit you see in the integrated model in step five below.

2: Volume Predictions over Time

Now it is time to forecast sales. Start with the same list of offerings used in step one above, and, together with your leadership, collaboratively predict the number of units you plan to sell per month for the next 12 months. Take a leap of faith, and make an educated guess. Feel the excitement of doing this, and don't worry about forecasting with immediate accuracy—*you can make changes later on.*

Once you have estimated volume sales for each offering for the first 12 months, total them up for the year. Next, ask yourself, "By how much do we plan to increase volume sales for each offering from year one to year two?" Consider your strategy, your plan, and the elements of the Customer Enrollment Funnel you plan to ramp up and invest in. What are your plans for increasing marketing and selling activities?

Once you have completed your volume forecast, you will see, in step five, where you integrate the list of offerings, the per-unit price, and the per-unit COGS for each, along with the volume you predict, to generate your forecasted revenue, COGS, and gross profit. If you are using the "Pro Forma Forecast and Budget" template, available online, you will be able to click over to the tab labeled "The Integrated Pro Forma Model" to see what your revenue and gross profit look like so far.

Consider these questions as you build volume forecast:

1. **What is your 10-Year Impact Goal?** Will you be making meaningful progress toward that goal in the forecast volume?

2. **Which offerings are you focusing on selling in year one?** Does growth shift or expand for any particular offerings in year two or three?

3. **What is your plan for growing your Customer Enrollment Funnel?** How much growth can you expect now, in six months, and in three years?

4. **Is your predicted growth per month and per year realistic?**

5. **What factors might affect your ability to produce or deliver the number of units predicted?** Can you produce the level of forecast sales? Are there bottlenecks in your supply chain that might constrain growth?

6. **Are there new offerings you plan to launch over the next three years?** If so, be sure to include them in your forecast.

3: The People You Will Need

Now that you know how many units of each offering you plan to sell, it is time to consider the administrative team needed to do so and the costs required to support them. This list does *not* include the people captured in your Cost of Goods Sold (COGS), those who directly deliver services that customers pay for. Instead, people captured here include everyone else needed to support sales, marketing, customer service, finance, technology, product development, research, etc.

Using the Pro Forma Budget and Forecast Generator, provided in the link above, list all of the current and future roles your company will need over the next three years in the tab marked "People." Forecast the cost of each by month for the first year, and by year for years two and three. Be sure to include any fringe benefits in this cost. The Pro Forma Tool provides a place for you to put an estimated percentage of wages to help you create a budget for fringe benefits.

If you plan to add administrative team members over the next three years, list those roles and the estimated costs for those members over time.

Consider these questions, and map out their costs per month and per year:

1. Who is your current team? What are their current roles, and what do you pay them?

2. For hourly employees, consider whether their hours will stay the same or increase over the months and years ahead. How will that affect your costs per month and per year?

3. Consider your strategy, milestones, and plans for growing your Customer Enrollment Funnel. Will you need additional people to support these initiatives?

4. Consider your volume growth. Will more people be required to support that growth? List the people you will need to add over the next three years.

The goal is to create a list of all the roles and costs by month for year one and by year for years two and three. These costs will all roll into your operations expenses, included in the next step.

4: Operations Expenses

Now it is time to consider your operations expenses. These are the investments you plan to continue making, plus any other resources, tools, equipment, technology, or office space you might need to fulfill your Purpose, 3-Year Milestones, or 12-Month Breakthrough Goal. This includes all your administrative employees, which you already budgeted in step #3, plus all the other costs of operating your company not included in Cost of Goods Sold (COGS).

Using the "Pro Forma Budget and Forecast Generator," list all of the current and future operations expenses your company will need to fund over the next three years in the tab marked "Operations Expenses." Forecast the cost of each by month for the first year and by year for years two and three.

If you already have a financial system in place, like QuickBooks, Intacct, or Xero, a great way to start this list is to have your CFO or accountant run an income statement by month for the last year, and then add in each of the expense accounts into the Pro Forma Tool in the tab marked "Operations Expenses." The Pro Forma Tool includes a basic list of business expenses as a template, but you are encouraged to model the expense list after your current chart of accounts. This will help you when it comes time to enter your finalized budget into your accounting system.

Questions to consider as you project costs:

1. **What did you spend last year for each expense type?** What will change this year to bring those costs up or down?

2. **Consider your volume forecast.** What will you need to do to support increases: customer service, production, supplies, space?

3. **What are your Customer Enrollment Funnel plans?** What new marketing channels and tactics will you employ over the next three years? How much will those initiatives cost?

4. **Will you need to invest in people or technology?** Will you need to purchase a new system, hire more service providers, or retain consultants to help you improve your current systems?

5. **What about facilities and equipment?** Do your 3-Year Milestones require new computers, office space, or other items?

The goal is to create a monthly budget for year one and annual budgets for years two and three for all of your expenses. This will allow you to see clearly the amount of gross profit you will need to fund your business operations.

5: The Integrated Model

The integrated model can come together now that you have built in all of the necessary elements—your offerings, sales volume, administrative team, and operations expenses. It will provide a summarized view by month for the first 12 months and annually for the first three years of the following:

1. Revenue

2. Cost of Goods Sold

3. Gross Profit

4. Operations Expenses

5. Net Income

Turn to the last tab, "Integrated Forecast and Budget," on the Pro Forma Budget and Forecast Generator. The calculations here will generate automatically after you have completed the other three tabs.

Once you have your first draft and see the results of your Integrated Model, you can start tweaking and validating. Ask yourself these questions:

1. **Do all of these estimates seem realistic?**

2. **Are you generating enough gross profit to cover your expenses?** If not, do you have a funding source (a line of credit, your own investments, or the investments of others) to cover the shortfall?

3. **Are you happy with the level of overall profitability of your company?** Based on industry trends, are your gross profit and net profit meeting standard benchmarks?

4. **What are the levers to grow faster?** To grow more quickly, could you acquire additional working capital through a line of credit, a loan, or an investor?

5. **Where could you reduce or delay costs?** What non-essential expenses could be delayed? Remember to fund what's most important first (12-Month Breakthrough), and find other places to delay or reduce investment.

6. **Where are you underfunded for the purpose at hand?** What are your options for overcoming those gaps?

THE POWER OF A WORKING MODEL

Congratulations! You now have a Pro Forma Forecast and Budget! Seeing your business through numbers clarifies how much you must sell, what you are budgeted to spend, and whether you have enough funding to get you through the next three years. The model also gives you a plethora of choices. With so many levers—volume, price, cost of goods, people, operations expense—there are endless ways to attain both Profit and Purpose.

UPDATE YOUR 4-PAGE GROWTH PLAN™

You now have the final piece of the puzzle for your 4PGP™! Once you add your Pro Forma Forecast and Budget, you are ready to implement your ideas and make them reality.

WRAPPING UP PART THREE

We are now exiting the third leg of our four-part system. As you prepare to walk forward into the final stretch of the journey, reflect on all that you accomplished here in Part Three:

1. You put words to your **Personal Definition of Prosperity** in terms of profit, freedom, impact, and security. You also considered your relationship with your company and what you plan to give and receive at each stage of your business. You began thinking about what you might need to do to ensure you have desirable options for the day you exit your company.

2. You took care to **Know Where You Are**. You articulated the current stage of your business (Existence, Survival, Scaling, or Impact) and collected Five Critical Reports and metrics for a Weekly and Monthly Dashboard.

3. You developed a **Focused SWOT**. You worked hard to unveil the most important details that are either supporting or constricting progress on your Impact, Scale, and Profit Goals.

4. You articulated your **Strategy and Milestones**, both chronologically and in terms of strategic priorities, to help you know how to reach 10-Year Impact, Scale, and Profit Goals.

5. You crafted a **12-Month Breakthrough Plan** that will take your company to a whole new level.

6. You created and refined your **4-Page Growth Plan**™. Drawing from all of the work done in every chapter leading up to this one, you completed a plan that integrates all of the key elements of the Force for Good System™ into a simple and easy-to-use format, including the key elements you will focus energy and attention on daily, weekly, monthly, and annually.

Now, you're ready to step boldly and confidently into Part 4.

PART 4
BE A FORCE FOR GOOD

"How wonderful it is that nobody need wait a single moment before starting to improve the world."

—ANNE FRANK

"Love is an action, never simply a feeling."

—IYANLA VANZANT

In the Meantime: Finding Yourself and the Love You Want

"Leadership is a matter of how to be, not how to do."

—FRANCES HESSELBEIN

Hesselbein on Leadership, Former CEO of Girl Scouts

"Leadership is about making others better as a result of your presence and making sure that impact lasts in your absence."

—SHERYL SANDBERG

Lean In: Women, Work, and the Will to Lead,
Former COO, Facebook

The last stage of the Force for Good Journey is all about you, the founder. It is about helping you discover your highest and best use as it relates to your business, today and every day going forward.

This is really the heart of what I want to talk to you about, but it was crucial to lay out the groundwork first. A strong foundation needs to be in place in order to pour your best self, your highest self, into these tools. In fact, all of the questions and activities before this point in the process have been about getting out of the solely analytical approach and accessing what I call "Your Knowing Self."

Again, to reiterate, the analytical matters. Without a clear forecast and budget, you can try to be wise, to be transformative, to be of highest and best use, but, in all likelihood, you're going to fall flat on your face. It's like learning the periodic table. You have to learn the structure of all the various elements before you can start connecting them to create elegant chemistry. But, at this point, we are ready! The time has come to get more fully into the most important piece. This section is no longer about *what* you're *doing*, but *who* you're *being*.

When I look back at my own entrepreneurial journey, it was the act of constantly asking myself, *"What is my highest and best use?"* along the way that helped me find clarity as I continued to track my own true north. It's easy to get stuck doing everything the same way you've always done it. It's easy to stick with what is safe and familiar. It's easy not to move out of the way when it is time to let others lead. But creating a company that can truly serve as a Force for Good requires all of this and more from you, dear founder. It requires you to evolve. Grow. Be wrong. It begs you to let go and allow the brilliance of others to shine.

When we start our beloved companies, we often wear every conceivable hat. And while we long for the day that changes, it is so often a struggle to relinquish control and break out of that initial role. The Force for Good System™ will help you understand how to do this, how to put others to work in deeply empowering ways that ease your own load while simultaneously enriching your business with the wisdom of many.

Asking, "What is my highest and best use?" will help you remember to evolve over time to meet the new and changing needs of your business, as well as your own shifting needs. In these remaining chapters, we will first address the essential role of implementing the system. We've covered all the Core Growth Elements that make up the transformational Flywheel that, when it's installed, will accelerate Impact, Scale, and Profit in your company. Regardless of which stage currently reflects your business—Existence, Survival, Scaling, or Impact—Chapter 17 will provide the details for how to build the Flywheel and then how to get it churning.

Most of the time, your highest and best use is simply to follow your 4-Page Growth Plan™ and conduct the Seven Rituals of Innovation. That's it. These two guides will inform you daily, weekly, monthly, and annually how you can be of greatest service to your purpose and vision.

The last three chapters answer the question, *"Who should I strive to be each and every day to cultivate a company that can fulfill the inspired vision within me?"* How should you behave along the way? Which qualities, called forth from within, will create the culture and team capable of delivering the many promises of your brand? Here we will discuss the three aims of a Force for Good leader:

- Be wise.

- Be transformative.

- Be of the Highest and Best Use.

CHAPTER 17
IMPLEMENT THE FORCE FOR GOOD SYSTEM™

"Never doubt that a small group of thoughtful,
committed citizens can change the world;
indeed, it's the only thing that ever has."

—Margaret Mead

Cultural Anthropologist

Now that you have been introduced to all of its elements, you can move on to implementing the Force for Good System™ in your company so that you can immediately start to experience the momentum and breakthroughs it offers. As an entrepreneur myself, I know how valuable your time is, which is why the instructions below are crafted to be expedient and efficient, aiding you in launching the first iteration of your system in just seven days. Without further ado, let's get into it.

BUILD YOUR TRANSFORMATIONAL FLYWHEEL

The Force for Good System™ is a Transformational Flywheel for your business, designed to accelerate Impact, Scale, and Profits. By defining the core elements in this book with your team, each becomes a spoke in the Flywheel that's going to propel your business forward. When combined with the Seven Rituals, discussed later in this chapter, momentum, strength, and sustainability in your business are givens.

To do this, you must empower your entire team—whether it's made up of 5 or 5,000—with awareness and knowledge of the Core Growth Elements at a level and format that is appropriate to their role. This will direct clarity, momentum, and focused action onto where it matters most. The rollout plan laid out in these pages will assist in allowing that to occur naturally. Remember, the Core Growth Elements make up the legs of the transformational Flywheel of your company. Each of them is summarized in the 4-Page Growth Plan™.

To review, here are the Core Growth Elements:

Part 1: Know Your Purpose	
Inception Story The story of how your company began and why its purpose is important to the founder(s).	**Core Purpose** The fundamental reason your company exists, the aspirational reason why your company is in business. It is the transformation your company aims to deliver to those it serves.
Company Vision A picture of the impact and goodness you intend to create for customers, employees, and the larger community you serve through living the Core Purpose and Core Values over a long period of time.	**10-Year Impact Goal** The specific 10-Year Goal inherent in the Company Vision—it's the specific transformation you want to deliver at a scale that will deliver the desired company profits.
Core Values These are the three to five ways you approach your business, the beliefs you and your team have about who you are and how you operate.	

Part 2: Know Whom You Serve	
Authentic Customer Avatar An avatar of a specific ideal customer whom your business is meant to serve. It is the fictional person you dedicate your business to serving.	**Who Your Customer Is** A clear description of your Authentic Customers, including the psychographics and demographics.
What Your Customer Needs These are the specific problems your Authentic Customer needs your company to solve, including wants, needs, desires, challenges, and points of pain.	**WHO + WHAT Statement** A simple, declarative short statement that articulates whom you serve and what they need. It speaks to the unique value your company brings to your specific customers.
Why—Trends and Triggers Trends are the larger market trends that validate the need for your company. Triggers are the specific moments in time when a customer needs your solutions. Knowing these helps craft customer experience and messaging.	**What You Offer** A list of core features and benefits your company offers to customers.
Core Competitors These are the other options available to Authentic Customers that most closely resemble your company offerings.	**Position Statement** A declaration that summarizes your brand's unique value and its promise to the market.
What Generates Profit? Empower your team with clear knowledge about which offerings have the highest profitability, which offerings sell the most, and which offerings to focus attention on for accelerated growth.	**Area of Chosen Greatness** The area you choose to be remarkable in as a business. The specific key strength featuring what is unique about your business *and* something your customer longs to receive. It is a specific aspect of your company you intend to build upon and devote 10X energy to being truly great.

Customer Journey Coming from the customer's perspective rather than the company's perspective. This is the 17-step experience your customer undergoes while being introduced to your company, deciding to become a customer, being onboarded as a customer, and being served long-term as a customer, including during any times of conflict, complaint, or disappointment.	**Three Feelings to Cultivate** The three feelings that you choose to deliberately create for your customer through every interaction, communication, written tool, piece of technology, or system.
Impact Mantras Three to five guiding phrases you repeat with your team and customers to remind everyone of your Core Purpose and method. These mantras will help keep what is most important top of mind, and they will give your team words they can use and embody to support the team purpose.	**Three Customer-Experience Improvements** At any given time, in the three areas your team is focused on making improvements to the customer or employee experience.
Growth Model Driven by Average Revenue Per Customer (ARPC), it is the strategy your company uses to grow. It is usually either market-driven or sales-driven. Examples are whale, deer, rabbit, and mouse models.	**Customer Enrollment Funnel** The five-step mechanism that automatically elevates your relationship with those you serve from suspect to prospect, to offers to new customers, to satisfied customers, and, ultimately, to loyal ambassadors.

Know Your Impact Plan	
Prosperity Goals The founder's goals for prosperity, including Profit, Freedom, Impact, and Security.	**Exit Strategy** The planned or preferred path for exiting the company.

The 4-Page Growth Plan™ The comprehensive plan guides daily, weekly, monthly, and yearly actions. It covers Four Areas of Crucial Alignment: Knowing Your Purpose, Knowing Whom You Serve, and Knowing Your Impact Plan, and their corresponding Core Growth Elements.	**Three Self-Assessments** The three assessments that help you assess where you are and what you need to focus on next: FFG Growth-Readiness Assessment, FFG Stage Assessment, and FFG Traction Assessment.
Five Critical Reports The five reports to look at monthly: Profit & Loss, Balance Sheet, Accounts Receivable Aging, and Cash Flow Statement.	**12+ Key Metrics Dashboard** The list of 12+ metrics you and your team review and innovate weekly and/or monthly, including metrics for Purpose, Growth, Profit, and Cash.
10-Year Impact, Scale, and Profit Goals These are the three measures of success, in terms of impact, scale, and profit, your company aims to achieve within 10 years.	**Customized Business Assessment** An assessment you and members of your team make to look at the strengths and weaknesses of your company. It is customized for your specific company to reflect your functions, systems, and processes.
Focused SWOT Undertaken at least annually, this is an assessment of the Strengths, Weaknesses, Opportunities, and Threats supporting or hindering progress on impact and profit goals.	**Chronological Strategy** The chronological three-phased explanation of how you plan to take your company from where it is now to the future place where it surpasses the 10-Year Impact Goal and Profitability Goals.
Strategic Priorities The three to five top priorities you believe will help your company reach Impact and Profit goals. They are a blend of Purpose, Impact, and Profit priorities that you intend to maintain in the years ahead.	**10-Year Milestones** A list of eight to ten other SMART goals to be completed at the same time your company reaches the 10-Year Impact, Scale, and Profit Goals. They may also include other key supportive and complementary outcomes you expect the company to deliver.

3-Year Milestones The list of eight to ten SMART goals you envision your company will hit three years from now on your way to achieving the 10-Year Impact, Scale, and Profit Goals.	**12-Month Milestones** The list of 8–10 SMART goals you envision your company will hit 12 months from now on your way to achieving 3-Year Milestones and 10-Year Impact, Scale, and Profit Goals.
12-Month Company-Wide Breakthrough Goal The single most important company-wide goal for the next 12 months. It is the goal that will move the company forward most profoundly.	**Functional MIGs** The Most Important Goal (MIG) set by each functional team. It is directly aimed at supporting the 12-Month Breakthrough Goal. It has a clear method for measuring its progress weekly.
Functional LEADs Each functional team selects three lead measurements (LEADs) to track weekly. These are three activities (throughout) that drive the MIG for that team.	**Quarterly Goals** Three company goals to complete each quarter to help actualize both the Breakthrough Goal and other 12-Month Milestones.
The 12-Month Breakthrough Plan The incorporation of all the 12-month elements into one plan that can be reviewed weekly and monthly.	**Pro Forma Forecast and Budget** Your 12-Month Breakthrough Plan and 3-Year Milestones translated into numbers forecasting volume sales and predicting revenue, COGs, gross profit, operations expenses, and net income over 3 years.

These Core Growth Elements reinforce and build upon each other organically. Additionally, while there is the upfront effort of generating and implementing the Force for Good System™, it is something that will be utilized through ongoing quarterly and annual rituals. Each element will be automatically used, refined, tuned, and integrated more deeply into your company, returning dividends on that initial investment.

SPIN THE FLYWHEEL—THE SEVEN RITUALS

After constructing your Flywheel, the next step is to get it spinning by implementing the Seven Rituals. If done consistently, these two forces will work together to remind you and your team of the primary goals you are aiming to achieve and what needs increased attention and innovation to accelerate the path to your 10-Year Impact, Scale, and Profit Goals, as well as the longer-term Company Vision.

The Seven Rituals, which will be described in detail below, are as follows:

1. Annual Retreats

2. Quarterly Reviews

3. Monthly Dashboards

4. Weekly MIGs (Most Important Goals)

5. Daily Huddles

6. Town Halls

7. Board Meetings

These rituals create the purpose-inspired space where elevated performance will emerge. Without these intentional respites from everyday operations, breakthroughs in performance—Impact, Scale, Profit, and other big improvements—will remain elusive. I feel confident that you will not see double-digit growth of any kind without creating intentional space for transformation in your business to be discovered, designed, implemented, and fine-tuned.

All too often, founders and leadership teams spend the majority of their time being reactive, with the squeakiest wheel claiming most of their attention and efforts. These Seven Rituals ask that—on a daily, weekly, monthly, quarterly, and annual basis—we look beyond the day-to-day challenges and instead give time to achieving our highest ideals, purpose, and goals.

Leadership must spend some dedicated time gazing at the loftier horizons if there is any hope of achieving the long-term goals of the business. For other members of the team, less time is needed at the more expansive horizons, but brief, consistent reminders of where you are headed are essential in keeping your vision, values, and goals top of mind each and every day.

1: Annual Retreat—50,000 Feet

Schedule time for you and your leadership team to meet offsite for two to three days every year, ideally at a hotel or some other accommodation where everyone can spend their days and evenings together. Going to dinners and scheduling a fun outing (for example, baseball game, sunset cruise, or cooking class) are important parts of the process. Sleeping away from home, where you and your team are free of distractions, can help you maximize time and effort, moving mountains in just a few days.

The Annual Retreat is dedicated to the **50,000-foot time horizon**, focusing attention and decision-making on goals that live 3–10 years away. It doesn't mean you won't put ample energy into 12-month and 3-year objectives at the Annual Retreat; it simply means that you will make sure the shorter-term goals you have are aligned and build toward the longer-term 10-Year Impact, Scale, and Profit Goals, and the 100-Year Company Vision.

For more details on the Annual Retreat, along with the other six rituals, download *The Seven Rituals Handbook* (link shared below).

2: Quarterly Reviews—10,000 Feet

Quarterly Reviews involve founders and leadership-team members, and are also best conducted away from the office. I recommend taking one and a half days, or about 12 hours. The ideal situation is to take your team away for a full day and night, so that everyone can immerse themselves in the task at hand. Sharing breakfast, lunch, and dinner brings everyone together, nurtures relationships, and provides a space for deeper conversations to emerge.

The Quarterly Review is dedicated to the 10,000-foot time horizon, with focus and attention going to the 6- to 24-month time period. The big-picture items, like Core Purpose, Core Values, and longer-term strategies, will also be reviewed quarterly to keep them front of mind, but no time will be spent refining or modifying them.

3: Monthly Dashboards—1,000 Feet

Monthly Dashboards focus on the 1,000-foot time horizon, directing focus and action toward the 30- to 90-day time period in the pursuit of monthly, quarterly, and annual goals. There are two types:

- **The Leadership Team Monthly Dashboard,** which looks at the data from all the functional teams of the company.

- **The Functional Team Monthly Dashboard,** which looks at the data from just one functional team and its team members.

Both types of Dashboards follow the same model, with some topics reserved for the Leadership Team Dashboard only (noted below). Carve out two to three focused hours per month for these Monthly Dashboards.

4: Weekly MIG Session—100 Feet

If the Weekly MIG Sessions are done wholeheartedly, they get your Flywheel spinning more than anything else. Because they involve brief-but-focused energy from every single person in your company, your Flywheel begins to whirl, almost without effort. The Weekly MIG Session is focused on making the biggest impact possible on the 7- to 30-day time horizon. This is partially achieved through aligning every single person in your company in knowing what is of Highest and Best Use for them to do this week and this month; the critical one-hour session celebrates wins, acknowledges successes, and innovates ways to achieve the Most Important Goals (MIGs) of your Company.

To break it down a bit further: each functional team has a single Most Important Goal (Functional MIG) aimed at supporting the larger 12-Month Company-Wide Breakthrough Goal. Then, supporting each Functional Team MIG, there are three LEADs (or leading indicators) that facilitate the actualization of the MIG. Thus, the primary focus of each Weekly MIG Session is making progress on the MIGs that facilitate the 12-Month Breakthrough Goal.

5: Daily Huddle—10 Feet

The purpose of the daily huddle is to connect with your team and help everyone know what they can do today to be of Highest and Best Use. This practice lives at the 10-foot horizon. It looks at how to serve the purpose, how to empower every individual to move forward, with the time and resources available *today*. Feel the power of the Flywheel starting to move!

6: Town Halls

The next ritual that will keep your team aligned, inspired, and motivated to keep that Flywheel spinning is the Town Hall, held monthly. Town Halls are the centerpiece of your company's internal communications, enabling you and your leadership team to connect with everyone in your company all at the same time in 60–90 minutes. This creates the opportunity to share the themes, mindsets, and core narratives of your company culture in a powerful way. Town Halls embody all of the previous time horizons, as they contribute to clarity and alignment on everything from today's actions through to 10 years from now.

Unlike the other rituals which are more formulaic, with a set agenda, Town Halls are each unique opportunities to disseminate information and inspire your team. The agendas can vary significantly from one to the next. They might be led by the founder, or by others. The unifying purpose behind these monthly Town Halls is to create engagement, trust, and belonging.

- **Engagement** is the emotional connection employees have with their work and the company.

- **Trust** is built as employees see and hear from their leaders regularly, something needed more than ever in our fast-paced, always-changing, quasi-virtual worlds.

- **Belonging** is a basic human need. When a team member feels she belongs, she is more likely to remain committed and present in the life of the company.

For more details on leading Town Halls, download *The Seven Rituals Handbook* (link shared below).

7: Board Meetings

All of the other six rituals are with your team. This ritual is one designed to help you, the founder, elevate to be your very best. All great companies lean on the support of an important circle of respected, trusted advisers. Whether you have a formal Board of Directors with fiduciary and governance responsibilities to investors and shareholders, or you have a less formal Board of Advisers, having a team of experienced confidants can help you grow and elevate the company, and yourself personally. You *will* be more successful when you implement the regular ritual of meeting with and providing transparent updates to the members of a board. This practice will tune your instrument and fuel sound decision-making like nothing else. It will also bring some much-needed kindred support to the often-lonely role of running a company.

The Seven Rituals of Innovation Handbook

Now that we have completed a brief review of what the Seven Rituals are, it's time to download this essential tool to transforming your company into a Force for Good. If you follow just one tool, this is the one that will make the greatest long-term difference in your business, because it connects every single person in your company with the opportunity to direct their brilliance to the most important breakthroughs and commitments of your company.

Access the Seven Rituals of Innovation Handbook in the FFG ToolKit:
www.aforceforgood.biz/book-bonuses

THE FORCE FOR GOOD QUICK-START PROGRAM

First: 7-Day Launch

You are ready to implement the Force for Good System™! Follow the link below to access the Force for Good Quick-Start Manual. It provides detailed instructions for drafting the 4-Page Growth Plan™ in 7 days, and then, over 90 days, implementing it throughout your organization.

Once you have completed the 7-Day Launch, the basic flywheel of your business will start spinning. With the Core Growth Elements drafted, the 4-Page GrowthPlan™ in place, and the Seven Rituals scheduled and started, the next 90 days will help you integrate the full system into your organization.

Second: 90-Day Reinforce and Refine

It is during the 90-Day Reinforce and Refine period that you will achieve these important goals:

1. **Continue to establish and follow the Seven Rituals**, ensuring the system continues to accelerate and transform your business. Making Daily Huddles, Weekly MIGs Sessions, and Monthly Dashboards happen without fail is the #1 goal of the essential 90-day period just following the system's launch.

2. **Conduct 12 training workshops with your team**, helping everyone experientially integrate the full Force for Good System™ into their mindset, behaviors, and actions. These workshops will allow you to both educate the team and refine the elements of your 4-Page Growth Plan™. All of this is covered in the Quick-Start Program below.

The Force for Good Quick-Start Manual

Use this step-by-step guide to implement the entire Force for Good System™, with its Core Growth Elements and Seven Rituals. Follow these instructions to expedite the process of accelerating breakthroughs in Impact, Scale, and Profit.

Access the Force for Good Quick-Start Manual
in the FFG ToolKit:
www.aforceforgood.biz/book-bonuses

GROWTH ACCELERATOR

Another way to quickly implement the Force for Good System™ is through our online Growth Accelerator. You can use this online journey to self-implement with your team independently, or with the help of a FFG Implementer. Visit **www.aforceforgood.biz/accelerator** to learn more.

CELEBRATE SUCCESS!

Once you have implemented the Force for Good System™, take a moment to celebrate. Express gratitude and appreciation for the hard work of everyone on your team toward implementing this new system. Give everyone the afternoon off; heck, bring in a food truck! This is the beginning of something big, and it deserves to be acknowledged!

Once you have defined the Core Growth Elements on the 4-Page Growth Plan™, implemented the Seven Rituals, and launched the Force for Good System™ using the Quick-Start Program, you have built the foundation for business acceleration. Staying focused on keeping the rituals not only going but also fresh and vibrant, has now become your most essential role. This will undoubtedly unlock increased Impact, Scale, and Profit.

Now that the system is in place, you must ask yourself what kind of leader you need to be to underpin the impact, breakthroughs, and special environments needed to cultivate lasting success.

CHAPTER 18
BE WISE

"Your essential self is the foundation of your being.
The more you connect with it, the more
genuinely you can live your life."

—MARTHA BECK

Finding Your Own North Star:
Claiming the Life You Were Meant to Live

"When we begin to listen from within,
we create a new way of seeing."

—CLARISSA PINKOLA ESTÉS

Women Who Run with the Wolves:
Myths and Stories of the Wild Woman Archetype

"The most important journey is the one within."

—REBECCA SOLNIT

The Faraway Nearby

"Only love is real."

—*A COURSE IN MIRACLES*

Y ou now have all the Elements and Rituals that make up the Force for Good System™. But the system is no more than an empty container until you and your team fill it with your collective wisdom, passion, and vision. Here, we come to the most essential question of all:

Who do you want to *be* along this journey?

The quality and energy of your being will make or break your enterprise. There are three states of being I invite you to bring to your business every day to create the impact and vision you've designed:

1. **Be Wise.** Cultivate what brings out the best in you.

2. **Be Transformative.** Nurture what brings out the best in everyone.

3. **Be of Highest and Best Use.** Seek purposeful action with impact.

LEAD WITH LOVE

While these three commitments bring forth different dimensions of leadership—and we will dive into each in the coming chapters—the underlying theme of all of them is:

Move from *fear* to *love*.

Being wise, transformative, and of Highest and Best Use all represent a clear departure from the archaic ways of fear-based, command-and-control leadership. For too long, business practices have been grounded in fear, motivated by scarcity, and perpetuated by a belief in zero-sum winners and losers. Yes, you can motivate and lead through fear. It can work—at least for a while.

But it is not a viable choice in the long term, particularly not in this day and age. We are living in a values-based era, with access to far more choices than ever before, as well as increased transparency through the availability of more information. Your team members have a choice about what company they are willing to devote their time and energy to, and your customers have many options when it comes to the enterprises they look to for goods and services. The reputation and values of an organization affect these decisions.

We, as business leaders, must align, not only to be morally upstanding, but to remain relevant. Businesses that lead with care and genuine social responsibility grow faster, maintain market share, and succeed in delivering the greatest value to all their stakeholders.

Leading through love is always the way forward. As such, we will move through each of these three ways of being, seeing through the lens of how each is an invitation to transcend fear into love.

BE WISE: CULTIVATE WHAT BRINGS OUT THE BEST IN YOURSELF

The third business I started was the Trust Leadership Institute. It was the result of an experiment I started in 2003 to see what would happen if I adopted a daily habit of pursuing inner guidance, plumbing my own mind and heart for direction. It was intended to be a 30-day experiment, but the series of guided-visualization exercises I developed and followed to help discern my inner voice and formulate an action plan was so life-changing that I stuck with the practice. Even now, I go through this ritual at least five days each week. The Trust Leadership Institute arose as a result of this deep impact I saw in my own life, providing a coach-certification program, along with other virtual programs for people around the globe. It was my aim to help leaders trust themselves more deeply, so they could transform their world more effectively.

The wisdom you already contain within yourself is the powerful—and often overlooked—ingredient that will make every aspect of your vision possible and propel your business to success.

My intention today is to open you to the idea and habit of calling upon the inner, wise part of you who "knows" what to do in every big decision you face—in your business and throughout your personal life.

Generally speaking, women particularly shine at bringing sensitivity and regard to the hearing and integrating of multiple needs from multiple parties. Given that, for a long time, it was not culturally acceptable for women to *demand what they want* in the same ways men were encouraged to, but rather to *be pleasing in their pursuits*, we possess the ability to be present to the many dynamics at play in a unique and valuable way.

Additionally, in our culture, the traditional experience has been that it's acceptable for men to have a more defined, one-note purpose: He goes out into the world, and he brings home the bacon to his family. A woman who is an entrepreneur, a wife, a mother is also bringing home the bacon while remaining cognizant of her many other responsibilities, thus developing the skill of being able to listen from different places to manage all stakeholders.

Imagine, then, the deep, rich well of wisdom that is readily available to women who know to mine for it! We've been practicing for years and years. And with the increasing transparency of our digital world, those who can think beyond their own experience and manage multiple stakeholders have a particular edge in the long term.

WHICH PART OF YOU KNOWS?

There are three parts of your being operating all the time:

1. The Thinking Self
2. The Feeling Self

3. The Knowing Self

All are available to consult for guidance. All are here to serve your highest good. The tricky thing is that, in business, we have overindulged in the first; often misunderstood the second; and, for the most part, completely forgotten the third. I offer that there is an important role for all three to play in a healthy and successful entrepreneur: By choosing to cultivate the likely underdeveloped Knowing Self, by electing to bring kindness and understanding to the Feeling Self, and by allowing the Thinking Self to take a break from time to time:

- A new sense of calm starts to emerge.

- People on the team feel lighter and more energized.

- Answers to puzzles seem to come more easily.

- Difficult relationships can soften and feel less challenging.

- Overwhelm gives way to certainty and clarity.

- You and your teammates are empowered to take actions you haven't taken before.

In short, when we integrate the higher purpose and gift of each of these parts of ourselves, we form and can tap into an elevated level of personal power. Let's take a closer look at each of the three components.

The Thinking Self draws from the power of intellect. It's the part of us that craves the chance to learn from others, read information, and absorb new skills and knowledge. It's best suited to help us analyze information, organize systems, learn new skills, apply tools to a problem, and make black-and-white decisions. The Thinking Self is most commonly associated with the head, a place in which I'm certain many of us spend much of our day.

The Feeling Self is the embodied part of us that experiences the world through our senses—touch, taste, smell, sound, sight, and emotions. The gifts of empathy, understanding, compassion, passion, conviction, and even outrage stem from this part of you. By inviting the Feeling Self into our work lives, we can embody our goals in our whole selves, rather than contain the effort to the boundary of our minds. We often associate the Feeling Self with the heart or the gut. Ask yourself: *Is this a part of who you are that you allow to show up in your work?*

The Knowing Self is harder to distill. It is liminal, a calm presence somewhere behind the thinking and feeling selves, who tend to run the day. We momentarily connect with this Self when we see a sunset and feel inspired, or when we pray for clarity and answers gently appear, or when we close our eyes and ask to hear the truth of our soul and are actually able to listen. It's a connection to the wisdom that springs from a source larger than ourselves: call it love, light, a higher power—whatever you choose. The Knowing Self can be experienced in many ways, but there's a certain visceral quality to it. It can be felt surrounding you, above you, or in a place deep within that transcends your physicality. Consider: *How often do you offer space and attention to this part of yourself?*

DIRECTING YOUR THREE SELVES

The Thinking Self is often confused with the Knowing Self, which cuts us off from a much larger pool of creativity, innovation, and possibility. Often in business, we allow the Thinking Self to direct the ship, guiding all of our responses. The Thinking Self is designed to manage risk and keep us safe; it tells us to build on what we already know and to search for answers in already explored territories. The Thinking Self does not want transformation. It is terrified of change. All of its efforts will be in the service of keeping things familiar and safe—even if your purpose and vision requires much more than that.

Becoming a transformative leader begins with assessing whether you are currently connected to higher wisdom or if you are stuck in the limited perspective of your mind. Notice how different the two voices sound:

Your Thinking Self Believes...	Your Knowing Self Knows...
The world is unsafe, and we have to protect ourselves.	Wisdom and love provide infinite clarity and protection.
We are happier when things are predictable, comfortable, and safe.	We are happiest when we are engaged in a purpose larger than ourselves.
There are limited resources, and we have to fight for what is ours.	At every moment, we have everything we need to take the next step.
People cannot be trusted and need to be carefully managed.	At their core, everyone is brilliant, strong, resourceful, and loving.
We need to move away from fear.	We need to move toward love.
Failure is bad.	Failure is a temporary teacher.

Another way to distinguish whether you are operating from your Thinking Self or your Knowing Self is to take a look at the emotions you most frequently exhibit.

When you connect to your Thinking Self, you feel . . .	Whereas, when you connect to your Knowing Self, you feel . . .
Logical	Elevated
Rational	Empowered
Reasonable	Loving
Contained	Abundant
Justified	Understanding
Defensive	Curious
Anxious	Grounded
Resistant	Open
Afraid	Brave
Angry	Conviction
Stress	Flow

Again, this is not to say that the Thinking Self is bad and the Knowing Self is good. Both have their proper place. Balancing these two Selves will help you move into greater levels of personal power. If you allow your Knowing Self to take the lead on the big picture, it will help you and your team discover a path forward that brings out courage, conviction, commitment, and curiosity. Once you have moved your team into an empowered state, you can direct everyone to employ their Thinking Selves to solve specific puzzles embedded in the bigger plan.

The Feeling Self is the amplifier. When you add feeling to any situation, the energy increases—for better or for worse. The Feeling Self will follow whatever you choose to believe in the moment. If you believe the world is unsafe, The Feeling Self propagates physical and emotional experiences of fear. If you believe instead that you and your team are wise and resourceful, the Feeling Self will release conviction and certainty. The Feeling Self, used properly and guided by the Knowing Self, will boost your purpose and support your team in feeling heart-connected and moved into greatness.

One of your most important roles as a leader is to guide the narrative playing out within the walls of your business. Your words and beliefs will direct thoughts that empower or disempower, inspire or deflate, calm or unnerve. Creating a narrative that is filled with wisdom will elevate what everyone believes, how everyone feels, and ultimately, how everyone acts.

THE KNOWING SELF CONNECTION

The Knowing Self Connection

To help you build a relationship with your Knowing Self, I have prepared a guided-visualization practice you can use as often as you like. If you want to see meaningful results and you want to see them soon, take the 30-Day Wisdom Challenge, and follow the guided visualization daily for a month. As you implement the inspired action that comes from the visualization, notice what shifts, opens, and transforms in your life.

- The Knowing Self Connection
- The Knowing Self Guided Visualization
- The 30-Day Wisdom Challenge

These resources are available in the FFG ToolKit:
www.aforceforgood.biz/book-bonuses/

WISDOM BUILDS TRUST

One of the most significant takeaways from my own 30-day Wisdom Challenge conducted more than 20 years ago was the incredible experience of embracing trust in several forms. Nothing has been more grounding and stabilizing in my life than this discovery.

First, I learned to trust myself. When you trust yourself, you know how to live. When you trust yourself, you believe you can do anything. When you trust yourself, you know your deep inner reserve of wisdom and safety cannot be taken from you. Self-trust is transformative for a leader, particularly valuable for one who aims to take the bold journey of following not just profits, but purpose and impact. Those who deeply trust themselves have the calm confidence needed to lead from faith and love, rather than fear and control.

Second, I learned to trust others. When you start to believe in yourself, you can begin to see others for who they are: brilliant, beautiful humans longing to contribute, make a difference, and feel valued and appreciated. By cultivating a deep security within yourself, you are free to let others be who they are. The fear that a great performer might leave or that an underperformer might make a mistake, is countered by the ineffable power of knowing there is a deep pool of wisdom surrounding you and your team to help guide the next step. You also know that, if a team member doesn't perform or lets you down, it's okay. There is freedom in letting others be who they are, giving them an opportunity to shine, and not taking it personally if it doesn't work out.

Third, I watched as others began trusting me. As I became more committed to hearing my wisdom, speaking my truth, and following my inner guidance, more and more people began to believe in me. Companies wanted to partner with me, customers wanted to work with me, and opportunities to create new kinds of businesses began showing up left and right.

Fourth, I found myself attracting the right people into my business and my life. This band of trustworthy people were the ones who would show up fully, listen to their own wisdom, and follow through with brave, wise action. I began attracting like-minded team members, partners, and investors—all with the same desire to build profits with purpose, and purpose with profits.

WHAT MAKES A GREAT LEADER?

What makes some leaders capable of guiding their people through impossible challenges? What is unique and special about those who can picture a brighter world and then lead others to it, like the strong examples like Mother Teresa, Susan B. Anthony, Indira Gandhi, Jane Goodall, Wangari Maathai, Frances Perkins, Wilma Mankiller, Shirin Ebadi, and Rosa Parks, to name a few? These are individuals who carry within them the seed of intellect, emotional intelligence, and embodied wisdom. Great, honorable leaders have all three—the thinking, feeling, and wisdom—working together, with the latter being the queen of the ship. Wisdom keeps us on course. It reminds us of what matters most. It keeps us sewn into the commitment of creating something good and lasting.

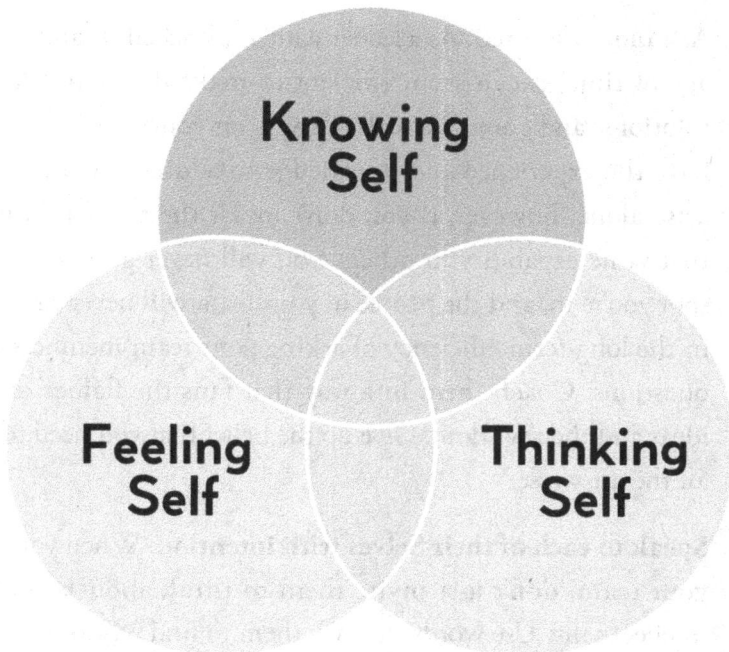

CREATING A CULTURE OF WISDOM

As you begin the process of more intentionally bringing the wisdom of your Knowing Self into your everyday life and work, it is important to invite your team members to do the same. Now, you might wonder: how do you, as the leader, cultivate an environment where personal wisdom is fostered and encouraged?

1. **Acknowledge valuable insights and ideas at every turn.** When someone comes up with a good idea, respond instantly with encouragement and praise. Support them in refining the idea and then taking the next step in the direction of implementing it. The key is to celebrate when people contribute, which makes them feel safe, seen, and valued, and thus encourages others to follow suit.

2. **Ask more than tell.** As a leader with a full schedule and a shortage of time, it can seem efficient to make decisions, develop solutions, and come up with answers on your own. You might have the experience and knowledge to address the issues that arise alone, however, if you don't invest the time in building that same capability in others, you will never grow out of the spot you're in, and the people in your team will never rise. Trust in the long-term efficiency of asking your team members more questions. Coach them in a way that fans the flames of their ideas and their wisdom. Give up the belief that you need to have all the answers.

3. **Speak to each of their Selves with intention.** When you guide your team, don't just invite them to think about a problem intellectually. Use words that ask them to find wisdom through

the parts of themselves that *feel* and *know* as well. Ask them questions like:

- What is your heart telling you?

- What would your wisdom say about this situation?

- What is the opportunity here that is available to us all?

- What would we do today if we could not fail?

- Beyond what we *think* we should do, what do we *know* is best and right?

Collaboration Amplifies Progress Better Than Competition

As you take steps to cultivate an environment where wisdom is encouraged, you will start to internalize this truth: *Collaboration amplifies progress better than competition.* Survival of the fittest has been overplayed as the guiding force in our survival and evolution. Neither in nature nor in business is competition the only way to sustain, persevere, and succeed. In nature, yes, there are examples where the strongest lion lives, but what about the even more prevalent set of examples where animals cooperatively survive, thrive and, together, can even shut down the lion? A herd of elephants loyally care for, protect, feed, and love one another; a hive of bees serves the higher purpose of collective survival; a colony of ants works together to build their complex community. Examples of powerful, effective cooperation abound.

It is far more critical to the success of each and every business to ask not what the competition is doing, but instead look to the bigger question of: what are *we* doing? Investing your time in aligning your team, products, services, and systems in what makes your company great will bear far greater fruit than trying to respond to whatever the other players in your market are doing.

Trade-Offs are Unnecessary and Shortsighted

Business is filled with competing needs, goals, and expectations. How do we create a quality product that is also profitable? How do we increase revenue and reduce costs? Should we invest in innovation or compliance? How do we attract and keep the best people and not increase prices? These questions make us believe that we *have to choose* among our stakeholders: customers, employees, vendors, community members, and shareholders.

This simply isn't the case! It is in these intersections between quality and profit, caring and efficiency, cost and benefit where we have the opportunity to shine. This is exactly where innovation is needed, and with our Knowing Self at the helm, we can guide our teams to finding revolutionary, transformative ways of bringing what appears to be competing needs into harmony. The more aligned we become in the service of our constituents, the more potent our power to elevate everything we do. The more we are guided by clear, authentic purpose, the more we will see our profit organically and sustainably swell.

FOLLOW YOUR WISDOM UNCONDITIONALLY

Think of the Force for Good System™ and the Seven Rituals that were laid out before this chapter as the scaffolding that must be in place in order to build a strong, proud building. What will actually make your building last is the wisdom you integrate into its actual construction. That is why, again, I implore you: As a leader, adopt the powerful practice of taking time each day to listen within for higher wisdom, and then watch your business—and life—soar.

CHAPTER 19
BE TRANSFORMATIVE: NURTURE WHAT BRINGS OUT THE BEST IN EVERYONE

"When we resist change, it's called *suffering*.
But when we can completely let go and not struggle against it, when we can embrace the groundlessness of our situation and relax into its dynamic quality, that's called *enlightenment*."

—Pema Chödrön

When Things Fall Apart: Heart Advice for Difficult Times

"Right now, there is a stronger, more vibrant, more inspired version of you that is wanting and waiting to emerge."

—Debbie Ford

The Best Year of Your Life: Dream It, Plan It, Live It

"Leadership is about recognizing that there's a greatness in everyone, and your job is to create an environment where that greatness can emerge."

Arianna Huffington

Co-Founder and Former Editor-in-Chief, The Huffington Post
Founder and CEO, Thrive Global

If we define "being wise" as what you need to cultivate within yourself as a *Force for Good* leader, then "being transformative" is the space you hold to bring out the brilliance, innovation, creativity, and expansion of everyone else—your team, customers, suppliers, investors, and your community at large. Entrepreneurs are creators. We start with an idea and bring it to life. Unlike an artist, however, who might create mostly alone and view the creative journey as an individual quest, being an entrepreneur, founder, and leader asks you to co-create masterpieces with others. This unique dimension adds to both the gifts and challenges of the journey; it must be considered and understood for you to manifest the vision, prosperity, and impact you desire.

Neither creation nor transformation follow a linear path. Rarely in business do you make a plan and follow it exactly. Intuitively, you *know* that building a company is just as much art as it is science. It is a blending of all your gifts to align everyone and everything to manifest a higher potential.

Embracing this important, intuitive aspect of leadership—naming it, clarifying it, and codifying how it works—will help you bridge gaps in performance, outcomes, and impact. Being transformative invites you to consider who you would need to *be* and what you would need to *do differently*, to hold the space for a new reality to unfold.

WHAT IS GENERATING YOUR CURRENT RESULTS?

You, your systems, people, and operations are generating the current results of your business. It is important to state the obvious. Unconsciously, we want to believe that a new result can be produced (more leads, prospect, sales, revenue, efficiencies) by continuing to do what we're already doing. That is insanity. I know, and you know, that a breakthrough of any kind won't happen without something changing, innovating, or transforming.

We know that *changes in behavior* are required: salespeople need to make more daily calls; customer-service reps need to respond faster to complaints; more products need to be shipped on time. We also know that *system innovations* are needed: a new CRM system is called for; we need to improve our customer-conversion rates; we need to increase the productivity of our service team. The question then becomes: Why *aren't* we doing those things?

Why is it that what we decide to do and what we actually do don't always align?

Until you confront the actual changes that need to occur within a human being to accept, adopt, and embrace change, you will continue to feel frustrated and disappointed in yourself and your team. I've heard countless times, "But I told Pam to do it this way!" "I trained Sylvia how to use the new system." "I reviewed this new policy three times with Jim." Yet, somehow, Pam, Sylvia, and Jim aren't changing. They are still "not doing what I told them." It is time to acknowledge and embrace what we already know: people resist change. They don't naturally feel safe trying new approaches.

And yet, actualizing your vision is going to require countless areas of evolution. To manifest the impact and vision of your business at its full potential, you must first expand as a leader to discover and cultivate what makes change, innovation, and transformation possible for your team.

THE THREE LEVELS OF EVOLUTION

In the Force for Good approach, I invite you to look at three Levels of Evolution:

1. Level 1: Simple Change
2. Level 2: Innovation
3. Level 3: Transformation

Moving forward, I am going to intentionally separate the word *evolution* from the word *change*, so as to illustrate the distinction between a *basic change*—the limits we typically have when we "*try to change things*"—versus the more expansive and elevated *innovation* and *transformation*. As I see it, the latter offers greater effectiveness and is dramatically different in practice.

Level 1: Simple Change

Simple change is the most basic level of evolution, utilized, ideally, for only minor shifts in behavior, habits, and mindsets, which don't require tremendous effort but are easily accomplished simply by asking yourself or others to do them. Examples might be:

- Asking Lois, your new customer-service rep, to change her hours by 15 minutes to accommodate a team need.

- Asking Joseph, a long-time sales rep, to send you an email after his meeting today, giving you a summary of what took place.

- Changing an ingredient from one brand to another in your manufacturing process.

In this case of *simple change*, simply asking for the change is enough.

But I Told Them What to Do!

If the change doesn't come, however, or if it doesn't last (after two weeks, Lois, the customer rep, starts arriving late every day, rather than 15 minutes earlier, as you requested), then I'm sorry to say that what you are asking for isn't really a *simple change*.

Pam, Sylvia, and Jim are not stupid when they don't do what you tell them, and they are likely not trying to be insubordinate. They likely want to do the right thing. As a leader, it's your job to help them do the right thing, to find a way to cultivate the adjusted behavior and secure the new outcome. The issue could also be that the adjustment or change you request occurs but does not produce the desired effect.

For example, you changed the flour in your world-famous cookie recipe to cut costs. There was no issue with the adjusted behavior. Your procurement team easily changed their process to order the new SKU from the distributor, and the person making the cookies used the new flour without hesitation. *But!* The resulting cookies were not as good as before. They were crunchy, when chewy is what you're known for, what you've won awards for, what your customers expect. This undesired outcome means the *simple change* did not satisfy the need. Yes, you and your team achieved the goal of using a less-expensive ingredient, but it failed to create the same quality of product.

Both of these cases—when people don't do what you tell them or when unwanted results ensue—illustrate how a *simple change* may not suffice. Something more comprehensive is required to create the new result you're after.

Level 2: Innovation

Often, we turn to *innovation* when we have a more complex problem that needs solving. It's the next level of evolution after *simple change*. It requires a bit more elbow grease.

The Seven Steps of Innovation

The whole Force for Good System™ is designed around innovation best practices and follows this simple Seven-Step Innovation Process throughout:

1. **Define.** First, clarify what you want to create, whether it is as straightforward as entreating your customer-service rep to arrive

15 minutes early, or as substantial as adjusting the long-term Vision for your company.

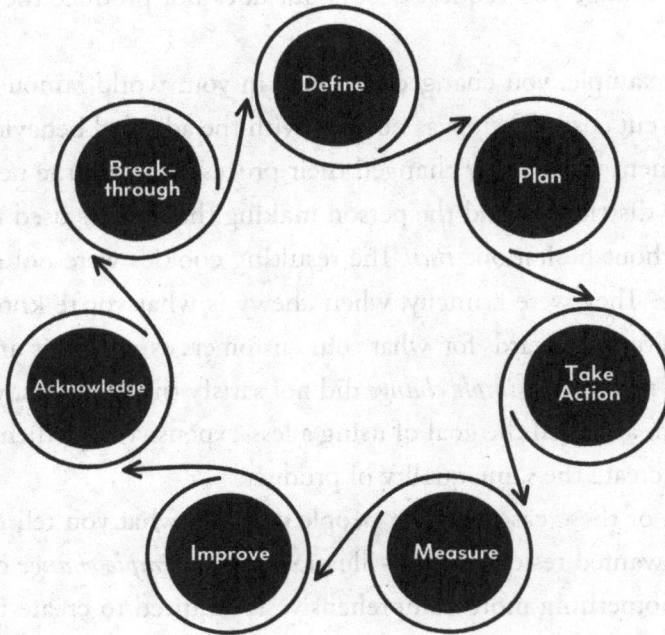

2. **Plan.** Next, create the path to your desired outcome. This could be the details for how you intend to encourage, incentivize, and hold accountable the customer-service rep to arrive 15 minutes earlier, for example. Within the larger Force for Good System™, your desired result is your Company Vision and Impact Goal. The "plan phase" includes the Focused SWOT, assessing your business, creating a strategy, crafting milestones, building a budget, choosing a breakthrough goal and a series of functional goals, and publishing your 4-Page Growth Plan™.

3. **Take Action.** Follow the plan. Do whatever is on the to-do list to support the sales rep in showing up early. In the larger Force for Good framework, this is following what is in the 4-Page

Growth Plan™, 12-Month Breakthrough Plan, and the actions inherent in your functional and individual MIGs and LEADs.

4. **Measure.** Having a system to track the customer-service rep's success in arriving each morning at the desired time, so that she can see that her percentage of success is one example of this. Within the larger Force for Good System™, the "measure" stage includes the Daily Huddles, Weekly MIGs, Monthly Dashboards, Quarterly Updates, and Annual Retreats, all of which provide a space where specific information is measured and progress updates discussed.

5. **Improve.** On the heels of measurement comes the topic of improvement. This is where you innovate specific new ways to make a system better. This could be strategizing with the customer-service rep about ideas to help her arrive earlier, like waking up earlier, taking a different route to work, or creating a more efficient morning routine. Within the overall Force for Good model, the Seven Rituals are designed to identify needed improvements in order to amplify and accelerate results. In each of the Rituals, the team is invited to think creatively about how to approach operations, systems, and activities anew. The Daily Huddle model provides 250 cycles (5 days a week for 50 weeks per year) of improvement, and the Weekly MIG model provides 50 cycles (1 time weekly for 50 weeks each year) of innovation.

6. **Acknowledge.** Every day, week, month, quarter, and year, there are reasons to celebrate. Progress is everywhere when you look for it. Acknowledging and expressing gratitude for small and large victories along the way builds positive, virtuous cycles of improvement—and nothing builds momentum more effectively.

7. **Breakthrough**. The final step is when the desired result takes place. The customer-service rep achieves 6 months in a row of 95%+ on-time results! Upon completion of the breakthrough, the process starts over again at the definition stage, where you and your team choose a new outcome you'd like to manifest.

In facilitating innovation and the subsequent breakthroughs, your most important role as a leader is to ensure that the journey is encouraging and positive for everyone involved and to build accountability into the process. Innovation is the product of knowing where you want to go, and then checking in regularly to ensure you are making the moves necessary to create new outcomes. And yet, while creating a positive space of accountability is one of the most powerful forces you can build into your business, you might still encounter challenges or setbacks that prevent you from achieving your breakthrough. This is what brings you to the next level of business evolution: transformation.

Level 3: Transformation

The Journey of Transformation—the third and most elevated form of evolution—is a topic I have been studying for more than 25 years. From that, I developed a program which I led from 2005 to 2009 through WorldChangingBusiness, a boutique consultancy I founded to support founders in scaling and growing early-stage businesses.

I developed the Journey of Transformation out of necessity. I was on a quest to answer big questions that had been plaguing me:

- What is stopping leaders from doing what they know would produce the desired results?

- Why are so many teams holding themselves back rather than elevating to the next level?

- How is it that even good strategies and plans so often fail to be executed? What I found is that there is often something that is holding a person, team, or entire business from moving forward—they don't feel like it, they can't find the time, they are held back by fear, they believe the change is unnecessary or stupid, or they're convinced they don't have the resources or capabilities. **Transformation is the force that frees people up to do the things they haven't done before and become a version of themselves more able to express their brilliance.**

So, to recap:

- **Simple Change** takes place by simply deciding to alter a behavior or system.

- **Innovation** occurs as a result of consistently measuring what matters, creating cycles of continuous improvement, holding people accountable for their commitments, and being disciplined about hosting the daily, weekly, monthly, quarterly, and annual rituals.

- **Transformation** happens when an inner shift occurs that sets a person (team or company) free to expand where they once felt small, take a risk where they long stayed silent, engage where they once felt skeptical, and commit where they once held back.

Being transformative is my favorite aspect of life as an entrepreneur. When you create a space where people can soar, they don't fly only at work. I've watched team members apply the tools of transformation at home in marriage, parenthood, family life, and beyond. This model of evolution will no doubt elevate the key performance indicators (KPIs) in your business, but, more importantly, it will uplift the lives of everyone your business touches.

THE JOURNEY OF TRANSFORMATION

Let's take a deeper look at the Journey of Transformation. It has been built to incorporate both the physical actions and behaviors required to harvest the *real-world* results you're after, while also looking deeply at the more-intimate *human* factors at play that determine whether someone is willing and able to take the prescribed action. There are many forces at work in one's mind, body, and environment that affect the level of ease, motivation, commitment, and determination one feels about a particular behavior or outcome. Being a transformative leader calls you to better understand and harness these considerations, thereby creating an environment that naturally brings out the best in yourself and others.

To enact effective transformation, we need to address those powerful forces: thoughts and beliefs; feelings and experiences; skills, aptitudes, and competencies. Transformation requires an integration of the thinking, knowing, and feeling parts of yourself, as the model will describe. All of the elements in the Journey of Transformation invite you to listen and integrate logic, intellect, analysis, feelings, intuition, and deeper knowing.

The Journey of Transformation

Now, I invite you to map out your own journey toward a desired outcome or breakthrough. A great goal to map is the 12-Month Breakthrough Goal. I'd like to direct you to two tools that will support you:

- Transformation Map™ template (pictured below)
- Journey of Transformation Process

These resources are available in the FFG ToolKit:
www.aforceforgood.biz/book-bonuses/

Below is the Transformation Map™, which is one of the three essential Force for Good Tools. It is a visual representation of all the change—inner and outer—needed to actualize a new goal or outcome. Often, it helps to unlock the hidden, unconscious reasons why we don't follow through, take new action, or allow ourselves to grow. It also enables us to uncover a deeper purpose for inner growth, which we can harness through each breakthrough journey we undertake. Refer to the Transformation Map™ as we move through the rest of this chapter.

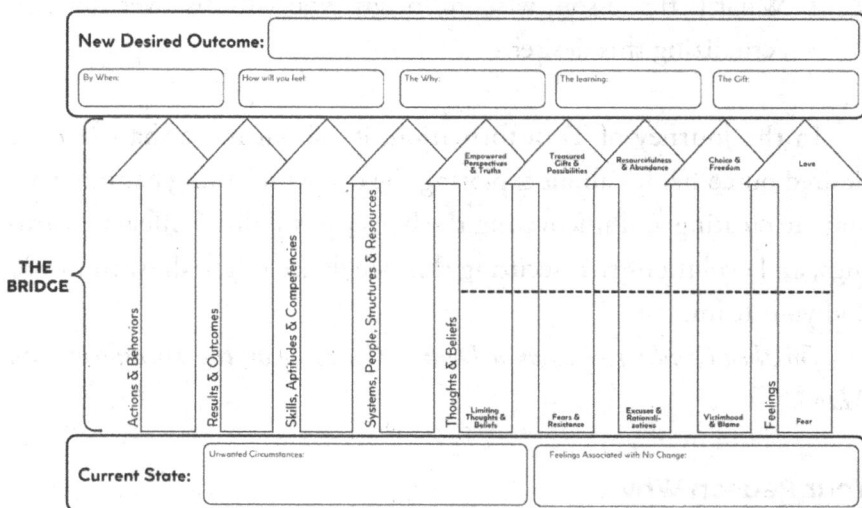

Your Desired Outcome

The first element in the Journey of Transformation is Your Desired Outcome, the clear picture of the result for which you're aiming. When you start with what it is you want, and ascribe the feelings and reasons around why it is wanted, you free yourself of whatever limits you might believe could get in the way. My friend and author of *Epic: The Woman's Power Play Book*, Carolyn Buck Luce, puts it like this: "If you know where you're going, any road will get you there." (Carolyn's eNewsletter, February 11, 2023.) Guided by your Knowing Self, begin by asking these questions:

- What is the desire?

- When would you like to have it actualized?

- When completed, how will you feel?

- Why is this desire important?

- What is the lesson, wisdom, or gift you will discover through actualizing this desire?

In the Journey of Transformation, it's about more than *just* the desired outcome. It's about exploring the deeper meaning behind what you are creating and uncovering the bigger possibilities, lifelong learnings, and evolutions that securing this one desire might draw from you and your team.

Go ahead and write down a Desired Outcome on the Transformation Map™.

Your Reason Why

For example, let's say your desire is to increase sales by 50% (from $50K to $75K per month) in 12 months. Articulating the deeper reasons why this goal is important gives it depth and meaning.

Perhaps this level of sales might finally generate enough scale to help your company break even and cover all of its costs, bringing you tremendous relief knowing the company is sustainable and can survive. Or it could mean that you can demonstrate a level of traction that would be more attractive to investors. Or it might be that these dollars make it so you can finally give your team (and yourself) a raise. Or it might simply be that you feel a deep responsibility for making your products and services available to customers so that you can fulfill the purpose and vision of the business. A defined purpose, or reason why, helps you more easily muster the strength, will, and courage to do what's necessary. Know why your desired outcome is important, as it can become the wind in your sails to help you follow through on the difficult-but-necessary actions required to achieve results.

Write down the reason why the New Desired Outcome matters to you on your Transformational Map™.

An Unmet Feeling in Disguise

One of my most cherished mentors, the late Debbie Ford (author of many books, including *The Dark Side of the Light Chasers*), used to say, "*A desire is an unmet feeling in disguise.*" There is great wisdom in this statement. The amazing power of this knowledge is that feelings can be cultivated anytime. Through the power of your mind, your energy, and your focus, you can elicit any feeling you like right now, this very moment—be it joy, faith, hope, or love.

One of your jobs in "being transformative" is learning how to cultivate the needed feelings within so that you can step into the person and leader you're meant to be. Once you're able to identify that the desire for increased sales is linked to the longing to feel relief, success, hope, and inspiration, you will be more equipped to manifest the outcome while cultivating these specific feelings along the way. Let me repeat that: **the key to manifesting your desire is to nurture the feelings you long for now**. I invite you to let go of thinking the feeling is tied up in the outcome. Instead, embrace that the unmet desires and associated feelings are what will guide you to where you need to be.

On the Transformational Map™, *write down two to three feelings you imagine you will feel when you actualize the New Desired Outcome.*

The Gift of the Journey

Last, the journey of actualizing every desire holds treasures far beyond the outcome itself, bringing about opportunities to heal and transcend. **Every transformative journey is meant to bring you into your power, help you discover more love (for yourself and others), and release fears, limitations, and victimhood from the past.** It can help to dedicate each transformative journey to a specific gift you would like to claim. Elevate the journey of increased revenues into a path of claiming your worthiness, discovering your inner strength, cultivating a remarkable team, or actualizing positive impact on the world.

Once you have articulated a particular desire, the deeper reasons why it is important, the unmet positive feelings you're meant to nurture, and the transcendent gift that will help you move from fear to love, you are ready to move onto the next element.

What is the Gift you will receive as you take this journey, overcome obstacles, and achieve the New Desired Outcome? Write it on the Transformational Map™.

Your Current State

Your Current State is a description of where you are right now, particularly in relation to getting to the destination you desire. In order to start generating that picture, consider these questions:

1. In relation to Your Desired Outcome, what are your current circumstances?

2. What are the biggest challenges or constraints you see standing in the way of the desired outcome?

3. What do you fear will happen if everything remains the same and you do not make progress toward Your Desired Outcome?

4. How do you feel when you think about your current situation, challenges, and constraints?

5. What are some of the positive aspects of your current situation? What's working for you? For what are you grateful? Sometimes we have to focus on the improvement and progress that we have just made, recently, right now, in order to feel like any progress has been made.

6. What are the strengths you have in your current arsenal you can call upon along the journey ahead?

When mapping out your Current State, it is essential to acknowledge what is working, and what is not; where you are worried, and where you are grateful. Honoring past progress while looking toward the next evolution allows us to celebrate where you are, while drawing in expansive possibilities to co-create with your team into the future. It releases the need to label yourself or others as wrong or bad about where you are right now. It honors and acknowledges what *is* while simultaneously giving you permission to move forward into the *next* stage of evolution.

Describe your Current State, including the Unwanted Circumstances and Feelings Associated with No Change, on your Transformation Map™.

The Bridge

The Bridge is the space between Your Desired Outcome and Your Current State, where the disrupting, dismantling, shifting, healing, rebuilding, and emerging takes place. It hinges on the conscious acknowledgment that your desire is a journey that will involve releasing what doesn't work and replacing it with something better. The elements of the Bridge can be broken down as such:

1. Actions and Behaviors

2. Results and Outcomes

3. Skills, Aptitudes, and Competencies

4. Systems, People, and Supports

5. Resources

6. Thoughts and Beliefs

7. Feelings

Movement in each of these areas will be required to bridge the distance between where you are today and the future Desired Outcome that awaits. Journeying through the Bridge is precious and sacred for everyone involved, with many gifts available along the way. It won't be easy. You and others will likely be triggered, *But as the leader, it is your duty to hold the space for the process of transformation to occur.*

Most of the time, we consider only items one through five on the list above, leaving out the important components of how we think, what we believe, and how we feel. The Journey of Transformation must incorporate these critical elements. Remember that as we now walk through each of the seven, with the Transformation Journey and Transformation Map™ available in the FFG ToolKit (www.aforcefor good.biz/book-bonuses/).

Take a moment to simply behold the many levels of change and opportunities for growth embedded within the New Desired Outcome you wrote down on your Transformational Map™.

Actions and Behaviors
Brainstorm all of the key actions you expect will need to take place to get yourself from Your Current State to your desired destination, and

do your best to map them out chronologically. As you assemble that list, consider:

- What will you and your team need to start doing that you are not currently doing?

- What must you stop doing?

- What are you already doing that you should amplify?

Let's return to the example of actualizing the desire to increase sales by 50% (from $50K to $75K per month) in 12 months. The actions and behaviors that need to take place over time include:

- Identifying and implementing 3 new ways to attract 200 more prospects each month

- Establishing new LEADs with each sales rep, empowering them to cultivate more sales presentations and create more sales

- Implementing daily huddles with sales reps to support progress and measure LEADs

- Developing weekly sales training to improve results

- Choosing to focus first on an activity that accelerates progress— like scheduling 10 sales meetings—before engaging in the never-ending list of emails.

List the Actions and Behaviors that will lead to the New Desired Outcome on your Transformational Map™.

Results and Outcomes

The next step concerns how you are going to track and measure the actions you laid out in the section above. What progress will you measure in your weekly MIGs and LEADs? What will grow on the Monthly Dashboard? How will your P&L and balance sheet change? Consider:

- What new, improved results will you achieve along the way to actualizing your Desired Outcomes?

- What specific milestones will you celebrate along the way?

- What activities are driving your results, and how are they increasing or improving over time?

Drawing on our example, here is a possible list of the sequential results and outcomes one might expect on the way to increasing sales by 50% (from $50K to $75K per month) in 12 months:

- Increase prospects to 500 per month.

- Sales team delivers 80 presentations in a month.

- Enroll 20 new customers in one month!

- Increase prospects to 550 per month.

- Sales team gives 100 presentations per month.

- Enroll 30 new customers in one month!

- Have a pizza party when we hit $60K in sales in one month.

- Increase prospects to 600 per month.

- Enroll 40 new customers in one month!

- Host a bowling celebration when we hit $70K in sales in one month.

- Increase prospects to 700 per month.

- Sales team gives 120 presentations per month.

- Enroll 50 new customers in one month!

- Host a big party on a boat to celebrate $75K in sales in one month!

The idea is to name and claim what progress looks like. The Results and Outcomes, along with Actions, represent the physical-world evolution and changes in behavior necessary to achieve Your Desired Outcome.

The remaining elements represent the internal aspects of change, innovation, and transformation we all encounter as we take new actions and generate progress.

On the Transformational Map™, write down the Milestone Results and Outcomes that will pave the way to your New Desired Outcome.

Skills, Aptitudes, Competencies

Sometimes a missing skill, aptitude, competency, system, or resource is keeping you from taking action.

- **A skill** is a learned practice that one is able to perform well.

- **An aptitude** is an ability, capability, or talent.

- **A competency** is the quality or level of dexterity to perform a specific skill, area of knowledge, qualification, or capacity.

Every role calls for all three to develop over time. Some are today's strengths that can be leveraged. Others are areas needing development. On the journey toward Your Desired Outcome, it is important to consider which strengths you (and members of your team) can strategically lean into, and which weaknesses might need to be avoided or addressed.

In this analysis, it is important to keep an open mind. If your desire and the actions required to get there call for you to spend your whole day in sales meetings and you are an introvert who longs to work in isolation, you might need to shift your plan. It is also important to identify which weaknesses you are willing and able to improve, and at what rate you can realistically level up as an extroverted sales champion and still achieve all the milestones in the plan. If the level of skills mastery required is not going to happen in the time you have, a new approach will be needed— one that *does* leverage the skills, aptitudes, and competencies you and your team already possess, and one that can realistically be improved upon. At this point, it's also important to consider how to bring in others from the outside to help you quickly build the strengths you need.

Systems

Also relevant to your ability to make progress on Your Desired Outcome are the surrounding systems and resources. Let's return to the sales example. It matters that you have a good way to track the number of prospects you attract or the number of calls a salesperson makes. Ask yourself: Is there a clear sales process or methodology everyone follows? Are there pre-built sales presentations that have been proven to work? Existing systems either facilitate or inhibit the actions that need doing and often need consistent improvements along the way.

Another important factor is whether the systems are inviting and intuitive. If your sales process requires sales reps to take burdensome actions (like emailing you with status reports every day) and they don't see the value in what you're asking them to do, their level of compliance will suffer. And, more than that, they will feel angry, which disrupts and slows progress. Systems need to be logical, efficient for your team members, and a clear value-add.

Questions to ask:

- What systems are already in place that will facilitate progress and completion of the Desired Outcome?

- What are the systems that are either missing or need improvement?

- By when would you need to implement new systems for greatest effect?

On your Transformational Map™, write down the Skills, Aptitudes, and Competencies that will be required and cultivated on your way to the New Desired Outcome.

People, Structures, and Resources
The current and needed people, support structures, and resources (time, energy, money) can also amplify or diminish progress.

As your plan (actions, behaviors, and outcomes) requires *time* dedicated to actualizing the New Outcome, are there activities that will need to be reassigned or delegated to someone else? Are there activities that you should stop altogether? Is there a new schedule that will support you? Perhaps scheduling time to complete your most important activities first thing in the morning, before you get sucked into the whirlwind of the day, will help ensure the most important tasks get done.

Learning new skills and taking bold actions take not only time but also *energy*—significantly more energy than doing a familiar task in your same old routine. Accounting for your energy peaks and valleys is essential to success, and acknowledging that you (and team members) might need replenishment along the way is to be expected. Aligning the most challenging actions of your day with the time slot during which you have the most energy will amplify your success. Making sure you have the best environment and people possible to support your energy demands is also important. If you need to make important phone calls, like ones to prospective investors or cold calls to prospective customers, you might need more time than makes logical sense, because of the energy required. On days when I do these kinds of critically important—albeit draining—tasks, it is critical I make sure the rest of the day is filled with more comfortable tasks or even rest.

The New Desired Outcome may involve *people*. There will be people who can help, as well as people who might resist. Articulating the team dynamics, how you can support them is important as you endeavor to create anew. Who can you enlist to support this new outcome?

Related to people are *supports*. Supports include anything that keeps you and everyone involved moving forward. Supports that create accountability, momentum, alignment, wellness, excitement, and inspiration can make all the difference. From a clear dashboard you can see and write on, to a personal daily tracker, to healthy food in the refrigerator, to creating a weekly accountability meeting—all these types of supports can help you succeed.

You will also likely need *supplies and equipment* on the journey ahead. Maybe you need marketing collateral, new office space, or mobile-enabled computers? When you celebrate victories, will everyone on the team get a special T-shirt? Will there be fun giveaways to your customers? Will you be ordering printed collateral that might be more affordable to create in-house with a new copier? Maybe you are altering your manufacturing or logistics system and need new equipment for these changes.

The next important resource is *money*. Does the journey from Your Current State to Your Desired Outcome require a financial investment? How will you fund a new technology system, specific supplies, or even additional people? Is this investment already in your budget, or will you need to modify it? Are you fully committed to making the financial investment in the timeline required? If not, it's okay, but write it down in your Transformational Map™. Ambivalence and reticence create drag on progress in the best circumstances, and in the worst case, can completely dismantle it. If you aren't sure about going all in on a particular investment, consider new pathways that break it down into smaller pieces and require less up-front investment. Talk about it with trusted leadership until you feel comfortable moving full steam ahead.

Consider these questions:

- What adjustments can you make in your schedule to dedicate more time to cultivating this Desired Outcome?

- How can you support your energy so that you have the inner fuel to learn and do new things?

- Are there new supplies or equipment you will need along the journey?

- What financial investments are you planning to make, and by when, to support actualizing the New Outcome?

On your Transformational Map™, write down the various systems, people, structures, and resources you can put into place to support the New Desired Outcome.

Thoughts and Beliefs

While traversing the Bridge between Your Current State and Your Desired Outcome, you will encounter areas of resistance that will hold you back unless you overcome fears, take new action, learn new skills, and evolve familiar habits. The mapping-the-Bridge stage invites you to preempt the thoughts and beliefs that might get in your way. Here, you are invited to expose familiar habits, disempowering behaviors, limiting thoughts, and unconscious beliefs that keep you where you are; additionally, consider the excuses, people you might blame, or situations you might believe have the power to keep you from having what you desire without intentionally shutting those thoughts down.

If left in the dark, negative thoughts and beliefs can keep you from the results you desire. By shining a light on these distractions, you are empowered to confront them head on and boldly stride past them with your team right on your heels.

Imagine how your thoughts and beliefs will organically evolve over time as you take new action, create small wins, and build confidence within your team. Acting from a place of "I am not sure we can get there" to "We are unstoppable" will transform the path ahead.

Creating something that doesn't exist (Your Desired Outcome) is a profound experience. It carries within it the opportunity to transform fear into love by confronting, healing, and overcoming everything that stands in its way. When you do what you haven't done before, elevate your skills to new levels of mastery, and create systems that bring out the best in everyone, given the framework, you can experience deep, empowering shifts in the way you engage with the world.

Fear stops us from allowing our greatness to shine through. When we step outside of that to manifest new results, we discover and own the inner gifts we are meant to receive and use along the journey.

Use the Journey of Transformation Process in the FFG ToolKit at www.aforceforgood.biz/book-bonuses/ to understand more about how you can elevate your thinking.

On your Transformational Map™, on the bottom half of the page, write down the Limiting Thoughts and Beliefs, Fears and Resistance, Excuses and Rationalizations, and Thoughts of Victimhood and Blame that might come up. On the top half of the page, write down Empowered Perspectives and Truths, Treasured Gifts and Possibilities, Resourcefulness and Abundance, and Choice and Freedom that you can discover along the way.

Feelings

I also advise that you map out how you (and others) might feel along the journey. Why is this important? Because as humans, most of us learned that uncomfortable feelings are bad and that pleasant feelings are good. I'd like to counter this: *uncomfortable feelings don't mean we should stop.* They don't mean we're on the wrong path. In fact, uncomfortable feelings are often a sign of progress on a Journey of Transformation. It is good to prepare to face uncertainty, vulnerability, fear, anxiety, overwhelm, and confusion, to name just a few.

The Cycle of Breakthrough

Taking big actions to create change requires you to go through the Cycle of Breakthrough, which looks like this . . .

CYCLE OF BREAKTHROUGH

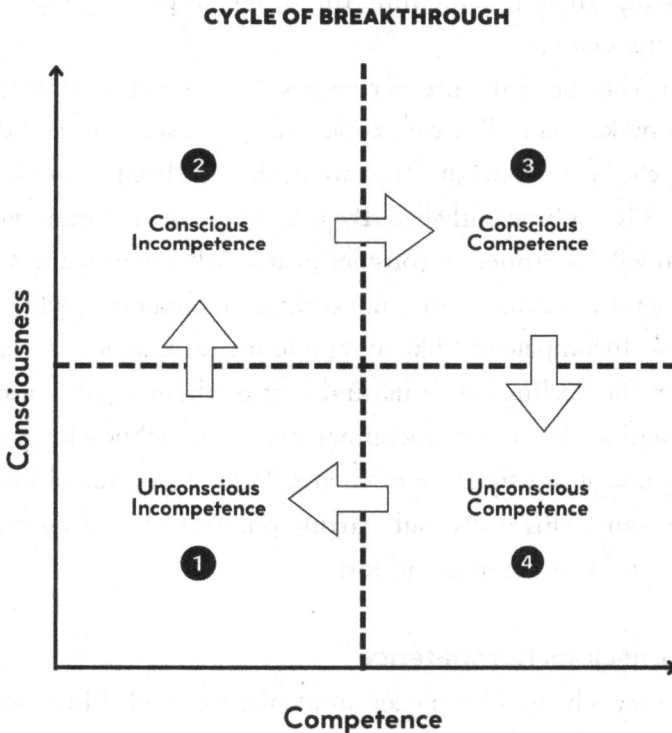

First: Unconscious Incompetence

This is the stage we live in most of our lives, by default. Ignorance is bliss. Sure, there are ways we might improve, but since we aren't focused on whatever "it" is—our low sales-conversion rates, our slow customer wait times, our level of nurse-documentation compliance—we are not bothered by it.

When in this state, how do you feel? Probably fine. Content, to some degree.

Second: Conscious Incompetence

This is typically the most uncomfortable stage of the journey. This is when you (or a team member) are suddenly aware that something is not working. There is something that needs improving—something that requires change.

When you suddenly discover results that are not up to snuff, how does that make you feel? Most people experience some level of discomfort, apprehension, concern, frustration, shame, defensiveness, or even anger. This is not inherently bad. By accepting that, and even preparing for it, you will be primed to consider instead what your team will need to feel, tolerate, and, as a result, not completely shut down when feeling consciously incompetent. I like to remind my team members that these uncomfortable feelings are a natural part of change, innovation, and transformation. Positivity, encouragement, and acknowledgment are super important during these moments. "You are awesome! Look how far we've come! This is just our starting point! And now we can build up from here" is the mindset to foster.

Third: Conscious Competence

At this point, changes have been implemented, and things are working, but we still need significant focus and energy to ensure that the positive results and trends continue. Here, accountability is essential. Continuing to measure results, celebrate wins, and foster continual small improvements on whatever the current goal looks like is key to ensuring the change sticks.

At this point, you and your team probably feel better than you did when you were consciously incompetent, but moments of frustration, annoyance, shame, and even guilt can linger here. It is essential to keep holding a positive space during this stage. Reflecting on what is good—incremental progress, lessons learned, and gifts of the circumstances—will help the team tolerate this stage. This is also where things can start to feel rote or boring. To avoid *"Enough* already—can't we focus on something else?" bring in fresh, inspired energy to keep things going. Plan celebrations for small wins to keep the momentum strong. Anything that builds fun, laughter, and humor helps at this phase.

Fourth: Unconscious Competence

By this final stage, a change or improvement that has been implemented will continue on without much effort. The level of mastery or performance has successfully been built into the operations of your business and is there to last.

What feelings might you expect at this stage? Celebration, satisfaction, and fulfillment *should* be what we feel, but so often these moments of success pass us by. Don't let them. This is the moment to shine the light on the team. Encourage everyone to see their own brilliance and to shout out and celebrate the brilliance of others.

On your Transformational Map™, name the range of feelings—from fear to love—to be expected as part of the journey to actualizing the New Desired Outcome.

Holding the Space for Breakthrough

Moving from Your Current State to Your Desired Outcome will likely involve many of these cycles of breakthrough to take place. You and your team members will sometimes ride out the experience together and sometimes asynchronously. As a leader, it is important to map out all the feelings that might come up and to hold tightly to the space for transformation to occur, supporting people through their uncomfortable feelings and facilitating the transition to the next and elevated level of brilliance.

The Hero's Journey

As you consider the full journey between here and Your Desired Outcome, identifying the many areas of change, innovation, and transformation needed, it is important to pause, reflect, and integrate these three things:

1. **The Why**—The core reason that the Desired Outcome is deeply and profoundly important to you, your team, and your company. Keeping this front of mind will fuel your strength, perseverance, and growth.

2. **The Learning**—Remain receptive to what you are meant to learn and change. There is always something you are *not* good at today; let that be an exciting challenge rather than a crushing blow.

3. **The Gift**—This is the wisdom you are meant to absorb along the way. As you take action, stay brave, overcome doubts, bounce back from setbacks, and make space for others to shine, a gift will be waiting for you. Be ready to receive it.

MAP YOUR TRANSFORMATION

Map Your Transformation

Now it is your turn. Download the tools to help you craft and map the journey from Your Current State to Your Desired Outcome. It can be used privately as a self-reflection tool, or it can be used collectively with a team.

- Journey of Transformation: Process Your Transformation Map™ template

These are available in the FFG ToolKit, located here: *www.aforceforgood.biz/book-bonuses/*

BUILDING HEROES

While mapping your own growth and transformation is undoubtedly empowering, make sure to hold space for the heroic journeys of your team members, customers, and partners as well. The reason I chose "Being Transformative" as the second Core Value of my newest business venture is that expanding the potential within others and the world at large strikes me as a huge part of being a Force for Good.

Imagine all of your team members now. Notice the incredible journeys they are each facing. Think of what might be holding them back and what is propelling them forward. What could you do today to support their transcendent journey? What could you do today to hold the space for their inner hero to unfold? This is what being a Force for Good is all about.

CHAPTER 20
BE OF HIGHEST AND BEST USE: *KNOW WHAT YOU ARE CALLED TO DO*

"Each morning we are born again.
What we do today is what matters most."

—Buddha

"The purpose of life is to be useful,
to be honorable,
to be compassionate,
to make a difference."

—Marianne Williamson

"Tell me, what is it you plan to do,
With your one wild and precious life?"

—Mary Oliver

"The Summer Day"

A **FORCE** FOR **GOOD**

> "True power comes from making choices
> that honor our highest self."
>
> —DEBBIE FORD
>
> *The Right Questions: Ten Essential Questions to Guide*
> *You to an Extraordinary Life*

In eighteen short months, Allumé had grown dramatically from its conception to a high-seven-figure business. Patients were reaching out daily, in need of our around-the-clock nursing services to enable them to come home from the hospital. Our office was filled with nurses interviewing, orienting, and training to provide Remarkable Care™ in the field. We had grown from a team of 4 employees to 150, and we were right at that point of breaking even, just beginning to see profits, when the pandemic erupted into all of our lives. I remember going to a regional emergency-preparedness meeting that I knew was important, but I didn't realize at the time just how monumental it would prove to be.

At that meeting, we were told that the state and federal government did not have enough personal protective equipment (PPE) for us and that we were encouraged to shut down our offices and shift all those in the field to a high state of infection control, in which everyone would be masked, gowned, and socially distanced. Marie, my colleague sitting next to me, and I looked at each other, dumbfounded. Within mere days, Marie and I implemented a plan to move our operations online—but that was only the first hurdle.

In the months ahead, the litany of challenges was endless. We worked desperately to have Tyvek suits handmade and distributed into the field, enlisted volunteers to make sets of cotton masks for nurses, and watched the news daily for new regulations and infection-control requirements being rolled out by the Center for Medicare Services and the Department of Public Health.

We had the responsibility of caring for 150 medically fragile patients and 150 clinicians. The weight of this commitment was, at times, overwhelming. But this was not the time to shrink in fear or to hide. I felt from the core of my being that this was our moment to rise and serve. We needed to be at the top of our game, and to do that, as the leader, I needed to be at my highest and best.

"What is my highest and best use?" was the question that rang in my mind during the days and weeks after the 2020 pandemic began. It became my inner compass, helping me sort out what was most critical for me to do each and every day.

At first, the answer was "to double down on Remarkable Care™." I focused on leading the team, reminding them of their purpose, providing everything they needed, and ensuring every nurse felt acknowledged and appreciated. Our leadership team hosted Town Halls, hired a person to deliver PPE, and sent care packages into the field. We reached out to patients and their families to ensure they knew all the ways we were there to keep them safe at home. I dedicated myself to our Core Values and leaned daily into making sure our team could see how important they were to our community.

Later in the pandemic, as I watched our volume of nursing hours shrink and our profits turn into red, the answer became, "to find ways to create a surge of sustainable volume." The pandemic had caused a total halt in new nurse applicants. We had no pipeline to fill more shifts. And our volume was shrinking. I needed a new strategy to boost our volume to keep us out of the red. After countless sleepless nights, I came to my business partners and told them we needed a change of plan. To weather this storm, we needed to buy, merge, or sell.

We couldn't cut our operations and still deliver our promise of Remarkable Care™, and thus we needed to scale by either buying another agency that would offer us the added volume we needed, merging with another agency in our market and consolidating our teams, or looking for an interested party who would like to buy Allumé.

In the months ahead, I worked tirelessly with my partners to source opportunities for all three. In the end, we chose to merge with another, larger agency in our market. All of this took more than a year, one that was full of thousands of challenging moments. Again and again, I asked myself, "What is my highest and best use?" Was I willing to give up the brand? Was I willing to give up operational control? What message did I need to deliver from meeting to meeting? What information did I need to share? What could I do today to make sure Allumé survives? To ensure each patient continues to receive care? To continue to provide jobs for our team of 150 nurses?

As the process of finalizing the merger extended from 3 months, to 6 months, to 12 months, and Allumé continued to bleed red and my partners and I continued to fund the business, I kept asking, "What is my highest and best use?" Each time, new instructions sprang up from within. It became clear that I needed to convince the state of Connecticut to increase our Medicaid complex-care nursing rates. I knew that if we had even a slightly higher rate, we could pull out of the red and stay alive. I put my heart and soul into writing testimony, calling my state representatives, and hounding the governor's office. I wrote an op-ed and called television stations. Amelia and I even went on the news. We collaborated with our state association for home-health providers and held a press conference on the stairs of the congress building in Hartford. Ultimately, after months of effort, this very focused work resulted in a much-needed 31.7% rate increase. That was more than we dared hope for and was absolutely game-changing. It gave us the resources needed to pay nurses more and give them better, more competitive benefits in the months after the merger.

This question, "What is my highest and best use?" has guided me in all matters, large and small. It often tells me what to do, and it sometimes tells me what not to do. On the quest to be a leader who can bring good into the world—who can synergistically materialize Impact, Scale, and Profit and can build a multi-million-dollar, profitable, sustainable business that others want to own—I have found that, more than any other resource out there, what I value the most is clear, empowered action.

To be a Force for Good, I shared the importance of being wise (Chapter 18) and the power of being transformative (Chapter 19) with my team during those tumultuous months. Here, in this last chapter of the book, my intention is to convey the same to you. I want you to walk away from here convinced of the power you own and the access available to you through wise, strategic, purpose-infused action.

The entire Force for Good System™, including the Core Growth Elements summarized in the 4-Page-Growth Plan, the Seven Rituals, your wisdom, and your transformative mindset will give you everything you need to know, each and every day, and will help answer what you can do to be of highest and best use.

The answer to that question didn't arise for me magically—or even by intuition alone—but largely from the strong foundation of the Force for Good System™ that I was standing on to ask it. It came from my well-oiled daily practice of listening for inner wisdom, the constant consideration of the 4PGP™, the Transformational Map™ I was standing in, and all the forces working for and against me.

You (and everyone on your team) are incredibly powerful creators. You are brilliant beyond measure. But if you keep all that brilliance locked up inside and don't take action to bring your creativity, innovation, and untapped potential into the world, nothing will happen. No breakthrough results occur. No impact transcends. No moments of greatness are released.

Action—new, gritty, courageous, committed, amplified, and focused—and sometimes deliberate non-action are what's necessary to create anything in the world, be it Impact, Scale, Profit, Purpose, or any other result.

HOW DO YOU DECIPHER WHAT IT IS?

Other ways to frame the question "What is my highest and best use?" include:

- **What does the company and your team most need from you?** Today? This week? This month? This year? This decade?

- **What can you do—that perhaps only you can do—to deliver the greatest possible impact?**

- **How can you elevate the company and team in the most meaningful way?**

To begin to answer these questions, we will:

1. Consult the Thinking

2. Consult the Feeling

3. Consult the Knowing

4. Turn to the Highest and Best Resources

As we move through each of these areas, I will be offering tools and contemplations for you to use personally. But please know that all of these concepts are also meant to be rolled out to *your whole team*, so that everyone in your organization can wake up each day and know what to do to bring the greatest impact to the organization.

CONSULT THE THINKING

The Key Results

First, it is important to employ the disciplined, analytical part of you (your Thinking Self) to hold the focus on the key results you need to achieve, even when the unexpected happens in the day-to-day life of your business:

- 4-Page Growth Plan™
- Company 10-Year Impact, Scale, and Profit Goals
- Company-Wide 12-Month Breakthrough Goal
- Functional MIGs (Most Important Goals)
- Functional LEADs (Leading indicator goals to facilitate Functional MIGs)
- Your Personal MIGs
- Your Personal LEADs

This first step might seem obvious, but in my experience as an entrepreneur, it is not. It is easy to get caught in the riptide of whatever hits when you open an email, receive an urgent, unexpected phone call from a client, or when the federal government declares an emergency, requiring all businesses to go virtual.

The squeaky wheel and today's fire will always steal your attention from your key goals. If you let it, weeks, months, or even years might pass before you lift up your head and say, "Now, where was I?" To be of highest and best use, your most important Company Purpose, Values, and Goals must be in focus, and your most potent actions must be aimed at those results.

Reflect on Where You Are

Next, regularly review what you already have, including these items that should already be entrenched in your thinking, knowing, and feeling:

- 4-Page Growth Plan™

- Progress on your 12-Month Breakthrough Plan

- Most recent Monthly Dashboard, including the 5 Critical Reports (Profit & Loss, Balance Sheet, Cash Flow Statement, Accounts Receivable Aging Report, and Accounts Payable Aging Report) and the 12+ Key Metrics Dashboard

- Latest data on Customer Enrollment Funnel

Notice what's working and what isn't. Notice where there's progress and where there's conflict. Where would you most like to see improvements next? What is the next priority to give your attention and focus?

Super-High Potency Impact

As you absorb and reflect upon where you are, return to the Pareto Principle, the theory that 80% of results come from 20% of actions. Also known as the "80/20 rule," this idea invites you to clarify which actions in your day are highly potent in accelerating New Desired Outcomes and which ones are not.

Choosing to be of highest and best use necessitates that you carefully select actions each day, so as to most potently move your results forward. Accomplishing some goals will give you a little boost to Impact, Scale, and Profit, while other goals being fully actualized will have a greater domino effect. Consider your 12-Month Company-Wide Breakthrough Goal, the goal you and your team believe is most essential for you to actualize this year. This is what you think will ease constraints and accelerate the greatest momentum throughout your business. It is, in itself, an exercise in the Pareto Principle.

With your 12-Month Breakthrough Goal in mind, do a quick audit of the actions you take in a typical day, week, and month: answering emails, making phone calls, writing documents, giving presentations, coaching employees, paying bills, fixing the toilet, etc. Some of those actions are supporting your 12-Month Breakthrough Goal, and some are not. It may be helpful to sort them into the following categories, relative to the achievement of a Desired Outcome:

- Constricts Impact

- No/Low Impact

- Medium Impact

- High Impact

- Super-High Potency Impact

Ideally, the LEADs, or leading actions that we discussed in Chapter 15, are themselves Super-High Potency. (And if they are not, the goal is to replace them with activities and habits that are.) Super-High Potency Impact behaviors, habits, and actions are the key to your Highest and Best Use. Deducing which actions really will set the organization free, grease the squeaky wheels, and catapult results is the constant, curious quest of discovering your Highest and Best Use.

The graph below is a framework for considering, with every behavior of your day, if you are falling prey to idle, unimportant activities, or if, in every moment, you are investing your time and brilliance in what is most worthwhile.

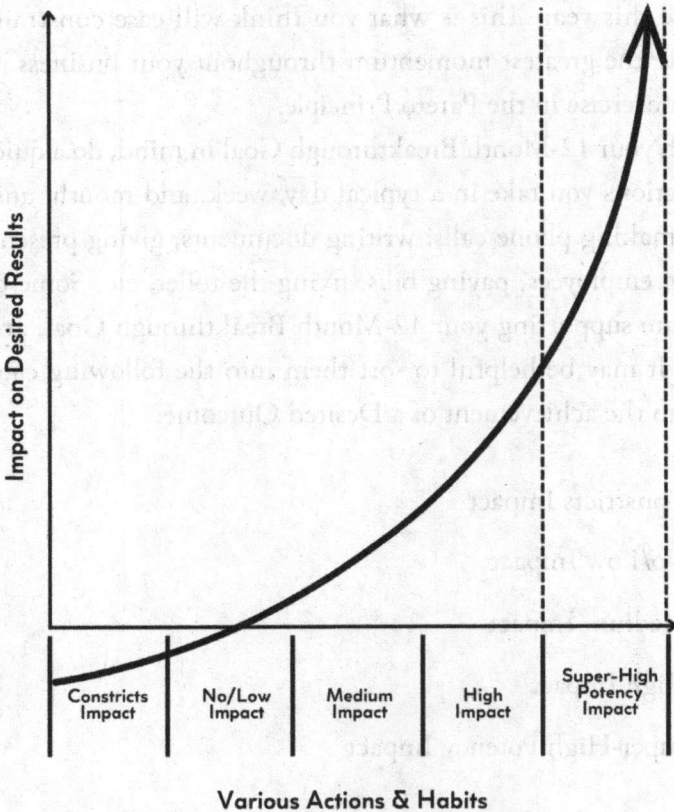

Impact on Desired Results

Constricts Impact

No/Low Impact

Medium Impact

High Impact

Super-High Potency Impact

Various Actions & Habits

Moving more and more of your actions from Low Impact to Super-High Potency won't happen overnight, but the Highest and Best Resources presented later in this chapter will help you accomplish this over time.

Habits and Actions

When seeking ways to achieve Super-High Potency Impact, there are two great places to examine: your habits and your actions.

High-Leverage Habits

Habits are those things you do regularly, be it daily, weekly, monthly, or annually. Certain things quickly come to mind when we think of habits: when you wake up, when you arrive at work, what you eat for lunch and when, etc. But it is also the repetitive behaviors you follow when you feel stressed, tired, bored, overwhelmed, anxious, or threatened: How often and why you feel triggered when checking email. The typical conversations you have and the people you regularly see. There are many habits that are running on autopilot in your life.

Some can be incredibly empowering in reaching your goals, while others are decidedly less so. In the quest to discover your Highest and Best Use, taking inventory of your habits and where they fall on this spectrum is incredibly revealing. What you do every day is the biggest predictor of your wealth, health, relationships, and level of perceived happiness.

In becoming of Highest and Best Use, look to implement High-Leverage Habits. These are habits that, when you act them out, almost guarantee the results you desire.

At Allumé, we implemented many intentional habits directly aligned with the results that were most important to us. For example, our biggest driver of success for a long time was hiring nurses, and nothing brought about that result more than interviews. Thus, we implemented the habit that every morning, Christine, our highest producer of interviews, would have protected time starting at 10 a.m., during which she did nothing but schedule and conduct interviews until she achieved her daily goal of ten. To support Christine in this most important goal, her coworker Taylor held her own daily habit of taking all the phone calls, emails, and issues that came in for Christine and handling them herself.

Another big challenge we faced in the early days of Allumé was billing in a quick and compliant way. In 2019, our Finance Most Important Goal (MIG) was to halve the time it took to bill and collect for services rendered, from 60 days to 30 days. Several habits were implemented to actualize this goal. First, we needed to reduce late nursing documentation, which was necessary for billing, so we adopted the daily habit of reviewing all visits from the days prior and reaching out to nurses with incomplete paperwork, imploring them to submit their electronic documentation. This habit—executed each morning and every afternoon—helped us improve on-time documentation from 80% to 98%. We employed this habit until our technology was updated so that it could automatically do what we had been doing manually. This habit of finding a problem that is constricting results, implementing a temporary process to immediately improve the system, while simultaneously innovating a more-efficient, permanent solution to fuel results more efficiently, is often the Highest and Best Use of any leader.

High-Potency Action

High-Leverage Habits are supported and furthered by High-Potency Actions, which are specific actions you choose to take outside of the regular list of your habits and plans. These "potent" actions boost your company and team in a measurable, intentional way.

Let's explore the story I told earlier in this chapter in greater detail. In 2021, right in the middle of the pandemic, our ability to hire nurses was at a standstill, and, yet, every day, hospitals were calling us, desperate to send home complex-care patients our way. As part of my long-term Highest and Best Use, I had become involved with the Connecticut Association for Heathcare at Home, an advocacy organization for home-health providers. We spent countless hours advocating for better rates and regulations so that we could serve our community better. In April of 2021, we learned that, despite initial hopes that we would increase Medicaid rates for complex-care nursing by 5–10% (after 19 years with no increase), we were shocked to learn that our increase was going to be only 1.9%, which would barely move the needle on our hiring woes. With such low Medicaid-reimbursement rates, we could not compete with hospitals and skilled-nursing facilities for nurses.

It was at this moment that I was called to a series of highly potent actions that, if achieved, might actually make a difference.

The first highly potent action was for me to write an op-ed that could be distributed, and hopefully published, in local media outlets. I had 48 hours to write a compelling article declaring the immediate injustice of our dismal rates and demand that our legislators take action. I'd never written an op-ed before, and I had plenty of other squeaky wheels to grease, but nonetheless I wrote late into the night and asked for the support of a dear friend and brilliant writer, Todd Johnson, to help me. Within a few days, the article was published in the *CT Mirror*.

The second Highly Potent Action was for me to reach out to every news source possible and pitch the story of how Allumé was founded to double the access of complex-care nursing to patients in Connecticut, all as inspired by our daughter, Amelia. I shared how babies and children were stuck in the hospital, unable to go home because there wasn't an in-home nurse available to care for them. I leveraged my network of contacts, and, within a few days, Amelia and I were interviewed on CT WTNH Channel 8 by Sarah Cody. Again, I'd never done anything like this before, but I didn't let that stop me.

The third Highly Potent Action was for our advocacy group to hold a press conference on the steps of the capitol building in Hartford, inviting legislators, home-health advocates, patients, and families to attend. With more than 40 participants and 20 members of the press, we made the news on several local stations.

The fourth Highly Potent Action was for all of us in the advocacy group to reach out to families and patients, asking them to call the governor's office to request higher rates. We had so many people calling the governor that one of his aides reached out, begging me to make it stop and asking me to help him understand exactly what our needs were.

A few weeks later, we were given a rate increase. It wasn't the 5–10% we requested. My jaw dropped when I learned they gave pediatric complex care a whopping 31.7% increase. For context, this was a 21% increase in our total top-line revenue. It finally gave us both the funding we needed to retain and attract nurses *and* the dollars we needed to be sustainably profitable. The value of our company increased by 40% overnight.

This is what I mean by *Highly Potent Action.* These are moves you can make that produce massive results. They change the game. They elevate the ecosystem. They generate real impact.

Every single day, we have the opportunity to do just that. Sit with that, and consider: How are you being called right now, with this day you've been given, to offer your Highest and Best Use to your company, your team, and to the world?

CONSULT THE FEELING

Now that you have consulted the Thinking Self, the next place to consult for clarity and guidance on how to be of Highest and Best Use is through your Feeling Self.

As I mentioned when we discussed the concept of Being Wise in Chapter 20, the Feeling Self is often a misunderstood source of wisdom. Using this simple set of questions, you can discover deeply supportive and powerful actions that will help propel your team toward success:

1. What are you feeling?

2. What is your team feeling?

3. To bring out the best in everyone, what feelings need to be cultivated?

4. What actions will cultivate those feelings?

Recall the importance of Being Transformative from Chapter 21. The Journey of Transformation demonstrates that each of us carries a complex set of behaviors, beliefs, habits, and feelings within ourselves. While taking a simple action may seem unremarkable—say, making 10 calls today—when you consider all the unconscious baggage surrounding each of us, taking action (especially new, transformative action) becomes much more complex. We are held back or accelerated forward on our way to a specific Desired Outcome, according to how we feel. When we feel empowered, hopeful, supported, competent, seen, and appreciated, we are much more likely to follow through with an action than when we feel disempowered, hopeless, unsupported, incompetent, afraid, invisible, or insignificant.

At every moment, a great leader must be cultivating the feelings needed for brave, wholehearted action. She first fosters those feelings within herself, and then within the environment of her team, knowing that that is energy well spent. Taking action that elevates agency and empowerment is often a significant portion of a leader's Highest and Best Use.

Cultivating Empowerment

Building a company is about building a team. Delivering remarkable products and solutions through collaboration is the purpose of a business. To work toward this effectively, most people need to have three specific feelings present to serve at their Highest and Best capacity on an ongoing basis:

- Safety

- Belonging

- Acknowledgment

Safety

Safety is the precursor to everything. Studies have shown that, despite old-fashioned command-and-control management styles used for eons to keep people in line, people do not perform at their best when they feel scared. Google recently conducted a two-year study on 250 high performers and found that psychological safety was far and away the most important factor for predicting high performance. The study showed that, when team members feel safe, they are more likely to admit mistakes, to partner with others, and to take on new roles. They are also more likely to harness the power of diverse and innovative ideas and bring in more revenue, and they are rated twice as effective by their managers. As if that wasn't enough, employees who feel safe are also much less likely to leave the company for greener pastures.[2]

In order for your team to be empowered, they need to feel safe. They need to know it's okay to be themselves. They need to believe that their ideas can be heard without ridicule and, if their ideas don't work, that they won't be shamed. They need to believe you and the team will support them when the going gets tough. Without this safety, team members will hold back, keep their mouth shut, and play small. This will not support the purpose of your company, the impact you long to deliver, or your vision waiting on the horizon.

Questions to inspire elevated action:

1. What can you do this week to cultivate a feeling of safety within the walls of your organization?

2. What could you do to invite people to speak their truth and feel safe doing it?

3. When might members of your team feel unsafe?

4. What could you do to reduce fear-inducing moments at your company?

---

2 https://hbr.org/2017/08/high-performing-teams-need-psychological-safety-heres-how-to-create-it

5. What could you do to ensure your team feels empowered to take risks, make mistakes, and safely fail?

Belonging

In a similar vein, people can't learn when they don't feel they belong. Neuroscience has shown that the brain shuts down to learning whenever someone feels rejected, judged, or marginalized in some way. However, when we humans feel a sense of belonging, our brain functions open up to uncharted levels of creativity, innovation, and exploration. Myra Landin, an educator and scientist, explains that, when we find ourselves in situations where we feel like an outsider, we use our mental energy to monitor for threats, leaving fewer resources for higher cognitive processes.[3] Conversely, studies show higher levels of motivation and performance are correlated with feeling a sense of belonging.[4]

Learning is an essential part of bringing your best forth each day, and it is a necessary ingredient for innovation. Thus, as transformational leaders, it behooves us to engage intentionally in building a sense of community and belonging on a daily basis.

What fosters belonging?

- **Acts of Empathy**—The extraordinary ability of empathy—understanding and sharing the feelings of another—is critical to creating belonging. Take action to foster an environment where it is natural and normal for team members to find out how others are doing and what helps them feel supported to do their best work.

---

3 Laldin, Myra. "The Psychology of Belonging (and Why It Matters)." *Learning and the Brain*, 11 Feb. 2016, www.learningandthebrain.com/blog/psychology-of-belonging/. Accessed 20 July 2024.

4 Walton GM, Cohen GL. A question of belonging: race, social fit, and achievement. *J Pers Soc Psychol*. 2007 Jan; 92(1):82-96. doi: 10.1037/0022-3514.92.1.82. PMID: 17201544.

- **Acts of Acceptance**—Acceptance is what allows each of us to feel as if we belong, even though we are all different. Actively choosing to point out the strengths and celebrate the quirks of others creates a place where everyone can be celebrated for who they are.

- **Act of Fun**—Building a constant stream of fun into your culture is time well spent. Team members soften with each other through laughter. This is why building fun rituals and celebrations that create energy, excitement, and humor allows members of your team to connect and belong.

- **Acts of Building Community**—As a purpose-led leader, creating community is one of your most essential functions. Together, you and your team are on a mission to make the world better. However you can connect with your team, through the common purpose of your company, allows you to build a true community. People who care about the same things and work toward the same good share a powerful sense of belonging.

Acknowledgment

When I founded Allumé, long before I had the required credentials to start serving patients, I began holding happy hours for nurses. I simply wanted to get to know nurses in my community, learn about who they were, and receive input on what I was planning to create. I asked what they most longed for within their workday and what they wished their employers would provide. The number-one response was that they wanted to feel acknowledged. Even more than higher pay, more days off, better health benefits, or tuition reimbursement, they wanted to know they were valued and appreciated.

This isn't something unique to the nursing profession. Humans have a deep need to feel valued, significant, and important. As transformational leaders, we are called to express gratitude, appreciation, and acknowledgment to everyone on our team in ways that are consistent, frequent, and authentic. Every time you acknowledge someone else in this way, it empowers them to keep going, keep growing, and keep bringing out their best.

Some members of your team will enter into the company and naturally succeed. Others will struggle. It is important to use the tool of acknowledgment not only to sing the praises of the superstars (who always get the praise) but also to bolster the rest—especially those who are struggling to succeed, struggling to take risks, or are scared they might fail.

There is power in acknowledging:

- **Small wins**—One of my mantras is "catch people doing the right thing." This is especially true for small improvements or victories. Someone struggling to learn a new function, improve a stuck result, or succeed at something scary needs validation along the way.

- **Brave Choices**—Thanking someone for coming forward with a difficult subject, for admitting they made a mistake, or for having a vulnerable conversation about something that's bothering them are all prime opportunities for acknowledgment.

- **Honesty**—One of the biggest possible barriers to success is team members who are afraid to tell you the truth. As a leader, and as the boss, people naturally want to please you. Someone on your team who speaks truth and reveals what no one else is willing to say is an incredible asset. Rather than shoot these brave truth-tellers, thank them. Acknowledge them. Let everyone know it is safe for them to tell you the truth, even when it's not what you want to hear. Nothing empowers a team quite like seeing someone deliver an undesirable-but-true message and having that message be received with gratitude by the leader.

- **Gifts of Failure**—You will change a person's life when you make it safe for them to fail. Acknowledge what was good about the process: the grit, the skills, the creativity, and the hard work. Acknowledge the wisdom and lessons derived from the experience. Do this both one-on-one and, whenever appropriate, within a group. Making space to talk about *all* results—even outcomes that don't turn out as hoped for—in a way that illuminates a silver lining will not just soften the blow—it will actually heal and restore any feelings of shame or regret.

- **Team Success**—While appreciating each individual for their individual strengths, contributions, and progress is deeply important, it is equally important to acknowledge the success of collective teams. A careful balance between team and individual acknowledgment will ensure that team members don't need to compete for validation. To build an organization that is a Force for Good will always hinge on the ability of team members to collaborate.

Highest and Best Resources

As we near the end of our Force for Good Journey together, my final parting gift to you is the Highest and Best Resources:

- High-Leverage Habits
- Activities and Habits Audit
- High-Potency Actions
- Constraints and Accelerators
- Financial Accelerators

These are all part of the FFG ToolKit, available here: *www.aforceforgood.biz/book-bonuses/*

GO MAKE THE WORLD
A BETTER PLACE

Your role as a leader, as a founder, as an entrepreneur, and as a team member, is to grow, transcend, transform, and heal. Your job is to find your light and let it shine, to use it to enlighten others and amplify their own glow. Your role is to be brave. Take risks. Purpose-led leaders are rare, but the world needs the elevated level of leadership that calls from within you today more than ever.

Join me in the quest to make the world better through business. Follow your instinctive quest to build organizations that elevate society, innovate products and services that transform lives, and create community with all your stakeholders, aligned with purpose and values. Know that just by bringing your whole heart to the journey, you are a *Force for Good*.

IT'S ABOUT GROWTH

The Force for Good vision is a world where business is elevated by the wisdom of women. The traditional model for leading and growing companies is outdated, based on a conveyor-belt kind of system that no longer exists. If you look at businesses from 50 to 100 years ago, most of their assets were physical: their land, their coal, their steel. Within this model, there were fewer stakeholders—and all you had to do was please them, really. There were no regulations in place to protect workers. On top of that, your workforce was replaceable; there weren't as many jobs, so everybody just had to bow to the man. Profit was king. Fortunately, that's changing. A power redistribution is in the works, and we get to be a part of it.

Business has become more complex and more transparent at the same time. There are many stakeholders, and, today, most companies' value lies in their people. As I see it, women's leadership is primed to be particularly poignant and powerful right now. Who better to lead in this new era than a group who was denied formal power for so long, while still shouldering the responsibility of managing things behind the scenes, despite that disenfranchisement? For hundreds of years, women have been helping from the second row, whispering the answers in men's ears while not getting credit. We're uniquely adept at reconciling multiple contradictory needs and getting each stakeholder what they require; we're able to leave our ego out of it, rally the team, and move forward with purpose. The men who are used to having the authority to declare, "Well, I said to do it, so go do it" don't have these additional skills and abilities that we as women—and all who belong to a group that has been undermined and underestimated—have and have honed over hundreds of years.

Getting more women in places of power, where they are leading large communities of workers and influencing many people, is something that only feels increasingly and urgently important to me as the years go by. It's really, really hard to be an entrepreneur. There's a reason most people work for someone else. But while it might be easier to go out and get a job, that is a soul-sucking pursuit if you're wired to be an entrepreneur. In other words, you are ready to embrace the challenge ahead simply because you must, in order to honor the voice inside, and you get to be part of shaping a brand-new era of business while doing so. Even though it's hard at times, once you build a business that is a Force for Good, you will keep at it because you must. You're not going to stop. Our souls are yearning to express and expand.

The world would undoubtedly be changed for the better in a landscape where at least half of the dominating corporations—the future Amazons, Targets, and Walmarts—are women-led. It is for this reason that, as I have gotten deeper into my investment journey, I made the decision to back only women-led ventures. With pitch after pitch, I have glimpsed a whole new economy—one that will be good for everybody, not just for women. When I hear the stories of these powerful businesswomen who are in portfolios of the venture firms that I'm investing in, they don't even have to say they are "purpose-led" or "mission-based." Invariably, they are, and it comes through clear as day as they talk about what they're doing. I see a whole new era of ingenuity and creation in spaces the former decision-makers didn't understand or think about. Helping women claim the power of creating and bettering offerings based on their own experiences is what I'm doing every day, and I wouldn't have it any other way.

Changing the framework, changing the rhetoric won't be easy. The status quo is deeply ingrained. Take, for example, the kinds of questions that men and women get asked while they're looking to secure funding. Studies have shown a man will likely receive queries around his vision for how far he can take his business, whereas a woman will hear, "What will you do if this doesn't go the way you want and things start to fall apart?" It's so important that women are coached and encouraged around how to not get stuck in the defensive during a pitch, how to push off questions like that and move back into, "And here's the vision. Here's where I'm going."

There are many reasons businesses don't grow. The founder doesn't have the knowledge—what needs to be done, what needs to be left alone, what order to do it in—or maybe they simply don't have the funds. They don't have the vision. Now that you've read this book, you know that the Force for Good System™ not only helps you fill these gaps but also provides the key piece many entrepreneurs are unaware they should even be straining for: it helps you be of your Highest and Best Use and, as such, tap into a transformation previously inaccessible to you. *A business can change only as much as the person who is running it and leading it is willing to evolve and grow themselves.*

I see business as creation. What's within you will project its way out of you. If what you're creating on the outside isn't what you want, the place to address first is the inside. That's why I say again that this is a soul journey. It will cause you to confront your own mistakes, your own failures. You will be alone at times and feel hopeless, and, at other points, things will unlock. You will be able to let go of the oars and watch as your boat goes right where it needs to go. Being of Highest and Best Use is that integration in action. That's when things happen. You won't make a difference in your business, you won't make a difference in people's lives, you won't see things shift until you are aligned in your purpose. Then, you're able to create a culture where everyone involved is able to discover their Highest and Best Use. That is profound, fun, and creative. It's like being in a beautiful dance—all people finding their Highest and Best Use and putting it toward accomplishing a purpose higher than themselves. What's better than that? Nothing. It is joy, distilled.

Just because our journey together on these pages has come to an end does not mean I will now leave you hanging. Instead, I'd like to invite you to our online Force for Good Growth Accelerator. There, you will find 12 modules that reinforce the entire Force for Good System™. The virtual accelerator is a microcosm of what the Force for Good System™ is all about: meaningful and sustainable growth. It's about growing yourself as a leader, growing your team, and growing your company—all with the buoyant force of a community of purpose-led businesswomen doing the same around you. See you there!

AFTERWORD

In the final days before *A Force for Good* went to press, I reached a momentous milestone: successfully exiting Allumé Home Care with the ideal acquisition partner. It has been quite the journey. Founded in 2016, Allumé merged with All Pointe HomeCare in 2021, and in June 2024, my partners and I signed an agreement to be acquired by Connecticut Children's Medical Center.

This moment is bittersweet. No other professional journey has enriched, enthralled, and fulfilled me as deeply as nurturing Allumé from her inception, helping her find her footing, and watching her flourish even without my daily involvement. Serving medically-fragile patients and their families has been the honor of my life. Their trust has been a privilege I will always cherish.

Being part of growing the Allumé and All Pointe team has been nothing short of a blessing. The work these incredible clinicians and administrators do is truly god's work.

As a purpose-led, vision-guided leader, this moment is poignant. On one hand, I could have continued this work for another twenty years. On the other, I knew our company needed a larger platform to reach its highest potential. I knew this day would come.

Over the last two years, as the healthcare industry continued to consolidate and regulations became increasingly challenging, I recognized it was time to find a partner who could carry forth our legacy of Remarkable Care™. We were fortunate to have many suitors, with several attractive offers, but Connecticut Children's Medical Center stood out as the perfect match for our purpose, vision, and values.

Our partnership is a testament to the virtues of following purpose, pursuing vision, being of Highest and Best Use, and making the world better. Back in 2021, while writing an op-ed and encouraging patients and families to call the governor's office, the CEO of Connecticut Children's Medical Center, Jim Schmerling, saw me on the news with Amelia. He was looking for a home health partner at the time. Two weeks later, my partners and I had dinner with Jim to discuss a potential partnership. Three years later, that partnership is now a reality.

Under Connecticut Children's Medical Center, the company I founded just eight years ago will become the pediatric home health platform, growing beyond the borders of what I once imagined possible.

So, what's next for me? What now is my Highest and Best Use? I'm focused on helping more women build high-impact, high-growth businesses of substance and scale. Through impact venture investing, helping women secure corporate board seats, connecting women founders with funding, serving on boards myself, and empowering as many women founders as possible with the Force for Good System™, I stand for a world where the wisdom of women can shape, heal, and elevate society. I see more women-led enterprises become tomorrow's Mercks, Microsofts, and Walmarts.

I hold the vision for *your* business to lead in both impact and profit.

Being a Force for Good leader will take you to extraordinary places. It will enrich, expand, exhilarate, and sometimes completely overwhelm you. But it is a life I wouldn't trade for anything. The benefits are never-ending.

Thank you for joining me on this incredible journey and for being a kindred spirit dedicated to making the world better through business. Your passion and commitment inspire me, and I'd love to learn more about you and your venture. Let's connect! Reach out to me at coco@aforceforgood.biz.

Together, let's go make the world a better place.

ACKNOWLEDGMENTS

I want to express my heartfelt gratitude to my beloved husband, Frank. You have been my unwavering supporter, my biggest fan, and the love of my life. Being married to a founder is never easy, but your steadfastness has been my anchor in every storm. Thank you for always being ready for every adventure and for being the love of my life. You are, without a doubt, my favorite.

To our precious girls, Amelia and Ella Pearl:

> Amelia, you are my role model. You always live your Highest and Best Use, bringing love, patience, kindness, and gentleness to everyone you touch. Your gentle soul inspires me every day.

> Ella Pearl, no one has a braver commitment to truth and wisdom than you. I wish I could see and hear the voice of wisdom as clearly as you. You are my forever inspiration and my faith in a better world.

> You both fill my heart with love and gratitude. Every. Single. Day.

Thank you, Jacquie, my strong and courageous mother. You always believed everything was possible, opened every door you could, and let my light shine brightly. Everything good I create is because of you.

Thank you, Zelma, my first angel and Grandmother. I am comforted knowing you are in heaven watching over us all. Your angel wings wrap me in safety and love every day.

Thank you to the rest of my Iowa family, Kassie, Reed, Greg, Amirah, Jayden, Jimmy, John, Linda, Jeff, Dan, Jessica, Bill, Vivian, Dan, and Alia. Uncle Jim and Aunt Jan, I feel your laughter, your rebellion, and your love always. I love you so much I *can* touch the sky.

Thank you to my entire Arizona family—Bub, Joeann, Richard, Dawn, Lily, Mia, Julia, Ricky, Marie, Sandy, Guy, Nancy, Ann Jennifer, Erica, Diana, EJ, Guido, Calib, Zack, Andy, Judy, Leah and Rusty. Your constant embrace, love, and celebration give me grounding and strength.

I extend my heartfelt thanks to everyone at Allumé Home Care and All Pointe HomeCare. Our work together has given meaning and purpose in my life.

Thank you, Christine, for everything you have done for me, my family, and the thousands of people you've cared for over the years. Your dedication is unmatched.

I am profoundly grateful to all the nurses, therapists, and caregivers. You make the world better every single day with your generosity, love, compassion, and commitment.

Thank you to all the patients and their families who have honored Allumé and All Pointe with your trust and faith over the years. I am deeply grateful for the opportunity to serve you.

A special thank-you to everyone who has served on the Allumé or All Pointe Governing Authority or Professional Advisory Committee, past and present.

Thank you, Wilson and Lili, for believing in me and investing in my vision. Thank you for holding the lantern in the darkest hours and bringing the caviar in moments of celebration!

Acknowledgments

To Nancy and Steve, thank you for being extraordinary partners through it all. I will always feel blessed, honored, and grateful for our journey together.

Finally, I am immensely grateful to everyone who helped me write this book: Stuart Horwitz, Emily Dalton, Constance Freedman, Jessica Goodman, David Kolker, Sara Santora, Jill Skilton, Lauren Donald, Katy Abrams, and all the other Cuba Ladies. Your wisdom and contributions have been invaluable.

Thanks to every single founder out there (yes, you!) who gives her heart, her soul, her resources, her brilliance, and her wisdom to making the world better through business. *You are a force for good.*

ABOUT THE AUTHOR

Coco Sellman believes business can be a force for good, especially with visionary women at the helm. With over 25 years of entrepreneurial experience, Coco has launched five companies and guided over 500 startups. As the Founder & CEO of A Force for Good, she leads an innovative ecosystem for purpose-driven women founders, helping them unlock exponential growth and prosperity.

One of Coco's recent triumphs is Allumé Home Care, a healthcare services company inspired by her stepdaughter, Amelia. Allume (now All Pointe HomeCare) provides round-the-clock nursing care for medically fragile children and adults. Under Coco's leadership, Allumé grew rapidly to eight-figure revenues, merged with another home health platform (All Pointe HomeCare), and achieved four-figure profits in under four years. Her advocacy led to a 31.7% increase in Connecticut's complex nursing Medicaid rates, expanding access for those most in need. The company completed a successful exit in 2024.

Coco's vision is to support the emergence of the next generation of businesses like Amazon and Whole Foods—founded and led by women. She created the Force for Good System™, designed to help women entrepreneurs (and wholehearted men) scale their ventures from $1M in annual revenue to $20M and beyond. Her approach blends strategy and analysis with wisdom and community.

As an impact-focused venture investor, board director, and advisor, Coco is dedicated to helping women-led businesses thrive. She's a Limited Partner of Moderne Ventures and How Women Invest, a member of 37 Angels, Entreprenista, Founders Collective, The KNOW, and Luminary, and mentors at Springboard and the Founder Institute.

Coco serves on several boards, including How Women Lead, The Connecticut Association for Healthcare at Home, Rise Children (formerly Worldwide Orphans), and the Oliver Wolcott Library. She divides her time between New York, NY, and Morris, Connecticut, with her husband, Frank, and their two daughters, Amelia and Ella Pearl, along with their Havanese doggies, Harry and Layla.

INDEX